Praise for
Climate Church, Climate World

"This is the book for which we have been waiting concerning the climate crisis. It is clear: the time for ambiguity is long since past. It is bold: deeply-rooted boldness is required to counter the forceful ideology of the fossil fuel lobby. It is institutionally realistic: this is no generic moral appeal, but a bid to the church to take up its primal mission. It is practical: it anticipates active ways for pastors and churches to get to it. This is a welcome must read."

—Walter Brueggemann, Columbia Theological Seminary

"Jim Antal's leadership and religious witness is legendary, and so is the power and beauty of his voice. This book will give you the courage, conviction, and practical tools you will need to be part of this movement!"

—May Boeve, executive director and cofounder, 350.org

"Antal argues that climate injustice is a force that amplifies every other social injustice, and that without a whole and restored earth we won't achieve a whole and restorative society. In urging the church to more deeply consider its obligation in calling society to action, this book will help Christians, both congregationally and individually, act in response to climate change and maintain an outlook of Christ-centered hope while doing so."

—Jim Wallis, president and founder, Sojourners

"Jim Antal is among the most knowledgeable and passionate advocates of creation care, and he captures the complete story in *Climate Church, Climate World*."

—James Hansen, director, Climate Science, Awareness, and Solutions Program, Columbia University Earth Institute

"Jim Antal's *Climate Church, Climate World* arrives at the perfect, most-needed moment. Tears came as I read it—tears of relief and joy that the church had found its voice in this time of crisis. Jim's brave, resounding summons to his fellow Christians comes as marching orders for us all."

—Joanna Macy, author, *Coming Back to Life*

"People of faith have been charged to answer the call of environmental stewardship in the twenty-first century. Too often a theological fringe element has silenced the compassionate and caring faithful serving in faith communities across this nation. Jim Antal's book is a profound answer to fringe and ethically suspect theological movements attempting to silence faith voices committed to creation care. This book is part manual, part theological reflection, and all prophetic witness."

—Otis Moss, senior pastor/servant, Trinity United Church of Christ

"Jim Antal's passion for eco-justice and his bold faith adhere in his emerging theological claim that faith communities have a new vocation: care for the Earth. This book breaks new ground in claiming that a faith not fully committed to the preservation of the planet loses its raison d'être."

—The Rev. Dr. John C. Dorhauer, general minister and president, United Church of Christ

"We must be honest enough to admit that religions originally acknowledged climate change with hesitation, even reluctance. Today, they embrace their responsibility in raising awareness about creation care. In this urgent vocation, Jim Antal has demonstrated unique leadership: proclaiming the gospel of the sacredness of God's creation, promulgating the dire effects of global warming on the most vulnerable, as well as practicing what he preaches in church and society. This book is the fruit of mature discernment and extensive ministry."

—John Chryssavgis, theological advisor to Ecumenical Patriarch Bartholomew

"Jim Antal is not preaching to the choir. He is preaching to all of us for all of us, summoning us and the church to an urgent new calling—to heal a creation broken by the ravages of global warming and climate disruption. His inspiring book and the stories he tells lift us up and prepare us for the great moral challenge of our time."

—James Gustave Speth, founder, National Resources Defense Council; former dean, Yale School of Forestry and Environmental Studies

"Antal braids science, testimony, and action plans into a strong tether between a planet sliding into climate disaster and a hope of creation restored. This book shows how we together can pull back from the brink. People of faith need to read this book—now!"

—Sharon E. Watkins, former general minister and president, Christian Church (Disciples of Christ)

"In his life and work Jim Antal has been a tireless Christian witness to the moral challenge of climate change. In this comprehensive book Jim brings together his compelling personal experience and his broad knowledge to assist other leaders in carrying on this great work. With his powerful prophetic voice he has done a great service to the cause of promoting climate awareness and climate justice."

—Mary Evelyn Tucker, Yale Forum on Religion and Ecology

"A growing number of calls plead for the church to address 'the long emergency' of the climate crisis. Few, however, say how to do so as people of faith who courageously take on the mantle of moral leadership. Jim Antal does both in his sure-footed and bracing way. *Climate Church, Climate World* is a gift."

—Larry Rasmussen, Reinhold Niebuhr Professor Emeritus of Social Ethics, Union Theological Seminary

"Jim Antal is a faithful and courageous advocate in the struggle to save the earth. I am thankful for his leadership. His new book is a must read for all who desire ideas and inspiration."

—Jim Winkler, president and general secretary, National Council of Churches

"Jim Antal has written an inspired and inspiring call to arms—inspired by his fervent belief in God and inspiring to all those of faith who respond to his call. The book charts the damage humankind is causing to its planetary home and points to the many ways in which humankind can change its ways—indeed must—before the damage becomes irreversible. A most timely and important book!"

—Bevis Longstreth, former commissioner, Securities and Exchange Commission

"For far too many mainstream churches, climate change is still considered a topic too hot for Sunday mornings. And yet, as the Reverend Dr. Jim Antal writes in this learned, heartfelt, and prophetic epistle to

American churches and people of faith everywhere, the climate crisis and the suffering it brings are the overriding physical and moral facts of the world that we as Christians are called to love and serve. Where, then, if not in our churches, must we engage this greatest of human crises? With candor, emotional honesty, and moral clarity, Antal offers a profound new vision for what it means to be a church, and a follower of Jesus, in the twenty-first century."

—**Wen Stephenson, author,** *What We're Fighting for Now Is Each Other: Dispatches from the Front Lines of Climate Justice*

"Antal pulls no punches, trenchantly calling people of faith to live beyond our denial and into our interdependence. Theologically grounding our call to action, he provides pragmatic ways for us to proceed as we seek to address the calamity at hand. He stretches us to live free from the limits of our fears. *Climate Church, Climate World* is an essential resource."

—**Alice Hunt, president, Chicago Theological Seminary**

"Jim Antal embodies the moral imagination that we so desperately need in order to rise to the challenge of the climate crisis. His book invites us to imagine a church that puts its principles into action in the twenty-first century and offers a wealth of resources for people of faith who are ready to answer that call."

—**Tim DeChristopher, founder, Climate Disobedience Center**

"For years we've been waiting for a book that has the power to awaken communities of faith to their high calling: to lead the way in preserving the web of life and averting climate chaos. We've been waiting for a book that gives us straight talk about the climate crisis, faces the terrifying facts without flinching, and provides its readers with the moral grounding, motivation, and tools for faithful and effective action. We've been waiting for a book that, in challenging us to take action on climate, skillfully articulates our moral and ethical responsibility and offers a humble, brilliant, and provocative reflection on the nature of hope. *Climate Church, Climate World* is that book. It is a joy to welcome it into print."

—**The Rev. Dr. Margaret Bullitt-Jonas, missioner for creation care, Episcopal Diocese of Western Massachusetts, Massachusetts Conference, United Church of Christ**

"As a pastor, a civil/human rights activist, and a psychologist, I find this book to be the best I have ever read at simply explaining climate change to the average person. It details the 'required action steps' to take if the Church is to assume its rightful place in saving and sustaining what God has entrusted to its care."

—Rev. Dr. Gerald L. Durley, vice chair,
Interfaith Power and Light

"Jim Antal reminds us that the climate crisis, while overwhelmingly frightening, recalls the church to its deepest vocation: incarnating the love that is God. The book describes a path forward, full of inspiration, scriptural grounding and science. It's also a path that leads to a world of peace, joy, and a more hopeful future."

— Richard Rohr, OFM author, ecumenical teacher, and founder,
Center for Action and Contemplation

CLIMATE CHURCH, CLIMATE WORLD

How People of Faith Must Work for Change

Jim Antal

An Alban Institute Book

ROWMAN & LITTLEFIELD
Lanham • Boulder • New York • London

Published by Rowman & Littlefield
A wholly owned subsidiary of
The Rowman & Littlefield Publishing Group, Inc.
4501 Forbes Boulevard, Suite 200, Lanham, Maryland 20706
https://rowman.com

Unit A, Whitacre Mews, 26-34 Stannary Street, London SE11 4AB,
United Kingdom

British Library Cataloguing in Publication Information Available

Library of Congress Cataloging-in-Publication Data
Names: Antal, Jim, 1950– author.
Title: Climate church, climate world : how people of faith must work for
    change / Jim Antal.
Description: Lanham : Rowman & Littlefield, 2018. | "An Alban Institute
    book." | Includes bibliographical references and index.
Identifiers: LCCN 2017059084 (print) | LCCN 2018001616 (ebook) | ISBN
    9781538110706 (electronic) | ISBN 9781538110683 (cloth : alk. paper) |
    ISBN 9781538110690 (pbk. : alk. paper)
Subjects: LCSH: Human ecology—Religious aspects—Christianity. | Climate
    change.
Classification: LCC BT695.5 (ebook) | LCC BT695.5 .A57 2018 (print) | DDC
    261.8/8--dc23
LC record available at https://lccn.loc.gov/2017059084

♾ ™ The paper used in this publication meets the minimum requirements of
American National Standard for Information Sciences Permanence of Paper
for Printed Library Materials, ANSI/NISO Z39.48-1992.

Printed in the United States of America

For future generations,
especially my two grandsons—
whose middle names are Muir and Roosevelt—
I write with hope . . .

CONTENTS

FOREWORD

Bill McKibben

This book is written with unusual authority because, for as long as there has been a serious climate movement in the United States, Jim Antal has been at the forefront. I have stood with him at a hundred demonstrations, languished with him in jail, sweated next to him in paddy wagons. I have listened to him preach the powerful good news—and bad news—about the energy and climate crises from pulpit after pulpit. And I've watched as his cheerful, insistent, relentlessly loving approach has allowed so many Americans to join in this fight. He is on the short list of heroes who have given their all.

And through it all he has learned what works—learned how to reach people who are not yet involved. That gives this compact and comprehensive book its power. It's not just one more guide to the problems we face, or the solutions we could choose. It's a guide to helping people grapple with the most urgent problem humanity has ever faced, a crisis that is close to overwhelming us. After decades of experimentation he has helped figure out some of the doors that need opening so that all of us can wholeheartedly engage in this work.

At first other clergy found it odd, I think, that Antal was so relentless in his efforts to raise the issue of climate. For religious people, the environment until fairly recently was a second-tier problem: for liberal Christians it was secondary to the "real" issues of hunger and war; to conservative people of faith it represented a way station on the road to paganism. Jim was indefatigable in his efforts to change that, circuit-riding his Massachusetts parishes to preach the word and urging all of his fellow parsons to raise the issue once a month from the pulpit. When we asked if he would organize people to ring church bells 350 times, he made sure it happened across the Bay State—I can remember standing at a small Berkshire church and tugging on the rope, listening to the tolling from above. He has been, in the first place, a very good educator.

But the deep problem for building a climate movement has always gone beyond mere recognition to what the sociologists call "agency"— the sense that the problem is so very large, and we are so very small, that nothing we can do will matter. That leads even people of very good heart to move on to other small problems that do seem soluble. But the exercises in this book will help one group after another recognize that they can indeed make a difference, and that they must. People of faith have been a crucial part of social change from America's beginnings, and we must stand up here—or, sometimes, sit down in front of pipelines and frack wells. Church can be behind bars.

What we can't do is slow down, not even in the blighted age of Trump. And Jim's never-ending witness is the best incitement to optimism that I can imagine. At first he was a voice crying in the wilderness, but now everyone right up to Pope Francis has begun to sing from the same hymnal. The world owes him a mighty thanks.

PREFACE

These pages are a guide for people of faith. We need to make God's hope our own as we respond to "the long emergency" known as the climate crisis. This book is founded on scripture: so many biblical passages make clear that God regards creation as good. It is informed by science, which tells us that in only a few generations, humans have severely upset the balance of life. And it offers a way forward for people of faith—individually and in our lives together—to repurpose the church and inspire humanity to engage a new moral era.

This is a book about vocation. It seeks to unpack "the great work" God is calling our generation to undertake. Individuals will find in these pages suggestions for how they can respond to God's call through new forms of witness and discipleship. I hope this book will prompt faith communities to listen carefully to how God may be calling their congregation to embrace a new vocation.

We follow God's call because we are inspired—filled with the Holy Spirit. The science conveyed in these pages makes it clear that God's call to our generation is not at all easy. But none of us are alone as we face this peril. Just as the church was born when the disciples were all together in one place, we will discern new directions by coming together in prayer and conversation. By reading this book with others, we stand ready for the Holy Spirit to open our minds and hearts to receive God's call.

Many pastors find preaching on climate change to be enormously challenging. In addition to devoting an entire chapter to our call to preach on climate change, the appendix offers a collection of over fifty preaching suggestions that are organized by the chapters from which they emerge.

Our task is to embrace our generation's challenge as a Kairos moment. God's helping presence is everywhere, and at every turning point. The gifts of the Holy Spirit empower us to accomplish more than we could ask or imagine. As urgent as our crisis is, God offers us the courage we need to address the greatest moral challenge humanity has ever faced. With God's help, we can do this, together.

ACKNOWLEDGMENTS

My father and older brother, an engineer and a scientist, found a way to devote their lives to science while retaining wonder, awe, and adoration. Their insight and questions accompanied me in writing these pages. For over fifty years, my stepmom Charlotte has lived a life of resilience, positivity, and gratitude amidst the toughest of life's challenges. Her ninety-six years illustrate so many of the qualities essential for our future. Living into that future are our sons, Luke and Mark. Always supportive of my work, their bold, courageous, and truthful feedback has given me both pause and encouragement.

At Princeton and Yale, Gene Outka and Margaret Farley welcomed my passion for environmental ethics before it was a field of study. Henri Nouwen showed me how to integrate spirituality and activism, while Bill Coffin stood as a model for my emerging call. More recently, Mary Evelyn Tucker and John Grim have inspired me (and countless others) as they examine the most important questions of our generation.

The United Church of Christ has provided boundless support for God's call in my life. For more than a decade, the Board of Directors of the Massachusetts Conference UCC has encouraged my vocation and this book, as have my staff colleagues. John Dorhauer, General Minister and President of the UCC, has added his creative and visionary gifts to several initiatives described in these pages. Our friendship has given me courage to take risks on behalf of the Gospel. In 2013 the organizers of the Craigville Colloquy honored me by asking me to prepare four lectures for their annual theological gathering. Feedback from that opportunity gave me the confidence to write this book. Cameron Trimble, Brian McLaren, and Alice Hunt have all provided invaluable encouragement along the way.

When the finish line was not yet in sight, a prescription written in 2013 by my physician, Dr. John Goodson, kept me going. He told me to "Go up to the mountain and bring back instructions for the church and humanity." That's also when I was blessed to meet Naomi Oreskes, whose friendship I now cherish and whose fierce resolve and uncompromising integrity give me courage and hope. I am indebted to both Karen Richardson Dunn and Margaret Bullitt-Jonas for their suggestions as they poured over earlier drafts, and for our partnership in this calling.

Amidst the flood of frightening scientific findings, the inadequacy of political resolve, and the machinery of denial, Bill McKibben's vision, voice, and embrace of his vocation have reminded me that the horizon of God's hope is beyond what any of us now see. I'm also grateful to Bill for introducing me to Gus Speth. Jail proved to be the perfect place to initiate a deep friendship with this gentle soul whose unconstrained vision helps me see new possibilities on even the darkest of days.

Over our thirty-five years of marriage, Cindy Shannon has been much more than the love of my life. Long before we outlined this book together, she spent countless hours improving my sermons and showing me more faith-filled approaches. Sharing her insights as a theologian and teacher, she has been a full partner in shaping this book. Its best parts come from our collaboration and her editorial suggestions. The public life and witness I have led would not have been possible without her affirmation, sacrifice, and support.

INTRODUCTION

More science and more technology are not going to get us out of the present ecological crisis until we find a new religion, or rethink our old one.[1]
—Lynn White

The world—each fragment as well as the whole—is a window into the love of God. Every moment we are given provides an opportunity to appreciate the gift of the world that God so loves. As God's children, we are entrusted with the responsibility to protect God's creation.

This book is for people of faith. I've written it for Christians, but I believe people of any faith perspective—as well as seekers and searchers—will find value in these pages. Likewise, I write as an American Christian, but the considerations of this book are not limited to an American audience.

This book focuses on why and how the church can address the present climate crisis. It seeks to invite people of faith—together with their faith communities—to accept that God has called us to bear witness in a time such as this—a time when the continuity of God's creation is in jeopardy. I suggest that the enormity of this moral crisis constitutes a theological emergency. To resolve this emergency, God is calling the church to initiate a moral intervention. As the church engages this calling, it will undergo what Brian McLaren calls a spiritual migration.[2] By repurposing our current social and economic systems, the church will prompt humanity to transition to a new moral era that honors and sustains God's gift of creation. Our current situation requires us to embrace what for many of us may be new forms of faithfulness, discipleship, worship, preaching, testimony, witness, and even hope. These pages show how people of faith and faith communities can embrace new opportunities that will inspire humanity to make the changes science says we must in order to preserve and protect God's gift of creation.

One of the bedrock recognitions that must be embraced by the thousands of human tribes is that we're all in this together, and that climate change intensifies every system of injustice, discrimination, and disadvantage. Near the conclusion of his profoundly moving letter to his son, Ta-Nehisi Coates laments this reality.

> This is not a belief in prophecy but in the seductiveness of cheap gasoline. Once, the Dream's parameters were caged by technology and by the limits of horsepower and wind. But the Dreamers have improved themselves, and the damming of seas for voltage, the extraction of coal, the transmuting of oil into food, have enabled an expansion in plunder with no known precedent. And this revolution has freed the Dreamers to plunder not just the bodies of humans but the body of Earth itself. The Earth is not our creation. It has no respect for us. It has no use for us. And its vengeance is not the fire in the cities but the fire in the sky.[3]

To reduce that vengeance, humanity must live into a new moral era.

Three commentaries that illustrate what that new moral era might require provide the frame for this book. The first is a resolution passed by United Church of Christ National Synod in July 2017 which sets out several imperatives for a new moral era. You can find it below.

The second commentary is an interlude between chapters 2 and 3. It takes the form of a letter from a pastor to her congregation written on Ash Wednesday 2070 on the occasion of the closing of the church. The church had been serving a city located on the eastern seaboard of the United States since the church's founding in the seventeenth century. Should humanity fail to engage a new moral era, this letter anticipates how a particular church might close its doors.

The third commentary is the epilogue. It takes the form of a speech given by a teenager to a gathering of the World Council of Churches in the year 2100. She is expressing her profound gratitude for her forebears in the faith who had the courage, imagination, and fortitude to initiate a new moral era that inhibited the worse consequences of climate change, and gave hope and promise to her generation.

I believe that people of faith the world over have the capacity to determine the trajectory of our common future. Here in America, if Christianity continues to emphasize personal salvation while ignoring collective salvation, if we continue to reduce the Creator to an anthropocentric projection who privileges and protects humanity, however alienated we may be from God's created order, then the practice of religion will continue to diminish and it will add little to the redemption of creation.

In contrast to that, when the delegates to the United Church of Christ Synod gathered in July 2017, they were confronted with two big asks. The first: to "resist all expansion of fossil fuel infrastructure and demand new sources of renewable energy that are accessible to all communities." The second: to write a new story for America—"a story that is not dependent on fossil fuel or on wealth for the few and misery for the many."

On July 3, 2017, the national Synod of the UCC voted not only to declare a new moral era but to name the current climate crisis as "an opportunity for which the church was born." The 700 delegates were voting on an Emergency Resolution responding to President Trump's announcement on June 1, 2017, that the United States would withdraw from the Paris Climate Accord. In less than a month, the resolution had been endorsed by almost half of the regional Conferences of the UCC, so it was not surprising that it passed the national gathering by 97 percent.

However, many will be surprised by the three moral imperatives named in the resolution.

Urging clergy to preach on climate change is the first moral imperative. As ecoAmerica has shown in poll after poll, clergy are regarded by their congregations as trusted messengers, and when they speak out, it matters.[4] God's creation is in jeopardy. The resolution declares that "those who follow Jesus will not back away from God's call to protect our common home." It is up to clergy to provide moral leadership so that church can be a safe enough place for people to share their deepest fears and hopes and then take action.

The second moral imperative—to "incarnate the changes we long for"—echoes one of Gandhi's well-known principles: we need to "be the change we long to see." But it calls for more than personal witness. It recognizes what (at least) 292 mayors representing more than 60 million Americans also recognize[5]—that the units of resilience going forward are towns and cities. When tens of thousands of congregations stand with their community leaders, committed to transition to a safe and sustainable future for their children, the church will reintroduce hope to a world gripped by fear and despair.

In keeping with the decades-long opposition by the UCC to environmental racism,[6] the resolution calls upon congregations and people of faith to undo "the disproportionate impact of climate change on communities of color, indigenous communities, and poor white communities around the world, even as we commit to hold all our religious, political, corporate, and global leaders accountable to do the same."

Truth is the focus of the third moral imperative—noting that we are now living in a John 18:37 moment. ("Pilate asked him, 'So you are a king?' Jesus answered, 'You say that I am a king. For this I was born, and for this I came into the world, to testify to the truth. Everyone who belongs to the truth listens to my voice.'" [NRSV]) The UCC believes that the role of the church in the public square is to provide a bold and courageous witness that fearlessly holds to the truth "we understand from our two Testaments and from the sacred book of nature, recognizing that when truth is compromised, only power prevails."

UCC congregations and members are urged "to resist all expansion of fossil fuel infrastructure and demand new sources of renewable energy that are accessible to all communities." How? "In the streets, at the State House, in the halls of power, with our phones, emails, technology and social media by committing our time, financial resources and prayers."

In essence, this resolution calls for the church to embrace a new vocation. Hours after President Trump announced that the United States would pull out of the Paris Climate Accord, the General Minister and President of the UCC asked me to write a resolution. Since this resolution represents a condensed version of the pages that follow, I offer it as a close to this introduction.

THE EARTH IS THE LORD'S, NOT OURS TO WRECK: IMPERATIVES FOR A NEW MORAL ERA

A Resolution of Witness Passed by United Church of Christ National Synod on July 3, 2017

SUMMARY

God's great gift of Creation—the context in which all life seeks fulfillment—is in crisis. Driven by material aspiration, humanity's use of fossil fuel since the Industrial Revolution has broken Creation's balance. The scale of Creation's demise is dramatically expanding beyond our comprehension. Never has the earth and the climate changed so quickly. While the leaders of every country in the world recognize this reality, our current Administration ignores science, defunds the Environmental Protection Agency, and withdraws from the Paris Climate Accord. As people of faith, recognizing that the earth is the Lord's, it falls upon our generation to embrace the imperatives set forth in this resolution—imperatives that constitute a new moral era. We view the current climate crisis as an opportunity for which the church was born.

BIBLICAL, THEOLOGICAL, AND ETHICAL RATIONALE
Psalm 24:1
The earth is the LORD's and all that is in it, the world, and those who live in it;
John 18:37–38
[37] Pilate asked him, "So you are a king?" Jesus answered, "You say that I am a king. For this I was born, and for this I came into the world, to testify to the truth. Everyone who belongs to the truth listens to my voice." [38] Pilate asked him, "What is truth?" After he had said this, he went out to the Jews again and told them, "I find no case against him."

TEXT OF THE MOTION

WHEREAS the leaders of over 190 countries have signed the Paris Climate Accord, acknowledging the critical role every country must play if the life-sustaining climate of the earth is to continue to sustain life as we have always known it;

WHEREAS the mayors of thirty American cities, the governors of numerous states, and leaders of hundreds of American companies have publicly committed the institutions they lead to reducing greenhouse gas emissions in compliance with the Paris Climate Accord;

WHEREAS, over the past fifty years, the UCC along with religious leaders from other faiths and denominations has issued countless statements on the goodness of Creation and our call to act as responsible stewards, all of which has been an insufficient witness;

WHEREAS the Core Purpose of the United Church of Christ states (in part): "we serve God in the co-creation of a just and sustainable world as made manifest in the Gospel of Jesus Christ";

WHEREAS this historic moment provides Christian communities with a powerful opportunity to bear witness to the sacredness of God's Creation and the urgent call to preserve it, and responding to this call expresses the new mission initiative of the UCC known as the Three Great Loves,[7] one of which is love of Creation;

THEREFORE, BE IT RESOLVED that the Thirty-first General Synod of the United Church of Christ raises its prophetic voice regarding the urgency of healing the climate of the earth, our home and God's gift for the future of all life, both human and all other life;

BE IT FURTHER RESOLVED that the Thirty-first General Synod of the United Church of Christ calls upon the whole of the church to prayerfully engage the following imperatives as we seek to initiate a new moral era:

Let our clergy accept the mantle of moral leadership

Now is the time for clergy to speak from their pulpits about the moral obligation of our generation to protect God's Creation. Let the world know that whatever the current American administration may say or do, we who follow Jesus will not back away from God's call to protect our common home. When the powers that be deny or obscure the truth, we followers of Jesus will proclaim the truth to protect our common home.

Let all of us incarnate the changes we long for

Now is the time for congregations and for every person of faith to set a moral example through our own words and actions. As individuals and as communities, let us commit to making decisions of integrity in our energy choices, undoing the disproportionate impact of climate change on communities of color, indigenous communities, and poor white communities around the world even as we commit to hold all our religious, political, corporate, and global leaders accountable to do the same.

Let us proclaim truth in the public square

We are now living in a John 18:37 moment in which we must hold to the truth we understand from our two Testaments and from the sacred book of nature, recognizing that when truth is compromised, only power prevails.

- Let our communities of faith be bold and courageous as we address one of the greatest moral challenges that the world has ever faced.
- Let us commit to resist all expansion of fossil fuel infrastructure and demand new sources of renewable energy that are accessible to all communities.
- Let us do all we can to change America's understanding of the story that our generation is writing. Let us begin a new story—a story that is not dependent on fossil fuel or on wealth for the few and misery for the many.

Accepting that it is up to us—we the people—whether in the streets, at the State House, in the halls of power; with our phones, emails, technology, and social media; by committing our time, financial resources, and prayers—let us pour ourselves out to bend the moral arc of justice, with joy in our hearts, beauty in our sights, and hope for the children.

QUESTIONS FOR GROUP DISCUSSION AND FURTHER REFLECTION

1. What other examples of crises can you think of that might be called "theological emergencies"?
2. Reread the quotation from Ta-Nehisi Coates. Discuss the parallels between plundering the bodies of humans and plundering the body of the Earth itself.

3. Name some examples of "the disproportionate impact of climate change on communities of color, indigenous communities, and poor white communities around the world."

4. Go to http://www.greenfaith.org and click on "Religious Teachings | Christian Statements on the Environment." Review and discuss the many statements linked to this site. How do they compare to the "Emergency Resolution" in this introduction?

I

THE SITUATION IN WHICH
WE FIND OURSELVES

I used to think that if we threw enough good science at the environmental problems, we could solve them. I was wrong. The main
threats to the environment are not biodiversity loss, pollution, and
climate change, as I once thought. They are selfishness and greed
and pride. And for that we need a spiritual and cultural transformation.
—James "Gus" Speth[1]

It was a preposterous idea. Imagine 350 churches each ringing their
steeple bell 350 times as a way of "sounding the alarm" that CO_2 in the
atmosphere was way over the safe limit of 350 parts per million (ppm).[2]

In June 2008, I invited each of the 400 UCC churches in Massachusetts to consider becoming a sentinel for their community.[3] Just as God
made Ezekiel to be a sentinel for the house of Israel (Ezekiel 33:7), I
suggested that God was calling the church to warn their communities of
the threat of climate change, and to lead their communities to respond.

We launched this initiative in support of the new climate activist
group 350.org, whose initial goal was to make 350 the most recognized
number on Earth. Over the next few months, many of us wore buttons
saying, "Ask me what 350 rings sounds like." Several local newspapers
covered the 40 or so churches that participated, although we fell far
short of our goal of 350 churches ringing their steeple bells.

What we told the reporters, as well as our curious and sometimes
disturbed neighbors, was that one of the reasons churches have steeples

with bells is to warn the community in case of an emergency. We wanted our communities to recognize that climate change represents the greatest moral crisis humanity has ever faced—a moral emergency of unprecedented proportions.

Why did relatively few churches accept this invitation to bear witness to their community? Of course, there were countless reasons. Perhaps first among them was this: most churches don't like change. The Sunday morning routines connect people with the timeless truths of their faith. The familiarity of the order of worship, the hymnal, where people sit, the rituals, rites, and prayers all provide comfort. Amidst an ever-changing world, church offers consistency that people can count on.

Because of this, not every church was ready to proclaim to their community that the world into which we had all been born was changing in profound, fundamental ways—and that we ourselves were responsible for these changes.

Since 2008, discussion of climate change has been drenched in disputation, denial, and despair. Also since 2008, many, many churches have embraced their calling as followers of Christ and communities of faith to be bold and courageous in proclaiming truth in the public square. This chapter—and this entire book—is a response to that calling.

WHAT HAVE WE DONE?

In the mid-1970s, my friend Mark and I ventured into the backcountry of Glacier National Park. About a week into our ten-day adventure, following the advice of a ranger, we went off trail and over a divide. From the top, we could see a storm brewing. We needed to get down in a hurry. But between us and the trail below was about 1,500 vertical feet of ice and snow on a 45-degree slope. After we had kick-stepped our way out about 200 feet, my friend Mark took off his backpack and unhitched his dense foam sleeping pad. Signalling the point of no return, he let his backpack slide down the snow and ice. We watched it pick up speed and then go airborne, tumbling and turning over and over again until it finally stopped about 1,000 yards from us. Watching that pack tumble was terrifying. Then Mark said, "Wish me luck!" Sitting on his foam pad, down he went. Fortunately, he didn't tumble. Then it was my turn—but I was frozen with fear. I lost myself for several minutes, staring at the glacier less than a mile away. Finally, I followed my friend's lead. Fortunately, I too went down safely—and we dodged the impending storm.

Since that eventful hike, my family and I have returned several times to Glacier National Park, and I hope to take our grandchildren there when they're old enough. But the snow and ice fall that helped us to safety—as well as the glacier—are now gone. In 1910, when Glacier National Park was founded, there were over 150 glaciers. As of 2016 there are 39, and over the past 50 years those glaciers have lost more than one-third of their ice.[4] Some experts suggest that by 2030, when I hope to take my grandchildren to Glacier National Park, there will be none.

Further north, there is still more change. Last Christmas (2016) the North Pole was above freezing—that's 50°F above "normal." The month before that, global sea ice was 25 percent below the median of the last 35 years.[5]

These excessively high temperatures are not limited to the far north. Throughout the United States, record high temperatures are outrunning record lows 20:1. These persistent high temperatures are wreaking havoc with our forests. Fire season is now seventy-eight days longer than it used to be,[6] and drought-related fires are breaking out in unexpected places like northern Georgia, North Carolina, and Israel.

The temperatures would be a lot hotter were it not for the oceans.[7] Oceans absorb over 90 percent of the heat created by global warming. As they absorb CO_2, the oceans are becoming more acidic at a frightening rate in excess of any change the world has seen in 300 million years.[8] The die-off of coral reefs is our canary in the coal mine. As the ocean acidifies, it becomes difficult for oysters and clams to build their shells. Fish have trouble breathing and the entire food chain of the oceans is being disrupted.[9]

As the oceans heat up, the water expands, ice caps melt, and sea level rises. The *New York Times* (4/19/2017) reports that parts of Washington, DC, now experience flooding thirty days a year, a figure that has roughly quadrupled since 1960. In Wilmington, North Carolina, the number is ninety days. It's hard to imagine, but some scientists and city planners call this "nuisance flooding." Not so in Louisiana, where the state's Coastal Protection and Restoration Authority provided a new Coastal Master Plan for 2017.[10] What had been the worst-case scenario for human-caused sea level rise in their 2012 plan is now their best-case scenario. On a larger scale, the Earth's temperature is already well into the range that existed during the Eemian period, 120,000 years ago, when sea level was twenty to thirty feet higher than it is now.[11] David Wallace-Wells reports that most scientists expect that within this century, sea level rise will overcome both Miami and Bangladesh.[12] Serious flooding will occur elsewhere as well. Nearly 500 US cities and towns, including 40 percent of oceanfront communities along the East Coast and the Gulf, could be "chronically inundated" by sea level rise by 2100, according to a report released by the Union of Concerned Scientists in July 2017.[13]

Fighting hunger has been a focus of the church since the first century, and thank God for the food banks that thousands of churches across the land provide for their communities! A photo of a hungry child motivates people to take action. Of course, if we had tried to take in the suffering portrayed in photos of 1.4 million hungry children and 20 million starving people around the world, we would be overwhelmed. In an extraordinary article focusing on Africa, professor Michael Klare writes, "Not since World War II have more human beings been at risk from disease and starvation than at this very moment."[14] Klare shows how climate change is primarily responsible for droughts as well as an increase in armed conflict, and that the people most affected are the poor, the marginalized, and those in countries already at or near the edge.

More than anywhere else in the world, the people in Africa live off the land. But climate change is increasingly rendering areas in Africa uninhabitable.[15]

Animals too are in trouble. In a few decades, children won't recognize many of the animals we today depict as going into Noah's Ark. That's because they will be extinct. The author of a 2017 study in the Proceedings of the National Academy of Sciences calls it "biological annihilation" and says, "It wouldn't be ethical right now not to speak in this strong language to call attention to the severity of the problem."[16] We are also experiencing the sixth mass extinction. Currently, species are going extinct at a rate at least one hundred times normal. Habitat destruction (for example, cutting down forests for agriculture) and pollution are the primary causes—and both are exacerbated by climate change.

All this is a tiny sampling of the ways in which our common home (as Pope Francis calls planet Earth) has changed over just a few decades. These changes prompted Bill McKibben to title his 2010 book *Eaarth*—deliberately misspelled—to signal that we have changed the planet so significantly that it has become a different planet.[17] (For a few years I included the word "Eaarth" in the title of my sermons, hoping to get people's attention. More often than not, the spellchecker would "normalize" this spelling, which made for an even more effective introduction to the sermon!) The first chapter of McKibben's book is so painful to read that it is hard to get through. In his 2015 book *Unprecedented*, theologian David Ray Griffin provides an even more detailed and updated account of the changes we have wrought on our planet and the risks that we are facing.[18]

Because the pace of change is accelerating, and science is improving, every few years someone will write a new account of the profound ways our common home is changing. Each of us needs to find a way, as upsetting as this material is, to stay up to date. I was encouraged to learn that five days after *New York Magazine* published David Wallace-Wells article "The Uninhabitable Earth," 2.5 million people had downloaded it, making it the most-read article in *New York Magazine*'s history. I was equally encouraged by the robust discussion of the article in various op-eds and by the responses from scientists and the Sierra Club (among others). Clearly, millions of people want to face the facts, and for many of us, that includes taking responsibility.

TAKING RESPONSIBILITY—THE ANTHROPOCENE

One of the most important roles of the church is to take responsibility for what it has done, and to help people to take responsibility for what they have done individually and collectively. My friend, Naomi Oreskes, professor of the history of science and affiliated professor of earth and planetary sciences at Harvard, understands what it means to take responsibility. In 2004, she published an article summarizing the scientific consensus on climate change. The shorthand version is this: climate change is happening, it's human caused, and it's getting worse.[19] Since then, she and others—including the World Bank—describe the scientific consensus as "unequivocal."[20] For example, between November 2012 and December 2013, only one of 9,137 peer-reviewed papers on climate change rejected human causation.[21]

The changes I have described—and dozens more I could mention—are of a scale we can barely comprehend. Once the Industrial Era began, it took us only two hundred years to upend millions of years of nature's balance. Never have the Earth and the climate changed so quickly. In fact, the scientists who oversee geologic time are on the verge of officially declaring that we have entered a new geologic epoch that they call the Anthropocene.[22] The Industrial Era, fueled by the unconstrained use of fossil fuel, qualifies as a planetary "event" on the same scale as the meteorite that hit the Earth 66 million years ago, wiping out the dinosaurs, ending the Cretaceous period and with it, the entire Mesozoic era.

One thing more. David Wallace-Wells reports that "more than half of the carbon humanity has exhaled into the atmosphere in its entire history has been emitted in just the past three decades; since the end of World War II, the figure is 85 percent."[23]

HOW LONG HAVE WE KNOWN?

Climate science began in the 1850s when John Tyndall first suggested that the emission of CO_2 could create a greenhouse effect—trapping the sun's energy and heating up the Earth's climate.[24] In 1938, Guy Stewart Callendar demonstrated that global land temperatures had increased over the previous fifty years.[25]

Over fifty years ago (November 5, 1965) scientists warned then president Lyndon Johnson of the risks associated with the buildup of CO_2 in the atmosphere.[26] In 1975 one of those scientists, Wallace S. Broecker, published a paper titled "Climatic Change: Are We on the Brink of a Pronounced Global Warming?"[27] The fifty-year projections he offered in that paper have proven to be remarkably accurate.

In June 1988, climate scientist James Hansen testified before the United States Senate Committee on Energy and Natural Resources. His testimony caught the attention of a young writer whose life was increasingly focused on social justice. In 1989, Bill McKibben published *The End of Nature*, the first book for a general audience about climate change.

ARE WE PAYING ATTENTION?

Let's face it: we can only change what we pay attention to. Has climate change gotten our attention? As it turns out, neuroscientists tell us that our brains are not suited to respond appropriately to long-term threats such as climate change. When we see an immediate threat, such as an innocuous garter snake crossing our path, our brain screams: YIKES!! But when we read that the United Nations has issued a new and scary report about the effects of global warming several decades from now, we y-a-w-n, and turn to the sports page.[28]

Andrew Revkin, former environmental reporter for the *New York Times*, puts it this way: "Climate change . . . violates all the norms of the kinds of things that we actually do pay attention to, which are usually near and now."[29]

In his comprehensive tour de force *What We Think About When We Try Not to Think About Global Warming*, Per Espen Stoknes ponders why the facts about climate change fail to compel appropriate action.[30] He identifies five psychological barriers to climate action, which he refers to as the five Ds: Distance, Doom, Dissonance, Denial, iDentity. Stoknes' suggestions regarding how to move through these barriers are well worth reading. In what follows, I want to examine more closely the barrier of denial.

George Marshall says it best. "The bottom line is that we do not accept climate change because we wish to avoid the anxiety it generates and the deep changes it requires."[31] Thus, denial is a form of self-defense. Rather than subject ourselves to fear and disruption, we align ourselves with others who share our position that nothing is wrong. We concentrate on holding to that position and ignore our strong instincts to defend the interests of our progeny. If a political leader confirms our position, we become a follower, because identifying with his or her position serves as a salve to cover over our underlying anxiety about the future.

This approach works for lots of people—including many who come to church every Sunday. By never discussing climate change, many churches allow denial to continue, unexamined.[32] Of course, we could pioneer a different path, and we'll get to that soon enough.

Even socially active congregations are not immune to denial. A few years ago, after I preached on climate change, dozens of parishioners wanted to engage me in conversation. About seventy of us crammed into an upper room for a stimulating exchange. Because these were knowledgeable, informed, and engaged individuals, I decided to take a risk. Knowing that they would soon be embarking on a very large capital campaign, much of which would address numerous deferred mainte- nance issues in their building, I asked a painful question. "I think it's great that you're about to raise millions of dollars to address this build- ing's deferred maintenance needs, and I'm completely confident your campaign will succeed. But what does it mean that everything we know about the impact of climate change in this area suggests that in thirty years or so, your church will be under several feet of water?" After a long, awkward silence, a few people mustered the courage to share that of course they were aware of this, but somehow, life had to go on. And with an exasperated sigh, someone confessed what we all knew: that most of us, most of the time, compartmentalize such long-term risks as climate change. Doing so is what allows us to get on with our lives. I left that conversation with enormous admiration for that congregation and since then, their leadership on the issue of climate change continues to be substantial.

Denial takes other forms. Given that most of the change brought about by climate change is gradual, my grandchildren will grow up thinking it's normal when "rain bombs" bring a "once-in-a-hundred- years storm" every few years. Hurricane Harvey inundated Houston with its third once-in-500-years flood in three years. Young people in Beijing think it's normal to wear dust masks. Peter Kahn, a professor of psychology at the University of Washington, refers to this as "environ- mental generational amnesia." (See Jon Mooallem's *New York Times* article: "Our Climate Future Is Actually Our Climate Present," April 19, 2017.) Two-thirds of the children growing up in impoverished areas like those near Houston's oil refineries understand that air and water pollution are environmental issues. But only one-third of those children believe that their neighborhood is polluted. (That may change after Hurricane Harvey.) If we are to resist accepting deprivation as normal, we must develop discipline and surround ourselves with like-minded, hope-filled companions. Or to put it another way: nothing shouts "interdependence" like climate change!

The denial of science is a relatively recent phenomenon. There was a time—not too long ago—when Americans marveled at science. Perhaps our admiration of science began with what some regarded as the "triumph" of the super-secret science initiative known as the Manhattan Project. A few years later, we couldn't get enough of the Mercury, Gemini, and Apollo space programs. Jacques Cousteau brought the wonder of the oceans into every living room. Twenty million Americans (10 percent of the population) participated in the first Earth Day in 1970. Carl Sagan's *Cosmos* (1980)—one of the most popular television programs ever produced—may have marked the height of that era. And mainstream Christians have long celebrated science and scientific achievement. In 2008, the UCC issued "A Pastoral Letter on Faith Engaging Science and Technology" that affirmed that "one of God's most provocative voices is science. We listen and respond, grateful that our theology is enriched by new ideas."[33]

Yet while Sagan was busy making *Cosmos*, the Love Canal disaster unfolded (1978)—giving rise to the creation of a federal Superfund (1980). Reporters Michael Brown and David Shribman together with courageous moms Karen Schroeder and Lois Gibbs used science to expose corporate culpability: an elementary school built atop twenty-one tons of toxic waste.

Meanwhile, during this *same* period of time, some of the most successful corporations in the history of money were beginning to tremble in fear. State after state had passed anti-smoking legislation. As a result, in 1979, the tobacco industry decided to declare a "war on science." No—that overstates it. As professor Naomi Oreskes outlines in exquisite detail, the tobacco industry decided to sow the seeds of doubt in the public mind and in our courts of law. Their two front-men repeatedly testified that the EPA's findings represented "junk science." You can read Oreskes' book *Merchants of Doubt* (or see the movie version) for more detail.

This is how America turned from championing science as a gateway to the American Dream to questioning science, distrusting scientists, and framing science as an optional "belief system"—with many Americans preferring to trust their religious faith instead of science in such matters as evolution and the origin of life.

Just as many Americans were beginning to turn against science, another fault line began to open: the issue of economic externalities. How much should tobacco companies pay for the lives taken by addiction to cancer-causing smoking? How much should chemical and mining companies pay for the lives and land decimated by their negligent practices? The same question is now being put to the most profitable industry the world has ever known: fossil fuel companies. How much should they pay to compensate for the life-destroying CO_2 that is the by-product of their activity, from which they profit immensely?[34]

In May 2015, Oreskes testified before Congress. The House Committee on Natural Resources heard her testimony; they also responded. Republican members of the committee denounced a wide range of scientific investigations related to the enforcement of existing environmental laws as being so-called "government science." What they meant by that derogatory term was that, by definition, such science was corrupt, politically driven, and lacking in accountability. The particular science under attack involved work done by—or on behalf of—federal agencies like the National Park Service, but climate science also came in for its share of insults.[35]

Since then, science denial at a level previously unseen in the administration of any country has taken hold in Washington, DC. Not only has the White House announced that the United States will withdraw from the Paris Climate Accord, it has also reassigned many of the best scientists working for the Environmental Protection Agency to positions as accountants and the like. EPA administrator Scott Pruitt is teaming up with energy secretary Rick Perry to formally challenge the scientific consensus that human activity is warming the planet—a consensus recognized across multiple presidencies, including Barack Obama's, Bill Clinton's, and George W. Bush's. Abandoning the normal peer review process, they suggest instead that a "red team" should write a critique of the scientific consensus, followed by a "blue team" that writes a rebuttal to that critique. The public would listen in on this political "debate" and then a commission would evaluate the exchange and write it up.[36]

It's important to note that we are the only major country whose leadership expresses this level of science denial. Why is that? First of all, for many of our most prominent global warming deniers, religion serves to reinforce their views. Senator James Inhofe (R-OK) is well known for his belief that global warming is a hoax. In an interview, he quoted Genesis 8:22: "as long as the Earth remains, there will be seed-time and harvest, cold and heat, winter and summer, day and night." Then he continued, "My point is, God's still up there. The arrogance of people to think that we, human beings, would be able to change what He (God) is doing in the climate is to me outrageous."[37]

Inhofe is not alone. In addition to dozens in Congress who share his views, Rush Limbaugh is doing his best to drive public opinion.[38] In August 2013, he declared: "See, in my humble opinion, folks, if you believe in God, then intellectually you cannot believe in manmade global warming . . . You must be either agnostic or atheistic to believe that man controls something that he can't create."

What's more, media shapes what we pay attention to. For years, the media treated climate change like a typical news story in which opposing views help illuminate the facts.[39] For example, if a species goes extinct or if a chunk of ice the size of the state of Connecticut breaks off from the Antarctic—these make the news. And if a single "scientist" who has no credentials as a climatologist questions the cause of these events or criticizes the latest United Nations report—a consensus document representing the views of almost 2,000 climate scientists—many media will give that so-called "scientist" equal coverage, and will forget to ask who funds that "scientist's" research.

In fact, according to a January 2013 *MediaMatters* report,[40] not a single climate scientist appeared as a guest on the influential Sunday morning television talk shows during the preceding four years, nor were any climate scientists quoted. Most of those invited to speak on global warming were either media figures or politicians, and, among the politicians, not a single one was a Democrat. Climate change deniers on the shows went unchallenged.

It's also important to consider what the media has not covered. Over the past fifteen years or so, as the science improved, as the scientific consensus has been clearly established, and as scientists' predictions have become increasingly dire, the media has yet to recognize, as one commentator puts it, that "Climate change isn't the news and it isn't a set of news stories. It's the prospective end of all news." Or, to borrow a phrase from the late Jonathan Schell, climate change is "anti-news."[41]

Just to be clear, all of that has nothing to do with "fake news." "Fake news" provides anyone inclined to deny climate change with exactly the support they seek. But here's the thing: even without the separate issue of "fake news" and deliberately falsified facts, the fossil fuel industry has too often gamed the mainstream news media by preying on their eagerness for "balanced news" that represents "both sides." *Mother Jones Magazine* (July 2017)[42] offers an impressive timeline—beginning in the 1990s—that summarizes scores of mainstream news media stories filled with climate misinformation.

WHAT'S AT STAKE? HOW URGENT IS THE CRISIS?

Imagine: since your childhood, you have suffered from asthma. You've learned to be disciplined about carrying an inhaler because your life depends on it. You might misplace your keys or your wallet—but you always know where you put your inhaler. Then, one day, your normal routine is interrupted—a friend you haven't seen in ages comes by unexpectedly, and the two of you rush out the door and head to a restaurant where you engage in a great conversation. And then you have an asthma attack—and in a panic, you realize that you left your inhaler at home.

What's at stake? How urgent is the crisis?

In 2015, I had barely ever heard of the island of Tuvalu. But when cyclones ravaged the tiny South Pacific nation, US churches were quick to respond to the crisis, providing emergency relief. As with the earthquake in Haiti and the tsunamis in the South Pacific, churches recognize an urgent, catastrophic crisis—even when it's halfway around the world—and churches respond generously.

In 2017, I had a chance to hear firsthand another story about Tuvalu. The leader of the Congregational Christian Church of Tuvalu, the Rev. Tafue Lusama, came to the United States to engage the national gatherings of both the United Church of Christ and the Christian Church (Disciples of Christ). It shouldn't be surprising that I found Tafue to be the most knowledgeable minister I had ever met on the science of climate change. After all, his country will be uninhabitable and underwater in only a few years.[43]

What's at stake? How urgent is the crisis?

It's urgent when an elite group of admirals and generals describe climate change as a "threat multiplier" and as a "catalyst for conflict" in a world with increasingly decentralized power structures. And it sure sounds urgent when the Center for Naval Analyses (CNA) Military Advisory Board (MAB) studies pressing issues of the day to assess their impact on America's national security. The introduction to their 2014 report on national security and climate change states "that climate change is no longer a future threat—it is taking place now."[44]

What's at stake? How urgent is the crisis?

For two hundred years, City Mission has been responding to the hardships facing residents of Boston. Since its inception, City Mission has helped the churches of metropolitan Boston engage God's call to overcome whatever social justice issue may be debilitating the lives of God's children. It has served as a model for countless church-affiliated social service agencies across the country.

Over the past decade, City Mission and hundreds of other social service agencies like them have realized that climate change is already amplifying every issue of social justice. As early as the 1980s, leaders of the United Church of Christ were connecting environmental concerns with issues of social justice—with a specific focus on environmental racism.[45] Pick a justice issue—hunger; homelessness; racism; immigration and refugees; conflicts and war; access to potable water; Israel/Palestine; health care; affordable housing; economic inequality—all of these injustices and more are made worse by climate change.[46]

One thing more: the people already suffering the most from climate change are those who did the least to cause it, and who have the fewest resources to deal with it.

What's at stake? How urgent is the crisis?

We must contend with the fact—as Adam Smith, the founder of classical free market economic theory, suggested in 1759—that while a person may be concerned if a hundred million people half a world away lose their lives in an earthquake, if that same person accidently cuts off his little finger, it will command his attention for God knows how long.[47]

We find ourselves born into a time when human activity and aspiration—if they simply continue without profound repurposing—will sentence our children to lives of struggle, not promise; skies of extreme weather, not rainbows; and landscapes of deprivation, not abundance. We know this to be true. People throughout the world have begun to see it happen and science corroborates it. Yet many cannot take in these truths. They deny the evidence that each day becomes more convincing. Some of us accept these truths, but we feel so small in comparison to the scale of the challenge.

ARE WE CHOOSING EXTINCTION?

The mathematician Brian Greene, in a 2017 interview by Krista Tippett, commented on the existential philosopher Albert Camus' book *The Myth of Sisyphus*. When Greene was young, Camus appealed to this budding scientist because he asked a number of scientific questions, such as whether there are only three dimensions. Then Camus suddenly pivoted and declared that there was only one true question worth asking—the question of suicide—the choice of whether to live or to die. As a young man, that made sense to Greene. But eventually, as he got older, his perspective changed: "I began to see things a little bit differently because, to me, the question of whether life is worth living, to me, is intimately dependent upon what life is and what reality is because ultimately your life is lived within reality."[48]

How we answer life's existential questions depends in part on how we understand reality. Scientists love reality. They also love those aspects of reality that continue to elude explanation—mysteries that give rise to conjecture. In his *New York Magazine* article, "The Uninhabitable Earth," David Wallace-Wells notes that several of the scientists he interviewed "proposed global warming as the solution to Fermi's famous paradox, which asks, If the universe is so big, then why haven't we encountered any other intelligent life in it? The answer, they suggested, is that the natural life span of a civilization may be only several thousand years, and the life span of an industrial civilization perhaps only several hundred." Carl Sagan makes this same point in his book *Cosmos*. He briefly refers to the "L-Factor" of the Drake equation. The "L-Factor" suggests that once an intelligent civilization gains the capacity for interstellar communication, at about that same time, they gain the capacity to destroy themselves.

Are we on that path? Over the past ten years, more and more frequently, climate change has been described as an existential threat. The human community is beginning to come to terms with the fact that continuing on the path of "business as usual" will lead us to extinction.

WE'RE ALL IN THIS TOGETHER

More importantly, we are beginning to recognize that just as each of us has agency which we demonstrate in the choices we make, we also have agency as a collective, all together. This was Moses' point in addressing the people of Israel in Deuteronomy 29–30. God set before them—not before this individual or that individual but before all of them together—the choice of life or death, blessing or curse. Collectively, they needed to make a decision. Would they continue to follow other gods (Deuteronomy 29:26) and thus bring about the devastation of the land God had given to God's people (Deuteronomy 29:22–23)? Or would they choose life? By choosing life, not only would they live, but so would their descendants (Deuteronomy 30:19). In this way, Moses intensifies the choice that is set before this generation: he emphasizes that what they choose will forever impact future generations (Deuteronomy 29:22; 29:29).

Fast-forward to our present crisis. The Paris Climate Accord embraces this same recognition: We're all in this together! On December 12, 2015, leaders from 196 nations adopted the agreement by consensus. However, for the agreement to take effect, fifty-five countries that produce at least 55 percent of the world's greenhouse gas emissions must ratify, accept, approve, or accede to the agreement. That threshold was crossed rapidly, on November 4, 2016, and the agreement took effect. Both China and the United States were among the countries that signed on. Four days later, the United States, the second largest greenhouse gas emitter, held an election. On June 1, 2017, the newly elected president of the United States announced his intention to withdraw the United States from the Paris Climate Accord. That withdrawal cannot take effect until November 4, 2020.

Are we all in this together?

Pope Francis and Ecumenical Patriarch Bartholomew, the spiritual leader of over 200 million Orthodox Christians worldwide, believe we must be. On September 1, 2017, they cosigned a declaration affirming "that there can be no enduring resolution to climate change unless the response is concerted and collective." They issued this first-ever joint statement on the World Day of Prayer for the Care of Creation.[49]

A few decades ago, US scientists and negotiators helped bring about the Montreal Protocol on Substances that Deplete the Ozone Layer.

After publishing a pivotal paper in June 1974, in December 1974 chemists Frank Sherwood Rowland and Mario Molina testified at a hearing before the US House of Representatives that the release of chlorofluorocarbons (CFCs) was causing the breakdown of large amounts of ozone (O_3) in the stratosphere. Since ozone prevents most of the sun's ultraviolet-B (UV-B) radiation from reaching the surface of the planet, depleting the ozone layer would lead to an increase in UV-B radiation at the surface, thus resulting in an increase in skin cancer and damage to crops and marine life.

Although their findings were attacked by the chair of the board of DuPont (who objected by asserting that the ozone depletion theory is "a science fiction tale . . . a load of rubbish . . . utter nonsense"), in 1995 they were awarded the Nobel Prize in chemistry. Despite industry criticism, they continued their research, funded by Congress through the National Academy of Sciences. In 1984, other researchers in Antarctica discovered an emerging "ozone hole." Just eighteen months later, the binding Montreal Protocol was signed. To date, 196 states and the European Union have signed the treaties, making them the first universally ratified treaties in United Nations history. Thanks to the success of these treaties, scientists now say that the ozone layer will return to 1980 levels between 2050 and 2070.[50]

Alarmed by skin cancer and more, the countries of the world, united in their recognition of scientific research, overcame the resistance of corporations and bound themselves, by international law, to drastically reduce the production and use of CFCs. Since it was agreed to in September 1987, the treaties have been reaffirmed eight times.

Kofi Annan calls the Montreal Protocol "perhaps the single most successful international agreement to date." There could be no finer proof that all the countries in the world are capable of restraining corporate profit in compliance with scientific findings that are universally accepted.

Yes, the nations of the world—all of them, including the United States—have shown that they can affirm that we are all in this together.

But the situation in which we Americans now find ourselves is strikingly different. What are we to do as citizens of the only country in which the science of climate change is so adamantly denied by our political leadership?

The answer is clear: Embrace the need for bottom-up initiatives!

One bottom-up response appeared four days after the United States announced in June 2017 that it would withdraw from the Paris Climate Accord. It took barely two months for more than 2,200 leaders from America's city halls, state houses, boardrooms, and college campuses, representing more than 127 million Americans and $6.2 trillion of the US economy, to sign the "We Are Still In" declaration—committing themselves to deliver on the promise of the Paris Agreement and America's contribution to it.[51]

Another bottom-up response comes from Bill McKibben. When asked, "What's the best thing an individual can do for the climate?" Bill responded, "Stop being an individual!"[52] Movements for social change are fueled by bottom-up engagement in which people identify with the movement and claim their collective power. Later in this book I will urge the church to recognize that scripture emphasizes collective salvation much more than it does personal salvation. You will also find background on the bottom-up movement to divest from fossil fuel companies, and you will come to understand the truth of Gandhi's observation, which can be summed up as: First they ignore you, then they ridicule you, then they fight you, and then you win.

One of the key functions of the church is to help people find meaning as they join together in pursuing a common purpose. The pages that follow are filled with suggestions for how local churches can fulfill this function as they respond to the moral emergency of climate change. As Mother Teresa reminds us: "If we have no peace, it is because we have forgotten that we belong to each other."

WE ALREADY HAVE EVERYTHING WE NEED

In his brilliant essay, "The Liturgy of Abundance, the Myth of Scarcity,"[53] Walter Brueggemann declares, "The great question now facing the church is whether our faith allows us to live in a new way." After unpacking the profound testimony to abundance found in Genesis 1, Psalm 104, Psalm 150, and Exodus, he points out, "The text shows that the power of the future is not in the hands of those who believe in scarcity and monopolize the world's resources; it is in the hands of those who trust God's abundance."

Brueggemann goes on to examine the Gospel accounts of the feeding of an enormous crowd (Matthew 14:13–21; Mark 6:30–44; Luke 9:10–17; John 6:1–14), a story in which "Jesus transforms the economy by blessing it and breaking it beyond self-interest." Brueggemann suggests that the miracle is that the people in the crowd "do not grasp, hoard, resent, or act selfishly."

In reading the story, we learn that in this moment of need—when thousands of people are suffering from hunger—Jesus felt compassion for the crowd. He suffered with them—which is what "com-passion" means. Jesus used what was available. He showed the crowd that they had a part to play in their own salvation; they needed to sit down on the Earth, to watch what he did, and to wait patiently while honoring one another. He gave thanks for what was available. He didn't ask for more. And he did this in sight of the hungry crowd, so that they could witness and participate in this expression of gratitude. Then Jesus broke the bit of food he had—a small portion of bread and fish. Surely Jesus himself was hungry, but he didn't eat. He broke the food, and gave the food to his disciples. And neither did his disciples eat. They served the hungry crowd. And everyone was filled.

The story leaves us with an unexplained mystery: How do those seven loaves and a few small fish provide enough food to fill the stomachs of thousands—with seven baskets of leftovers? However we interpret what happened, the message of the story unfolds as each person in the crowd recognizes that his or her personal prospects are bound up with what happens to everyone else. Scripture doesn't record it, but as Jesus takes the food, gives thanks, breaks the food, and gives it to the disciples, I hear the voices of person after person on the hillside declaring:

"O.K. I'm in!"

"Even though I don't understand how this is going to work, I'm in!"

"Even though I could hoard the bit of food in my own pocket, I'm in!"

"Even though I don't know 99 percent of these people, I'm in!"

"Even though I haven't eaten in thirty-six hours, I'm in!"

"Even though my spouse was expecting me to show up two hours ago, I'm in!"

"I'm in. My life depends on you. And I accept responsibility that your life depends on me."

In this time of environmental demise, and moral peril, Jesus' ministry depends on us. Humanity's challenge is no less than our call "to live in a new way," and no greater than the challenge of feeding the multitude with seven loaves and a few small fish. Let us rejoice that we have been given everything we need to meet this challenge!

FORWARD MOMENTUM

It's been ten years since I called upon 350 churches to each ring their bells 350 times—and only about 40 responded. Since then, a lot has happened—much of it encouraging. Interfaith Power and Light, GreenFaith, Creation Justice Ministries, ecoAmerica, and many other regional and national organizations are all doing excellent work to assist congregations as they engage this crisis. I am grateful for local organizations like Faith in Place as they inspire faithful people to care for the Earth. One of their programs is the George Washington Carver Garden at Trinity United Church of Christ on the south side of Chicago.[54] Trinity's entrepreneurial and inspirational leader, the Rev. Dr. Otis Moss III, understands the importance of making real the intersectionality of all justice issues.

Sometimes we learn that people are more responsive than we expect. The first Ecumenical Lenten Carbon Fast was held in 2011. Sponsored by New England Regional Environmental Ministries (NEREM), we would have been satisfied with a few hundred people receiving our daily emails containing action suggestions and reflections. But when a reporter released a story about this initiative on Religious News Service, we ended up with over six thousand participants representing every state in the union and fourteen countries.

The story of the UCC passing the Emergency Resolution in response to the US announcement of its intention to pull out from the Paris Climate Accord is told in this book's introduction. If someone had told me on May 31, 2017, that in five weeks, 97 percent of the delegates to the national UCC Synod gathering would vote to embrace preaching on climate change and resisting new fossil fuel infrastructure, I would have responded, "You're dreaming!"

The human community already has all the solutions we need to address climate change. For example, in 2009 Stanford professor Mark Jacobson proposed—and later proved—that each of the fifty states—and virtually every country—could transition to 100 percent renewable energy by the year 2050.[55] Most people don't realize that the cost of solar in 2016 was less than 1/200th the cost of solar when Jimmy Carter installed it on the roof of the White House in 1979. And it costs even less than that today. One thing more: people are amazed to learn how much energy is actually available from the sun. Using only solar panels (not wind, hydro, tidal, etc.), if we covered only three-tenths of 1 percent of the Earth's land area (the size of Spain), we could power all of humanity's electricity needs. The one-time cost would be 10 percent of world GDP (gross domestic product) or about $5 trillion (which is less than what we paid to bail out the banks in the last recession).[56]

Having said that, we must be clear: most scientists now concur that we will fail at limiting the rise in Earth's temperature to below two degrees Celsius. But if we were to fully implement the complete range of solutions humanity is already utilizing here and there, we could assure significant intergenerational continuity.

What could keep us from embracing these solutions? Habit—yes. Fear of change—yes. Ideology—yes. Lack of vision—yes. Vested interests—yes. Profit for the current generation—yes.

None of these roadblocks are scientific constraints. Rather, all of these roadblocks can and must be understood as moral shortcomings that can be healed and transformed.

This is why it is essential for religious leaders to engage this challenge, and bring to it the same prophetic imagination that led to the defeat of slavery, the passage of child labor laws, the passage of both the Civil Rights Act of 1964 and the Voting Rights Act of 1965, the defeat of apartheid, and the dawn of marriage equality and LGBTQIA+ rights.

You and I are called to proclaim Good News in a time of moral peril. In the pages that follow, I hope you will find strength and inspiration to claim your God-given gifts and to offer them in service of witnessing on behalf of and healing God's creation.

QUESTIONS FOR GROUP DISCUSSION
AND FURTHER REFLECTION

1. Have each person in the group share a brief story about something you value, something you love . . . and how that treasure is—or will soon be—in jeopardy, vanishing as a result of climate change; and how, because of this, your children will be denied this pleasure.

2. Share with a partner your thoughts about your legacy—what you want to be remembered for by those in the future. How might your legacy connect with climate change? Those interested in this question will find great value in this article: "We Need Stories of Dystopia Without Apocalypse," by Emmalie Dropkin, https://electricliterature.com/amp/p/73b3c15b5ee.

3. With a partner, share an example of how—in your thinking or behavior—you have recently exemplified one of the five psychological barriers to climate action: Distance, Doom, Dissonance, Denial, iDentity.

4. Share with one another your views on why you think climate denial persists. Climate scientist and evangelical Christian Katharine Hayhoe is one of the authors of a recent 600-page climate report. In a tweet on August 11, 2017, @Khayhoe points out that all of that complexity can be summarized in one tweet: It's real. It's us. It's serious. And the window of time to prevent dangerous impacts is closing fast.

5. Have each person in the group share one behavior or activity that is the best example of your commitment to restore creation. After everyone has had a turn, go around again and this time, name one behavior or activity you are not yet doing but are inspired to undertake thanks to this conversation.

2

A LOVING GOD FOR A BROKEN WORLD

Once Jesus was asked by the Pharisees when the kingdom of God was coming, and he answered, "The kingdom of God is not coming with things that can be observed; nor will they say, 'Look, here it is!' or 'There it is!' For, in fact, the kingdom of God is among you."
—Luke 17:20–21 (NRSV)

What if it's true? What if we already have everything we need? What if the answer to every question echoes Jesus' response to the Pharisees, "In fact, the kingdom of God is among you" (Luke 17:21). What if life is nothing more—and nothing less—than an opportunity to be in right relationship to creation, to one another, and to a loving God—a God who creates, redeems, and sustains; a God who set the universe in motion and breathed life into it, and continues to abide within it?

You've probably already figured out that I have spent much of the time God has given me focusing on the harm that humans have inflicted on God's creation and on each other. Of equal importance to me are the moments I have treasured—every single day of my life—"lost in wonder, love, and praise" as Charles Wesley puts it in the hymn, "Love Divine, All Loves Excelling" (first published in 1747).

FINDING GOD IN A BROKEN WORLD

As a denominational leader in Massachusetts, one of the least religious states in the United States, every day I hear testimonials about people's relationships with God and involvement—or lack of involvement—in church. While there's not a monolithic, single narrative, these stories do form several trend lines. One of those narratives is associated with people who once were churchgoers but no longer attend. Many of them say that they no longer feel connected to the God proclaimed by the church. For them, evidence of a loving God is scant, victories of a just God are few, and experiences of a transcendent God are—at best—fleeting. Jesus' assurance that "the kingdom of God is among you" simply doesn't resonate with their experience.

That's one narrative. Diana Butler Bass offers another in her landmark book, *Grounded: Finding God in the World—A Spiritual Revolution*. She writes not only as a sociologist and commentator on religion and culture but also as a searching disciple, journeying through a profoundly changing religious landscape. The narrative she identifies and masterfully unpacks is a simple one: God is with us.

> God is the ground, the grounding, that which grounds us. We experience this when we understand that soil is holy, water gives life, the sky opens the imagination, our roots matter, home is a divine place, and our lives are linked with our neighbors' and with those around the globe. This world, not heaven, is the sacred stage of our times.[1]

Years ago, in anticipation of Earth Day, I invited my congregation to email or bring in a photograph of their favorite place on Earth. I arranged the photos as a collage that became the worship bulletin cover for our service. The cover offered no indication of who was associated with each photo. The impact on the congregation was profound. As people entered church and were handed a bulletin, their hearts were immediately touched by the beauty of the Earth depicted on the cover of the bulletin. But these photos were not random. This collage testified to the loving relationship that individuals had with particular places on God's good Earth. The response to the collage spoke volumes about the loving relationships everyone in the congregation felt to one another, and thus to each of these sacred places. The liturgy and sermon focused on our love of the Earth and the theological truth that love is the most powerful force on Earth—powerful enough to motivate us to make the changes scientists all over the world insist are necessary to address the climate crisis.

Imagine leaders of all faith traditions speaking to those in tens of thousands of houses of worship across God's good Earth. Imagine them inviting their congregations to acknowledge how much they love the Earth and how they fear for its future. Imagine clergy knowing enough science to articulate with passion the frightening realities toward which our current unrestrained choices are leading. Imagine hearing scripture from each faith tradition proclaiming our duty to protect the Earth so that future generations can flourish. Finally, imagine religious people the world over embracing a call that resides in every faith tradition—a moral call to resist greed in favor of sharing and even sacrifice.

SHOULD WE TRY TO KEEP OUR HEARTS FROM BREAKING?

If we allow ourselves to be lost in wonder, love, and praise as we contemplate the universe, we will find ourselves all the more heartbroken each time we learn that a new pipeline is being built or that a regulation or policy that protects the web of life has been cancelled. I believe that heartbreak for the world we are breaking is an essential part of our generation's vocation.

How do we keep our hearts from breaking? Not by protecting them! We can only fully become the persons God wants us to be if we connect deeply with the awe-inspiring gift of creation. And if creation is wounded, if it is scarred (as it most certainly is), and if we are the generation that must right this wrong, then we must stay connected with our emotional lives, however painful that may be.

How do we keep our hearts from breaking? The short answer is: we don't and we shouldn't. Having been given the capacity for empathy and compassion, God calls our generation to hear creation crying, to feel heartbreak and grief for our damaged world. God calls us to be compassionate—to "suffer with" the world as Jesus did—to share in the pain we are inflicting on creation. If we allow ourselves to feel this pain, we can gain strength from knowing that we do not suffer alone. God's heart is the first to break when harm is done to God's creation.

GRATITUDE FOR A GOD OF LOVE

The spiritual discipline that has most shaped my life is the discipline of gratitude. Every morning, gratitude is my first waking thought—gratitude that God has given me at least one more day to serve, one more encounter with the incomprehensible beauty of creation, one more opportunity to inquire and testify, one more chance to seek and bear witness to the truth as I see it.

It's the spiritual discipline of gratitude that allows me to take in and process the reports—new each day—of the ways we are destroying God's great gift of creation. Only by renewing my connection with the God of Love—many times each day—am I able to face the ways our generation continues to reverse Genesis, de-creating the living world and unraveling the web of life. Only by reminding myself, again and again, that "God so loved the *world*" (John 3:16) do I have the stamina to defend that beautiful world against all who would exploit it.

I join Ecumenical Patriarch Bartholomew and Pope Francis in recognizing that God is calling for nothing short of "a change of humanity" in which we "replace consumption with sacrifice, greed with generosity, wastefulness with a spirit of sharing." We must "learn to give, and not simply give up . . . [and to move] gradually away from what *I* want to what God's world needs."[2] Like Pope Francis, I am convinced that we are "intimately united with all that exists" and that "we were made for love."[3]

HOW DO WE REMAIN FAITHFUL?

To remain faithful during this frightening time, we must embody a "both-and" approach. Our spiritual maturation must be guided by engaged "com-passion." We must allow ourselves to be increasingly vulnerable as we take in the pain, suffering, and destruction of our breathtakingly wild and beautiful home. As we do this, we must also open ourselves to a loving, creator God who is at our side, joining us in our heartbreak. With God at our side, we experience an expanded capacity to absorb the horror of what we have done and what we are doing to life itself.

All of that prepares us for the miracle of faithfulness amidst discontinuity. God does not abandon us in our despair. Quite the contrary. The more deeply we take in the lifelessness of drought and clearcutting, the choking exhaustion of heat waves, the helplessness of rising waters, the loneliness of extinction—the more receptive we are to miracle. Nothing we have done—nothing we can do—can extinguish the Holy Spirit who breathes into us renewed conviction and fresh courage that nothing can take away.

The church, seeking to be faithful in a time such as this, will facilitate this kind of preparation among its members and throughout its community. Inspired by the Spirit, we the people will take action by engaging the powers and principalities, whoever they may be. We will do so, not because we expect victory, but because—in our deepest places—we are connected to a loving God and can do no other.

JULIAN BOND'S TESTIMONY IN HANDCUFFS

On February 13, 2013, I experienced that kind of clarity.[4] I had cuffed my wrist to the White House fence alongside the cuffed wrist of Robert F. Kennedy Jr. Our nation's chief climate scientist, James Hansen, stood next to me; actress and activist Daryl Hannah sat in front of us; fellow clergy and leader of the Hip Hop Caucus, Rev. Lennox Yearwood, stood two persons farther on. A few feet away, also cuffed to the fence, stood civil rights giant Julian Bond beside Bill McKibben and Michael Brune, executive director of the Sierra Club. Altogether, forty-eight of us came from all over the United States to obey our consciences. The days of safety and silence were over. A day of reckoning was at hand.

And it was Ash Wednesday. When I mounted the platform to address the rally that preceded our civil disobedience, many were unaware that Lent was beginning. In the context of climate disruption, anyone who cares about creation can embrace the significance of Ash Wednesday. It's a day of conscience, repentance, and conviction; a day when we take stock of our lives and our life together on the planet; a day when we confess our self-indulgent appetites, our intemperate love of worldly goods and comforts, and our obsession with consumption of every kind. For Christians, Ash Wednesday is a day to acknowledge that we are accountable to the God who gave us life and who entrusted the Earth to our care.

"Ash Wednesday is a good day to be arrested," I told the crowd. "It's a good day to realign our lives with God's desire to preserve this good creation." I invited any who wanted to receive ashes as a sign of their repentance to approach me on their way to White House.

Dozens did, including those who would soon be arrested, supporters, camera technicians, and journalists. The mood was a striking mix of sober, joyous, serious, grateful conviction.

As we slowly approached the White House fence, President Obama's State of the Union address from the night before echoed in my mind: "If Congress won't act soon to protect future generations, I will. I will direct my Cabinet to come up with executive actions we can take, now and in the future, to reduce pollution, prepare our communities for the consequences of climate change, and speed the transition to more sustainable sources of energy."

One such action to protect future generations—an action that the president then and now has the power to take—was to stop the Keystone XL pipeline. For a moment, while I held the cold iron of the White House fence with my left hand, it seemed simple. Such an action by President Obama would give hope to the world, and would be regarded by future generations as a hinge on which history would swing towards hope.

We cheered the name of each person as the police cut the plastic cuffs attaching us to the fence. Then, threading our hands through new plastic cuffs, they tightened them and escorted us to the police transport vehicles. I greeted two of the police whom I had met back in August 2011 when 1,253 of us were arrested, and 63 of us spent three days and nights in jail. We remembered our friendly conversation.

Hope became tangible for me during the two hours I spent jammed in the police transportation vehicle, hands cuffed behind me, shoulders aching, and wrists in pain. Two hours is a long time.

Hope emerged—as it so often does—from conversation. To my left was writer and now full-time activist Mike Tidwell, founder and director of the Chesapeake Climate Action Network. We had been arrested together in August 2011. Across from us was our friend and inspiration, Bill McKibben. Sitting on my right was Julian Bond, former chairman of the NAACP and the first president of the Southern Poverty Law

Center, whose first act of civil disobedience was in 1960 at a lunch counter in Georgia.

Hope grew as I began to take in Julian's resolute courage and as I realized that less than fifty years had passed between Julian's first arrest and Obama's first election. Much had changed in that time. From all that he shared, what most stuck with me was Julian's testimony that the single most important ingredient in social change is persistence.

When I emerged from the two-hour confinement in the transport vehicle and stretched my legs, my soul was aglow from conversation laced with hope. Two-and-one-half years later, along with tens of thousands of others, I wept tears of gratitude for the life and witness of this inspiring prophet who had moved on to his great reward.

THE MINE AND THE SNOW GEESE—A STORY FOR OUR TIME[5]

> Even though you intended to do harm to me, God intended it for good.
> —Genesis 50:20

The Industrial Revolution required something more than fossil fuel—it required electricity. Electricity required wires—thousands of miles of copper wire. For five decades, a single mine provided one-third of the copper needed by the United States and one-sixth of the copper needed by the rest of the world. In the 1940s, the price of copper plummeted and traditional mining became unprofitable. A new form of mining emerged when, in 1955, they blew off the top of the mountain just outside Butte, Montana.

The Berkeley Pit soon became the world's largest open-pit mine, until Earth Day 1982, when the mine was closed. The ore was no longer profitable.

There was a problem: the pit was filling with rain, snow, and groundwater. Without anyone paying to operate the pumps, a lake began to form. Not just any lake, but an unspeakably dangerous brew of acid and metals from the ore: copper, cadmium, zinc, and arsenic, among others. Nothing could grow there. Life was not possible. The killer lake kept growing until its volume made it one of the largest lakes in the United States.

And so it was not entirely surprising that on a stormy, wintry night in November 1995, a flock of over three hundred snow geese landed on the lake. For the geese, in a snowstorm, it was an obvious place to land. They were behaving like normal geese—slaking their thirst and resting up so that they could find food in the morning. But there was nothing normal about this lake, and morning never came. Throughout the night, people living nearby could hear lots of honking. By dawn the geese were silent. The first to arrive at the edge of the pit saw acres of floating, lifeless bodies. The sulfuric acid had eaten out the insides of the helpless geese.

Long before the geese landed, the lake had been deemed a Superfund site. One day, a man carrying a stick with some green slime on it came into the lab of two biochemists at the University of Montana. He had retrieved the stick from the lake. The professors were shocked. The slime was alive, having adapted to the life-cancelling conditions of the lake. They called it an extremophile—a kind of life no one had ever seen before. This impossible slime launched the careers of professors Andrea and Don Stierle.

Not long after that, the Stierles came across a small pile of black slime—yeast actually—with some very special properties. Prior to that, they had found a few organisms that actually consumed metals. If you put the algae in a beaker of pit water—voilà!—10 to 15 percent of the metals in the water are consumed by the algae. But this new, black, slimy yeast performed this miracle on a different level. It absorbed 85 to 95 percent of the metals!

Since the professors knew of nothing like this, they contacted their colleagues around the world to find out if this yeast was known to exist anywhere else. Finally, a veterinarian got back to them. The one place they could find this yeast, he told them, was in the gastrointestinal track of snow geese.

The 342 snow geese that had each died a horrible death had left a gift behind. A common yeast from their intestines had not only defied death in the acid bath—that yeast had actually thrived! Using the snow geese's gift, the scientists could help life to return to one of the most lifeless places on Earth. These innocent geese had taken into themselves the very worst that humanity had to offer, and in dying, had returned to humanity something that might actually restore this most forsaken and wounded corner of God's creation.

THE STORY OF THE MINE AND THE SNOW GEESE: A POSTSCRIPT[6]

> The summer is ended, and we are not saved.
> —Jeremiah 8:20

The late fall in 2016 had been unusually warm in northern Canada and the arctic. Sensing that they had overstayed their welcome, hundreds of thousands of geese took flight heading south, as the first cold winds began to blow. As they flew over Montana, the temperature plummeted. Of the tens of thousands flying over Butte one night, 3,000–4,000 were exhausted and had to land. Since the smaller lakes were frozen, they landed on the acidic wastewater of the Berkeley Pit. The people working at the Superfund site went into action. They desperately did everything they could to shoo the geese away—including deploying the Goosinator, a large remote-controlled boat designed to frighten the geese. But the geese weren't moving. They had landed because they were exhausted. They would move no more. By morning, the lake was covered with thousands of carcasses.

"The die-off in 1995 should have been a wake-up call," a county official said. "Instead, we hit the snooze button."

The mine is the mire we have made of creation. Rising a foot each year, the lake may soon contaminate the groundwater for at least 120 miles down the Clark Fork River to Missoula, Montana. The geese are God's surprising gift—soaring above the muck—reminding us of the generativity of creation.[7] They offer us a way forward and possibly a way out of the mess we have made.

Yes—God has given us everything we need. The climate scientists who have overcome ridicule and stayed focused on this issue will one day be known as heroes. So will the politicians who have shown courageous leadership by calling for the profound changes that are necessary in our nation's policies, regulations, and way of life. And so will the business leaders who are stretching the time horizons of their business plans from months to generations, as they search for a more sustainable way of doing business.

But it's up to the rest of us to decide how we direct our energy, focus our attention, invest our capital, and release our imagination. We can choose to continue our rapacious assault on our common home, motivated by a mistaken understanding of progress, seeking to benefit only a narrow understanding of family. Or we can embrace the fact that we really are all in this together, and that God is urgently calling our generation to make wise use of the gifts and mysteries of God's good Earth so that we may begin to restore God's glorious gift of creation.

QUESTIONS FOR GROUP DISCUSSION AND FURTHER REFLECTION

1. Share with the group an example of when you experienced heartbreak upon learning one or another example of irreversible harm to God's creation done by humans. After everyone has spoken, share with one another your views on lament. These days, many people insulate themselves from lament, often asking "what good does it do?" But scripture includes the Book of Lamentations for a reason. What might that reason be?
2. Spend a day immersed in gratitude. Let it be an ordinary day—keeping your normal calendar and commitments—but focus your inner voice on gratitude as much as you possibly can. Be guided by wonder and uplifted by awe. After the group has shared with one another their various experiences and what it was like, ask one another why don't we spend all our waking hours immersed in gratitude?
3. Share with one another an experience of discontinuity during which you struggled to remain faithful to a commitment or principle that was being undermined or attacked. Albert Camus' *The Plague* offers an example of this struggle.
4. Share with the group your truest beliefs about whether persistence will succeed in reorienting human behavior and aspiration so that our grandchildren will not be relegated to an unlivable world. What critically important virtues would you add to Julian Bond's acknowledgment of persistence?

INTERLUDE

If We Fail to Heed Our Calling

The Earth is sufficient for everyone's needs but not for everyone's greed.[1]
—Gandhi

As I write in the fall of 2017, humanity is making only insufficient, incremental progress in addressing climate change. Few scientists believe that either goal[2] of the December 2015 Paris agreement will be met. The year 2016—like 2015 and 2014 before it—was the hottest year on record. Our global temperature for the first half of 2016 was 1.34°C above pre–Industrial Age averages.[3] This rate of increase, far above expectations, suggests that even the most aggressive action will at best "succeed" at limiting the temperature rise to between 3°C and 4°C.

Should humanity fail to make the changes needed to preserve continuity of creation,[4] what of the church? Under these conditions, I expect two patterns from the early twenty-first century will continue: interest in institutional religion will keep declining and interest in religious fundamentalism will continue to grow. By 2025, the devastating consequences of climate change will be more widespread. Some writers and even some clergy will suggest that belief in God has become less and less viable as "God's creation" is experienced by many as an enemy of civilized life. By 2050, political leaders will have been forced to put all their resources—military and otherwise—into crisis management and border control. This will further deepen the general public's despair, even as it swells the ranks of fundamentalists. By 2060, the institutional church will have dwindled to only a remnant of the halcyon days of the mid-twentieth century when the first warnings of global warming were issued. The once-elevating conviction that the role of the church was to animate the conscience of the nation will be abandoned. While despair decimates the church's ranks, the remnant will look to the prophets and the defiance of the early church for solace and inspiration.

What follows is an imagined a letter from a pastor to her congregation written on Ash Wednesday 2070. The church had been serving a city on the eastern seaboard of the United States since the church's founding in the seventeenth century. The pastor mentions the frequent catastrophic weather events, the endless border wars, the hundreds of millions of refugees fleeing flooded cities, the permanent deployment of military to protect the interests of the rich, and billions of people dying from uncontrollable disease, drought, and starvation. These conditions will have caused the world population to drop from its peak in 2040 of about 9 billion people[5] to a huddle of survivors in 2070 numbering about 2 billion.[6] This letter paints a picture of how a particular church might close its doors.

A LETTER FROM A PASTOR TO HER CONGREGATION ON THE OCCASION OF THE CLOSING OF THE CHURCH ON ASH WEDNESDAY 2070

Ash Wednesday, February 12, 2070
    Beloved in Christ:

Grace and peace to you. It was good to see so many of you at our final service. Thanks for making the effort. After all our tearful hugs, I realized that it was important for me to reach out and offer a final farewell to those of you who were unable to join us.

Today, as I marked each of you with a cross of ashes, I said, "From dust you have come and to dust you shall return." I am so grateful that Ellen suggested Ash Wednesday as the closing date for our church. The liturgy, as we adapted it, seemed so fitting.

After everyone had received ashes, I was caught off guard when Mark respectfully asked me to let him hold the urn of ashes. (For those of you who may not know Mark, he grew up in our congregation, and then spent the past twelve years in the Army. Like millions of other soldiers and members of the National Guard, in 2059 he was reassigned to try to contain the Great Conflagration in Canada, Montana, and the Dakotas. He returned home about three months ago.) As I handed him the urn, it dawned on me that he had spent his whole adult life amidst ashes and fire. If anyone understood Ash Wednesday, it was Mark. He prayed silently for a moment, as if he were summoning all he had learned from his years amidst the fires, and then he reached into the bowl of ashes and used them to "mark" the altar, the pulpit, and the chancel. With each mark, he repeated, "From dust you have come, and to dust you shall return." Stirred by his profound witness, we all joined him in unison the third time. Truly, this felt like the closing of our church.

Since the Great Flood in 2037, our church and neighborhood have been under water six times. At first, we did all we could for the neighborhood. But the Third Flood in 2051 was such a catastrophe—and our membership had dwindled to so few—that for the past twenty years we've focused on keeping our once-beautiful building open in order to carry out funerals and other liturgical responsibilities. Last year's Category Six hurricane made it clear to the dozen or so members who were still trying to live in the neighborhood that it was time to close the church.

My greatest regret is that over the past few decades—in our time of greatest need—faith in God has become as extinct as the elephant, tiger, panda, and the other thousands of species whose extinction we have mourned each St. Francis Day. Many have suggested that humanity's abandonment of God is due to despair over the widespread increase in war, the persistent killings along the national border barriers, the unforgiving mosquito-borne viruses that have now invaded even Canada, and so on. My own view is that, as God's creation came to be experienced as the destroyer—not the sustainer—of civilized life, people could no longer believe in a loving God.

Thanks be to God that our congregation has resisted this view! Many of you credit one of my predecessors, the Rev. Dr. Jill Smith, for her clear and courageous leadership over her twenty-three years of ministry

(2017–2040). More than any voice in America, she urged all who would listen to embrace a new set of values. As our congregation adopted these values, we were both cheered and jeered. I have marveled at the stories of how, in 2022, over half the congregation made an "Acts 2:44 commitment" to hold all things in common. Not long after that the congregation undertook a year-long study of the concept and practice of ownership of land. Recognizing that "The earth is the Lord's" (Psalm 24) the church voted to turn the church property into a land trust—and dozens of members did likewise with their own (previously) "private" property. We still use many of the life-changing liturgies Jill wrote that helped this congregation expand the Golden Rule to include unborn generations of people and creatures as our neighbors.

Thankfully, these changes kept us connected with the compassion that God is always pouring into our hearts (Romans 5:5). As all of you know, a few months after my son was conscripted into the Army, he was killed while protecting our border from climate refugees. Although I had only been your minister for a few months, your caring, compassionate support saved my life, and over the years we have become family for one another.

Not a day goes by that I don't cast my mind back to 2015—the year Pope Francis issued his Encyclical "On Care for Our Common Home" and when 193 nations signed the COP21 Paris Climate Agreement. Although I was only twelve years old at the time, I'll never forget the hope I felt that the grownups were going to own up to having trashed God's creation and were now undertaking the necessary changes to make things right. But at that young age, I didn't realize that the politicians would only make these changes if forced to do so. Throughout history, one of the voices that compelled the end of slavery, the guarantee of civil rights, and LGBTQIA+ rights and the end of apartheid was the voice of the church. But darker forces than I could imagine at the age of twelve had already made certain that the church would mostly stay silent on climate change because climate change was a "political issue."

What if the leaders of every faith community the world over had done what Jill did? Looking back, I just don't understand why religious leaders failed to recognize that the conflict over climate change was a moral conflict—a conflict of values. Was it a lack of personal courage? Did they really think that religion had more to do with personal salvation and little if anything to do with collective salvation? Was the uncritical acceptance of personal gain so universal that it was unthinkable for a pastor to insist that everything we have comes from God? Did the blasphemous idea that God gave us the Earth to plunder for our own benefit become so embedded in our economy that our obligation to future generations was forgotten or dismissed?

Jill was a great moral leader because she never lost her moral compass. She knew that God had not called her to embrace an ideology of the status quo. She was not afraid to ask us to become living examples of the values needed to sustain life as it had evolved on this planet. And you responded! Over the past twenty years, every one of you has shared with me your testimony—the more you lived your lives for one another and in service to the dying world, the more satisfied you became with your own life.

But now all of that is past. I'm reminded of the Prophet Jeremiah's comment: "The harvest is past, the summer is ended, and we are not saved" (Jeremiah 8:20).

In the coming months, I expect most of you will join the others who have relocated to higher ground. Now that the world population is less than a quarter of what it was thirty years ago, you will likely find a place. Among our many lamentations is the abandonment of the once-elevating conviction that the role of the church is to animate the conscience of the nation. In its place, I hope that each of you will continue to respond to God's call to be ambassadors of the beloved community. I hope that each of you will make whatever community you join become more resilient. And, as has been the focus of our life together here, I urge you to bring to your new community a new understanding of hope, rooted in the Prophets and the Book of Acts.

The theologian from whom I have learned the most—Walter Brueggemann—introduced me to Jeremiah, Ezekiel, and Isaiah. Like us, these prophets lived in a period when their "known world" (Jerusalem) was assaulted and finally disbanded.[7] They told their people, and they tell us today, that we have two tasks: to let go of the world we once knew, and to receive from God a new world. As Isaiah says, "Do not remember former things; Behold, I am doing a new thing" (Isaiah 43:18–19).

Only by fully grieving all that we have lost can we enter into the new tomorrow that God is preparing. We have so much to mourn: personal grief over loved ones lost and homes destroyed; ubiquitous grief over the long emergency that has straight-jacketed our lives; and anticipatory grief over the catastrophe that we are handing over to our children. I hope that our life together over the past twenty years has allowed you to grieve in the deepest possible way. What I am certain of is that your tears, your outpourings, and your honesty have allowed me to pour out my grief without reservation. Your love and compassion have given me hope that scripture's promises of forgiveness are true.

Because of this, and thanks to you, I go forth in hope, trusting that you do so as well.

QUESTIONS FOR GROUP DISCUSSION AND FURTHER REFLECTION

1. After reading this letter, try to have a conversation about personal grief (such as grief over loved ones lost); ubiquitous grief (experienced when a community is subjected to severe constraint by long-lasting emergency); and anticipatory grief (concern, regret, remorse over the catastrophe we are handing over to our children).

2. With this letter in mind, discuss the possible importance of people of faith publicly expressing our grief over creation's demise. Is it possible that by making our expression of grief public and visible, we will expose the denial that has held so many of our political leaders captive for so many decades? Does public grief amplify the urgency of a crisis? Can you recall any examples of social change that were prompted by public expression of grief? Can the public grief of a faithful remnant give voice to our still-speaking God whose compassion, pain, and suffering allows for new and unimagined possibilities to emerge?

3

THE CHURCH'S VOCATION TODAY

The subject of ethics is how we and others are to survive and flourish. So when a turning point arrives and a time of transition from one way of life to another intrudes, moral inertia no longer suffices and all that belongs to the present moral life must of needs be engaged anew.
—Larry Rasmussen [1]

WHAT'S CHURCH FOR?

When one of my staff meets with one of the several hundred United Church of Christ congregations in Massachusetts that we oversee, things don't always go as expected. Most of our congregations are over two hundred years old; several are over three hundred years old. We typically meet with our congregations when they are going through a transition. Centuries-old systems tend to resist change. However, when a transition upends the normal life of the congregation, a window of opportunity opens.

"Begin with the end in mind." This is our mantra as we work with congregations. Three years from now, what will be different in your neighborhood and in the lives of those connected to your congregation as a result of your congregation's witness? What is your vision? What is your purpose? What's church for?

Our congregations are often struck by how relentless my colleagues can be as we invite the congregation to enter a visioning process that will provide them with clear responses to three crucial questions:

- Who are we right now (our skills, character, gifts, historical trends, and DNA)?
- Who is our neighbor (in our community and our commuter radius, along with our neighbors around the world)?
- What is God calling us to become and to accomplish in this current time and place?

My colleagues press these questions for a reason. The landscape of ministry is undergoing profound changes. All denominations are experiencing a seismic shift as many of our churches shrink and others close their doors, including some that have been around for centuries. Across much of America, attending church is no longer the norm. People are finding other ways to fulfill the needs that attending church once met.[2] These changes represent a profound discontinuity with the past. Many pastors lack the training and skills to provide leadership in the context of such unanticipated and fundamental change.

This is why it's crucial to engage all of our church leaders in addressing foundational questions. Only by deeply probing the question of purpose can a congregation gain the perspective it needs in order to be able to explore a new path and to embrace opportunities for renewal. More often than not, this involves exploring new kinds of worship experiences.[3] More fundamentally, congregations must ponder anew how God may be calling them to advance God's mission.

But here's the thing. As consequential as these trends may be for thousands of congregations, as well as for entire denominations, there is something even more momentous going on. Creation itself—the context in which life as we know it has evolved—is experiencing severe discontinuity.

Because Christians regard God as Creator, the church must proclaim God's love for creation and work to stop humanity from running Genesis in reverse.

Over the next decade, some churches in the United States are likely to be directly upended by creation's discontinuity. Some may burn down, because fire season is now 19 percent longer than it used to be.[4]

Some may be washed away, destroyed by high winds, or irretrievably flooded. Many more churches will be incrementally affected as they pay for air conditioners and use them with increasing frequency year by year. Still more churches will find themselves responding to the mounting challenges their members face from deadly heat waves and extreme storms, from rising rates of asthma and tropical disease, and from food insecurity caused by local, regional, and national changes in weather patterns.

Although climate change will affect churches in varied ways, members of every church will experience the often unspoken dread that burdens our hearts and brings tears to our eyes. Already, many people are feeling the existential threat of climate change as we come to realize that in just two hundred years we have upset millions of years of nature's balance and have set into motion processes that could bring human civilization to an end.

In the context of such massive upheaval, what is church for?

Bill McKibben told me in 2007 that climate change was an opportunity for which the church was born. If he is right (and I believe he is)—if God is truly calling the church to a new vocation—then the church will have to repurpose itself in several significant ways. Before getting into that, it's worth exploring how the church's history might illuminate the unprecedented situation in which humanity finds itself today.

HISTORY'S LESSONS FOR AN UNPRECEDENTED TIME

How did our ancestors in the faith respond when they faced radical social discontinuity caused by the misuse of their God-given freedom? What guidance and encouragement can we glean from our history?

Consider this bit of history supplied by Sister Joan Chittister.[5] In the sixth century, not long after the founding of their order, Benedictine monks began to focus on the fact that, with the collapse of the Roman Empire, the farmlands and forests of Europe had been destroyed. This new religious band of brothers believed that God was calling them to respond lovingly and constructively to this environmental horror. Over a period of many years (presumably decades), the monks set out to replant the forests, recreate the watersheds, restore streams and ponds, and reintroduce composting. For these Benedictine monks, working to restore the land and water was a spiritual practice, a faithful response to God's call. Seven hundred years later, Cistercian groups again devoted themselves to the reforestation, replanting, and reclamation of some of the most damaged land in Europe.

During the years that these monks became arborists, do you think they were any less prayerful—any less devoted to God? Were they living out their vocation as monks any less faithfully during the decades in which they worked as arborists to restore the forests and farmlands of Europe? Of course not! They had correctly read "the signs of the times" and had responded with Spirit-filled dedication and clarity.

Another example of repurposing the church in a time of discontinuity is the seminary that was founded by the twentieth-century German pastor, Dietrich Bonhoeffer. While its official name was the "Emergency Teaching Seminary of the Confessing Church," the seminary came to be known simply as Finkenwalde. For two years, Bonhoeffer trained a new generation of church leaders whose allegiance to the church was uncompromised by the German Christian movement and by Hitler's efforts to nazify the church. Starting with twenty-three students in 1935, Bonhoeffer created a "mostly improvised community"[6] that boldly sought to initiate "a new manner of being a Christian" distinguished by dissent, resistance, spiritual discipline, sacrifice, and an expanded moral imagination.[7] Bonhoeffer invited these aspiring pastors to read scripture with new eyes, unafraid to draw conclusions that would oblige them to disobey the state. He prepared them, and they prepared one another, for the cost of discipleship that they would all soon pay.

From its beginning, the Confessing Church had no official state sanction as a church. In 1936, the Gestapo began arresting Confessing Church pastors. The association of these pastors with non-"assimilated" (non-Nazi) churches had been declared a crime, and their personal association with Bonhoeffer was tantamount to treason.[8] Over the next many months, almost one hundred of them were arrested. In September 1937, the Gestapo closed Finkenwalde.

What can today's church learn from Bonhoeffer and the witness of the Emergency Teaching Seminary at Finkenwalde? Two lessons come immediately to mind. First, at times of profound and unjust discontinuity, members of the church will respond in divergent ways. Many will retreat to a personalized understanding of faith and thus dodge the social and collective implications of discontinuity. However, a remnant of the church will look reality in the face and ask, "How can the church as a collective body remain faithful amidst the dislocation we are now experiencing?" This was, of course, how Jeremiah responded, as did Bonhoeffer. Second, those who resist the destructive powers and principalities by "driving a spoke into the wheel" of injustice (Bonhoeffer's metaphor capturing the role of the Confessing Church) will risk being discounted, marginalized, or crushed.

What would it look like for today's church to become a witness on behalf of God's creation? What impact could the church have if we were to speak out on behalf of the complex, interdependent ecosystems and species that have no voice and whose lives are now being threatened or extinguished by humanity's unconscionable greed? What if we took seriously our moral responsibility to our human neighbors already suffering acutely from the effects of climate change, to say nothing of our responsibility to human generations yet unborn? What if we took seriously our moral responsibility to our nonhuman brother and sister species?

The discontinuity created by the Nazi rise to power prompted Rabbi Abraham Joshua Heschel, another great witness, to speak out. In March 1938, just before Hebrew Union College brought him to America, Heschel addressed a group of Quaker leaders in Frankfurt am Main, Germany. He titled his brief talk, "The Meaning of this Hour."[9] In 2008, when a rabbinic scholar at the Shalom Hartman Institute in Jerusalem introduced me to Heschel's address, I was profoundly struck by how much of what Heschel had to say about his own times applies just as well to our situation today. Here is a sample of Heschel's courageous reflection:

> We have profaned the Word of God, and we have given the wealth of our land, the ingenuity of our minds and the dear lives of our youth to tragedy and perdition. There has never been more reason for man to be ashamed than now.
>
> We have bartered holiness for convenience, loyalty for success, love for power, wisdom for information, tradition for fashion.
>
> Let the blasphemy of our time not become an eternal scandal. Let future generations not loathe us for having failed to preserve what prophets and saints, martyrs and scholars have created in thousands of years.

God is waiting for us to redeem the world. We should not spend our lives hunting for trivial satisfactions while God is waiting constantly and keenly for our effort and devotion. The almighty has not created the universe that we may have opportunities to satisfy our greed, envy and ambition.

Heschel concludes with this challenge: "The mountain of history is over us again. Shall we renew the covenant with God?"

This provocative question echoes through the generations, even as it challenges church leaders today. The tragic consequences of ignoring this question are described in a letter written to a Bonn pastor shortly after WWII by a then little-known Konrad Adenauer. Adenauer had just been released from a concentration camp. A short while later, he would become the first postwar chancellor of West Germany.[10]

I believe that if all the bishops had together made public statements from the pulpits on a particular day, they could have prevented a great deal. That did not happen, and there is no excuse for it. It would have been no bad thing if the bishops had all been put in prison or in concentration camps as a result. Quite the contrary. But none of that happened and therefore it is best to keep quiet.[11]

Serving as a denominational leader in a time of profound systemic injustice and increasing discontinuity, I hear Adenauer's words resonating with my own conviction that God is calling the church to speak with a clear, bold, truthful, and prophetic voice in a time of climate crisis.

Throughout history the church has played a decisive moral role in society on numerous occasions. In the nineteenth century, hundreds of American congregations made the Abolitionist Movement the focus of their life together. In the 1970s and 1980s many churches in South Africa added their voices to the call to end apartheid, often at great sacrifice. For instance, funeral liturgies for people killed in the struggle were frequently repurposed as protest marches in which the coffin was carried through the streets. Grieving families willingly set aside their need for the comfort of a church service so that the coffin of their loved one could become a rallying point to advance the struggle for justice and equality.

What is church for in a time of disruption and discontinuity? Are we here to comfort the brokenhearted in their time of grief? Of course! Are we here to address the countless other pastoral needs that are multiplied under such conditions? Absolutely! But just as important is our call to partner with Jesus in his supreme work to reconcile us to God, to one another, and to all of creation.

WITH GOD, THERE ARE NO EXTERNALITIES

One of the most significant ways many Christians impede reconciliation with God is to embrace a fiction that our behavior does not have consequences for ourselves, for others, and for our relationship with God. This kind of self-deception shows up in countless forms. Scripture is peppered with people who act as if God is somehow unaware of or doesn't really care about their actions and motives. These men and women seem to be convinced that God is somehow "off duty" when they engage in behaviors they know to be wrong. They act without moral scruples or conscience, and they think they can get away with it. What we fail to realize is that everything matters to God, because each choice shapes the person we are becoming. God constantly invites us into right relationship and reconciliation. Every time we ignore or reject that invitation, God knows—and weeps. God sees the harm we do to ourselves when we choose selfishness over love, narcissism over altruism, dominance over justice, wrong over right.

For two million years of human history, individuals who step on others to advance themselves have been—with various degrees of success—held accountable by the laws and customs of their tribe or society. When communities, armies, or nations behave this way, other communities, armies, or nations have tried to hold them accountable. Multinational corporations that engage in harmful behavior are among the newest threats to civilization, and people all over the world are struggling to determine how to hold them accountable.

It may not be obvious, but there is something very important and perhaps distinctive about God-fearing people. People who try to be faithful to God acknowledge that everything is known to God. Hiding is impossible. Eventually the truth will come out. Whether quickly or slowly, what is hidden will be revealed. Recognizing this fact is like having a life preserver in a sea of self-deception, or like having a compass when we are lost. To be a person of faith means to be committed to seeking the truth and to overcoming our natural human tendency to dodge uncomfortable facts.

Facing the truth is extremely "inconvenient" when we consider how humans have damaged the environment. For the past 10,000 years, humans have regarded the oceans, lands, and atmosphere as a dumping ground. For the first 9,800 years or so, the material consequences of this behavior seemed insignificant. But over the past 200 years, as humans increased exponentially in both numbers and technological power, the damaging consequences of our treatment of God's gift of creation have become undeniable. Because of this, as Pope Francis points out in his recent Encyclical, "The earth, our home, is beginning to look more and more like an immense pile of filth." [12]

For the past ten generations, humanity has been engaged in a dangerous experiment, testing whether the Earth that is entrusted to our care can sustain a substantial increase in population, consumption, waste, and material aspiration. Human beings have always resisted limits, as the biblical stories of Adam and Eve and the ancient tower-builders in Babel teach us. We have lived as if unlimited growth is possible—as if we can drill, mine, drain, burn, excavate, and consume to our heart's content. If problems arise, we have trusted that the market-place would magically take care of everything.

By now we don't need a degree in economics, biology, or physics to recognize that the expectation of endless growth is a dangerous fiction and that the assertion that the marketplace will correct all imbalance is a lie.

As Gus Speth, one of the most-respected environmental leaders, puts it, "Today's market is a strange place indeed. At the core of the economy is a mechanism that does not recognize the most fundamental thing of all, the living, evolving, sustaining natural world in which the economy is operating." [13] "The source of this failure is what economists term an externality. . . . Many of our environmental resources are unprotected by the appropriate prices that would constrain their use. From this perspective, it is hardly surprising to find that the environment is overused and abused. A market system simply doesn't allocate the use of these resources properly." [14]

What can the church bring to this economic, moral, and environmental calamity? The answer, while simple, goes straight to the heart of the need to repurpose the church: With God, there are no externalities!

Whatever a person may mean by God, God cannot be deceived. No amount of cleverness on our part can hide our motives from God. Before God, we (as individuals and as a community) are accountable. God brings a comprehensive understanding to all circumstances. Nothing is off the books.

This understanding of God represents a moral perspective. But a person need not believe in God in order to hold to a moral position that shuns self-deception and that insists on a comprehensive, unflinching look at the facts regarding our use and abuse of nature. This moral stance makes use of the most recent and robust science as a tool of full disclosure.

A church repurposed for a climate change world would recognize and embrace God's call to conscientization. The church finds itself in a world where "the sacrifice of the environment to economic growth . . . has unquestionably been a feature of economic development at least since the birth of industrialism."[15] In church, we honor God as Creator, and give thanks for the Earth—our common home—through which our Creator graciously offers humanity hospitality. But when we return to our everyday lives, we routinely steal from our host and Creator, gorge ourselves on the abundance God has provided without regard for those who will follow us, and foul our nest by upsetting countless parts of the interdependent ecosystem. In response to this perilous situation, week in and week out, the church must reawaken in people the moral clarity and resolve to build our lives—and our life together—around God's promises and gifts as we model a way of life and advocate for laws that hold humanity accountable.

This is just what Bill McKibben is doing as a spokesperson for the report by Oil Change International, which makes clear that we must immediately end all exploration for new oil, gas, and coal.[16] It is exactly what Citizens Climate Lobby has been doing for years as they continue to build a movement to persuade Congress to put a price on carbon by implementing a carbon fee and dividend system.[17] And this is at the core of the United Church of Christ's 2017 Synod vote "to resist all expansion of fossil fuel infrastructure and demand new sources of renewable energy that are accessible to all communities."

GOD CALLS COMMUNITIES, NOT JUST INDIVIDUALS . . . WE ALL LIVE AT THE SAME ADDRESS

Another cornerstone for a repurposed church is the recognition that God calls communities, not just individuals. If you read scripture, you can't miss this emphasis. But when my colleagues and I are working with congregations to discern God's call, the idea that God might be calling the congregation—as a unified community—to embrace a particular mission is often dismissed. It's as if it never occurred to a whole lot of Christians that God might call "us" to join in common cause to fulfill God's mission.

One of the most distinguishing features of the American ethos is our centuries-long emphasis on rugged individualism. The church's concentration on personal salvation has amplified this theme considerably. While there was a time when this emphasis served an important purpose, we now realize that all of life—not only with other humans but also with the rest of creation—is characterized by interdependence. The lives of all living things are woven together in a common destiny. A repurposed church will focus as much theological attention on collective salvation as it will on personal salvation.

A familiar way of saying this is to say that we are all in this together. But this expression is so common that it doesn't get people thinking. One of the ways I get at this is by pointing out that every person on the planet (along with every creature) is our neighbor because the distinctions between this neighborhood and that one—between this country and that one—are insignificant compared to the fact that we all breathe the same air. I like to say that we all live at the same address. Our common address is—as I write this—407: that is, 407 parts per million of CO_2 in the atmosphere.[18] And then I add one thing more. This place in which we are all living—this place with the number 407 emblazoned on every door and dwelling—this place is no longer "home." Home is a place where the number on the door is 350 or less. Home for Mozart, Mary and Joseph, and the earliest humans living in caves was even less; their address was 275. Yet by the time my grandchildren reach my current age, their address will likely exceed 450ppm, a result of what scientists call "committed warming" or "climate lag."[19] This is likely to become the frightening reality even if this very day we were to close every coal plant, immediately stop burning gas and oil, and instantly trade in our gas-powered cars for bikes.

This is the predicament—the systemic injustice—created by the actions of about seven generations of humans. We have fundamentally altered life as we know it, for ourselves as well as for the whole of creation. In a repurposed church, that systemic injustice will receive fierce and unflagging attention, alongside the more apparent systemic injustices of hunger, homelessness, poverty, bigotry, white privilege, usury, and so forth—all of which are connected to how we treat the Earth.

Furthermore, climate disruption is amplifying all the other injustices. Our efforts to advance God's mission and to build a just world at peace are undermined by the fact that the Earth's life-systems are no longer stable. We have set in motion global conditions which assure that the people least responsible for the problem will suffer most from the consequences. For example, a once-in-a-hundred-year flood will wipe out the *poor* neighborhoods, not the rich. Not only that—the effects of a disrupted climate are intensifying year by year, and will continue to do so for generations to come.

Recognizing this reality, a repurposed church will inspire its people to regard salvation in this world and the next as a function of how we live together, building the beloved community for this and all future generations. A repurposed church will help lead a just transition to a sustainable economy by taking its cues from leaders like Jacqueline Patterson, director of the NAACP Environmental and Climate Justice Program.[20] In a repurposed church, the first question people will ask about climate change will not be: How will it affect me? Instead, it will be something like: How can I help my neighbors to thrive? How can I build a more resilient community? What changes can I make in my life so that generations to come are more likely to inherit a habitable world?

OUR COVENANT WITH GOD: FOR ALL TIME—WITH ALL CREATURES

Another cornerstone for a repurposed church is the covenant found in the ninth chapter of Genesis. Its common name—the Noahic covenant—is misleading. The text is clear that God makes the covenant not only with Noah and his sons, but also with all of their descendants, as well as with every living creature and even with the Earth itself ("the covenant between me and the earth," Genesis 9:13). Lest anyone wonder about the duration of this covenant, it is "for all future generations" (Genesis 9:12)—an "everlasting covenant" (Genesis 9:16).

The force and implications of this covenantal declaration conflict with the anthropocentric interpretation of scripture that has been championed throughout much of the church's history. A repurposed church will follow the lead of Thomas Berry, Larry Rasmussen, and others (including Václav Havel) who recognize the need for humanity to anchor our morality in the recognition of our deep connection with the entire universe.[21] Not only does Holy Scripture testify to this truth—environmental science and ecology repeatedly show us that life on this planet is interdependent in the most fundamental of ways.

GOLDEN RULE 2.0

A final cornerstone for a repurposed church concerns the most basic moral instruction of both the New Testament and Hebrew Scripture—a moral instruction found at the core of every world religion. We are called to love our neighbors as ourselves; and on this new E-a-a-r-t-h (see page 13), we must recognize that future generations are no less our neighbors than those who live next door today. We can think of this as Golden Rule 2.0.[22]

Make no mistake—this represents a revolution in human values. For thousands of years, civilization has been shaped and well served by the Golden Rule. But the development of nuclear weapons served notice that humanity needed a new moral standard. Suddenly, humanity had the capacity to significantly alter—or even to end—life as we knew it. However, this threat would only become reality if nuclear bombs were used. Not long after the first nuclear explosion (with the repulsive code name "Trinity"), scientists began to sound an alarm about the greenhouse gas effect. It turns out that the CO_2 "bomb" has been quietly exploding since the beginning of the Industrial Age. Simply by continuing with business as usual, we are guaranteed to leave a ruined world to our children.

To make this point, climate scientist Jim Hanson reports that humanity's current use of fossil fuel is adding energy (heat) to the planet's oceans, atmosphere, and earth that is equivalent "to exploding 400,000 Hiroshima atomic bombs per day, 365 days per year. That's how much extra energy Earth is gaining each day."[23] Think of the enormous media attention given to each horrific terrorist attack or mass shooting when specific people are wounded or killed. In contrast, almost no media attention is devoted to enhance public understanding of the fact that using fossil fuel to manufacture and transport goods, to power our vehicles, to heat our homes, and to provide meat for our meals dramatically increases the heat in our oceans, atmosphere, and earth with the equivalent of three Hiroshima-sized nuclear bombs every second.[24]

We need a moral compass that points to the fact that ordinary human activity—if it continues unchanged for another decade or two—will sentence future generations to lives that never experience nature in the way that people have for thousands of generations. No longer can we claim the moral high ground when we treat only our nearby human neighbors as ourselves. No longer is it morally adequate to expand our understanding of justice to include in the circle of neighborly treatment more distant neighbors. We must recognize that all people, indeed all creatures alive and all those yet to be born, are our neighbors. As the Rev. Dr. Martin Luther King Jr. said, "We are caught in an inescapable network of mutuality, tied in a single garment of destiny. Whatever affects one directly, affects all indirectly."[25] God is calling us to reorient our hearts, our lives, and our laws so that we honor and respect the interdependence of all of creation. We are called to confess the harm our generation has done to the Earth and to future generations. Such honesty and repentance can set us free to take action that will help future generations to survive, perhaps even to thrive.

OUR CHILDREN'S TRUST

One of the reasons our world has not yet engaged such a moral revolution is that our situation feels so overwhelming. Perhaps that's why tears fill my eyes every time I learn more about the work of Our Children's Trust. This is a group of teenagers whose hope is like that of the young shepherd David as he quieted his trembling hands so that he could gather up a few smooth stones before facing the giant Goliath. Their confidence is like that of the carpenter's son who assured those around him that they could move mountains and that the truth would set them free.

The courage of the young people involved in Our Children's Trust enables them to sustain their focus. It allows them to see that continuity-of-life is in jeopardy, that most of the grownup leaders are unwilling to take appropriate action, and that many of those leaders deny that there is even a problem.

These fearless teenagers display unstoppable hope by taking action. Teaming up with attorneys, scientists, and filmmakers, they have built a legal case to protect the climate, based on the public trust doctrine. This legal doctrine, which stretches all the way back to Roman times, is well established in American law and in many other legal traditions around the world. Its universality in the law is not unlike the universal acceptance of the Golden Rule across diverse moral systems. The doctrine states that it is the duty of the government to protect the natural resources essential for our collective survival and prosperity. Rivers, groundwater, the seashore—and in this case, the atmosphere—cannot be privatized or substantially impaired because these natural resources belong to everyone equally—including those not yet born.

Our Children's Trust has taken legal action in almost all fifty states. In April 2016, US magistrate judge Thomas Coffin of the federal district court in Eugene, Oregon, decided in favor of twenty-one young plaintiffs, thus mandating that their federal case—*Juliana v. United States*—be heard.[26] These young people, now aged ten to twenty-one, come from all over the country. They are suing the president and various federal agencies, alleging that the US failure to protect their right to a future not wrecked by climate change is a violation of the Constitution.

Not surprisingly, the fossil fuel industry initially intervened in the case as defendants, joining the US government in trying to have the case thrown out of court. After their two appeals were denied, Judge Coffin released the fossil fuel industry defendants from the case. As of this writing, the government is continuing the appeal process. Nevertheless, a trial date has been set for February 5, 2018, before Judge Aiken at the US District Court of Oregon in Eugene.

In a repurposed church, as the time of trial approaches, tens of thousands of congregations would hear sermons on this future-shaping witness—and many of those sermons would be delivered by teenagers.[27]

Not only is the work of Our Children's Trust built upon legal principles that are thousands of years old, these young people are also calling us to embrace the universal moral principle of the Golden Rule by expanding it to recognize future generations as our neighbors: Golden Rule 2.0.

CONFRONTING THE END OF CONTINUITY

Ours is not the first generation to live with the fear of discontinuity. In the late 1970s and early 1980s our fear of nuclear war was frequently in the news and central to political debate. It brought a million people to the streets of New York City and millions more to their TV screens to watch *The Day After*. Commentaries by Yale professor Robert J. Lifton and Harvard professor John Mack were studied and discussed. Perhaps one of the most lasting and best outcomes of this unsettled period was the early work of Joanna Macy.[28] Although nuclear weapons have generated real fear and anxiety, when it comes to triggering discontinuity in all of creation, thus far (thankfully) nuclear weapons have posed only a threat.[29]

In the early church, many Christians focused much of their faith on the apocalyptic passages in scripture. More recently, tens of millions have been drawn to writers like Tim LaHaye in his *Left Behind* series, whose message combines Christian triumphalism with American nationalism. While Lutheran theologian Barbara Rossing does an excellent job of showing that Tim LaHaye's books are in no way based on scripture,[30] unfortunately her compelling case for a scripture-based countervision has not succeeded in reaching anything like the same audience.

The fact that our brains are wired for fear means that much of the time we don't discriminate between something we should really avoid, and something that poses no danger even though it arouses fear. What really gets our attention, as George Marshall brilliantly demonstrates, are "threats that conjure up strong images or that are communicated in personal stories."[31] Thus, when we have before us the possibility of massive discontinuity—whether by nuclear war, the rapture, or climate change—our wired-for-fear brains will be drawn to whichever account offers strong images communicated in personal stories. Marshall goes on to say, "We have still not found a way to effectively engage our emotional brains in climate change."[32]

The last time I checked, preaching that effectively engages a congregation often includes strong images that are communicated in personal stories. A repurposed church would focus people's moral attention on climate change and inspire them to take action.

A KAIROS MOMENT—TIME FOR A MORAL INTERVENTION

I join Archbishop Desmond Tutu and numerous others in describing our current situation as a "Kairos moment," an opportune moment fraught with God-inspired possibility. The church now has an unprecedented opportunity to shape the future of life on this planet. By embracing the suggestions presented in these pages, a repurposed church can welcome the theological shifts and spiritual practices that will make this opportunity a reality. I now turn to theologians Thomas Berry and Larry Rasmussen to make the case for why such a significant change is essential.

Over the past 170 years, humanity has shifted the fulcrum on which all life hinges, so that, as Thomas Berry puts is, we've moved from "an organic, ever-renewing, land-based economy to an extractive, non-renewing, industrial economy." This economic shift has allowed a tiny percentage of the human population to grow unimaginably rich at the expense of the balance of creation itself. Ethicist Larry Rasmussen asks a pointed question: How have the ministries of the churches responded? They have, he charges, "tagged along, as though on a leash."[33]

In contrast, over the past many decades, scientists have made almost unimaginable advances in providing humanity with a thorough understanding of the consequences of what we call "progress"—and have done so despite the war being waged against them by the most powerful people on Earth—those who benefit from the status quo. And yet, as Rasmussen points out, in itself "science 'does not teach us what we most need to know about nature'—namely, 'how to value it.' Religion and culture do that."[34]

Can communities of faith do more than tag along as though on a leash? I believe they can. And they must. Doing so, as I have suggested, will require the church to embrace a new vocation. I am not alone in that belief. Here is how Larry Rasmussen puts it:

> Morality rests in the constructive work to be undertaken when one way of life must of needs give way to another. The subject of ethics is how we and others are to survive and flourish. So when a turning point arrives and a time of transition from one way of life to another intrudes, moral inertia no longer suffices and all that belongs to the present moral life must of needs be engaged anew—cosmology; community of reformation of human character and conduct; the understanding of what is morally normative; and the shape, behavior, and outcome of systems, structures and practices. All of these belong to the work of human responsibility as the way is forged from the industrial-technological era to an ecospheric one.[35]

For the sake of humanity, the world, the ecosphere, and countless generations of unborn children and creatures, our present social and economic system needs a moral intervention. And so does the church. It's time to declare a new moral era.

QUESTIONS FOR GROUP DISCUSSION AND FURTHER REFLECTION

1. Review the history lessons from early in the chapter. Share with your group what for you stuck out most.
2. Invite those in the group to each share their examples of how climate change exacerbates virtually every other social justice issue.
3. If in three years the progressive church in America will focus on climate to the same extent the church focused on abolition in the 1830s–1860, what do we need to do now to get there?
4. If religion is perhaps the best—and possibly the only—aid which has the power and promise to restore a right relationship to God

and creation, what might be a next step your congregation could take to move your community in that direction?

4

THE MARKS OF THE CHURCH
IN A CLIMATE CRISIS WORLD

Leaders and spiritual communities are not needed to comfort people feeling lost in times of change. Instead, spiritual leaders need to help transform [the] fears [of their congregations] into urgency and courage.[1]
—Diana Butler Bass

Churches succeed for lots of reasons. Many succeed because they have established a niche that not only appeals to their members but also attracts those in the community who would not otherwise be interested. I have had the privilege of visiting scores of thriving churches. No two are alike. Most have a niche. Over time, that niche can change. Led by the Spirit that spoke to Isaiah 43:19 ("Behold, I am about to do a new thing"), a congregation may vote to become "Open and Affirming"; or it may welcome the homeless for a week through Family Promise; or it may install solar panels and become carbon neutral; or it may call a new pastor. By distinguishing themselves in an appealing way, the church hopes to be faithful to God and to attract new members.

In addition to creating a distinctive niche, churches succeed because they excel at what strong churches have done for centuries. They engage people in authentic worship. They proclaim Jesus' life, death, and resurrection and invite people into a meaningful relationship with God. They create a safe and caring community. They pour themselves out for others in service of the world. These four classic marks of the church are often identified by their Greek names: Liturgia, Kerygma, Koinonia, and Diakonia.

Seeking to be faithful, from time to time church leaders attempt to identify the marks of a faithful and healthy church. In my role as a denominational leader, I have seen many such lists. Today, a new generation of church leaders is imagining and creating new communities that are gathering and serving in fresh ways. The General Minister and President of the UCC, John Dorhauer, has reflected on the emerging church in his book, *Beyond Resistance: The Institutional Church Meets the Post-Modern World.*

But here's the thing. No matter what a church's distinctive niche may be, no matter how effectively a church may be living out the classic marks of a faithful and healthy community of faith, no matter how innovative and creative a postmodern gathering of Christians may seem, every church faces a daunting new reality: we can no longer depend on the continuity of God's creation.

Not only that—consider this: It is *"God's* creation" that is being destroyed. If any segment of the human race were going to face up to what human beings are doing, one might expect that it would be people of faith who realize that humanity is trashing what does not belong to us—the Earth belongs to God. It seems to me that when people of faith grasp this truth, the alarm of climate change will finally ring out in every church and cathedral, in every mission outpost, and wherever two or three are gathered in Jesus' name.

In 1968—a very tumultuous year—a song was born, "They Will Know We Are Christians by Our Love." Written by Peter Scholtes, a Roman Catholic priest, the song inspired countless Christians to choose love over war. It's time to add a stanza. It's time for the world to know that we are Christians by our love for the Earth and for all living things—by our willingness to sacrifice for God's creation—by our commitment to join Jesus as he works to reconcile us to God's creation.

I believe that communities of faith can be the "delivery vehicle" for a redeemed Earth. Indeed, strategically speaking, I believe that the only hope we have for a redeemed Earth is the wholesale transformation of what it means to be religious. While that transformation requires us to increase our energy conservation and efficiency, and to use more renewable energy by installing LED lights and solar panels, these practical steps mark only the beginning of our transformation. A successful climate crisis church will embrace a life together that is distinguished by the following characteristics, new marks of the church.

OUR ROLE AS KEEPERS OF CONTINUITY

We've all heard a great deal about the critically important role of the church upholding timeless moral teachings and principles that are as true today as they were two thousand years ago. Countless preachers—especially those serving more orthodox or conservative churches—emphasize unchanging moral values as the focus of their sermons in times of so-called culture wars, when traditional social mores are challenged by competing moral visions.

The continuity of creation and the viability of life for future generations are now threatened by two constituencies that benefit from creation's demise. The first constituency is a tiny group of people who are becoming staggeringly rich by extracting fossil fuel. Fossil fuel companies are the most profitable industry in the history of money because society has not yet made them pay for the damage to the Earth caused by their product. They have sought to extend this benefit by spending hundreds of millions of dollars on a public relations campaign to discredit science, and by lobbying lawmakers.

The second constituency that benefits from trashing creation is the majority of people who are alive today—particularly those living in advanced industrial countries. Many people believe that the only way to maintain their current lifestyle requires that they continue to extract and burn oil, coal, and gas. As President George H. W. Bush put it at Earth Summit in Rio de Janeiro in 1992, "The American way of life is not up for negotiation. Period!"[2]

Elsewhere in this book, I discuss the emerging Davids who are taking on the Goliaths of the fossil fuel industry. Here I want to make a simple, though by no means obvious, point. At various times over the past two thousand years, the church has played an enormously important role as a keeper of continuity. Creation is crying out for the church to play that role again.

The previous chapter drew attention to several of the ways that creation itself is presently imperiled. Already, the most vulnerable places in the world are experiencing disruption related to conflict over scarce resources such as potable water and arable land. As these and other conflicts related to essential resources escalate, tribalism, racism, and xenophobia all increase. As society edges towards breakdown, humanity will need the church more than ever to uphold continuity of such traditional moral values as justice, mercy, nonviolence, human rights, welcoming the stranger, and so forth. In other words, as the continuity of creation breaks down, humanity enters into a time of moral discontinuity as well.

Upholding the ancient values that protect God's people and the whole of God's creation must become a core mark of the church in a climate crisis world. Such a commitment would increase the chance that future generations will receive an inheritance as bountiful as what we ourselves were given.

BUILDING RESILIENT COMMUNITIES

If you want a great example of a church committed to building resilience, have a look at Trinity United Church of Christ on the south side of Chicago. While Trinity's senior minister, the Rev. Dr. Otis Moss III, is one of the most brilliant preachers in America, he recognizes that not all preaching is done in the pulpit. As an example of a message that needs to be shouted from the rooftops, Trinity is growing carrots . . . on its roof! It's part of a renovation to align Trinity's campus with their theology, which affirms our role as stewards of God's creation. Ninety percent of the contractors used to create these rooftop gardens were African American. In addition, the church engaged in "hyper local hiring"—by using firms that traditionally do not get opportunities on large-scale projects and by hiring returning citizens (persons coming out of prison). The Rev. Dr. Moss points out that not only will the church renovations raise property values in the community because such improvements on anchor properties lift all boats, the rooftop gardens absorb water and thus reduce flooding in his community.

Over the past several decades, many communities of faith across the United States have joined together to amplify their town's resilience during times of tragedy, disaster, or threat: 9/11 in New York City; Hurricane Katrina in New Orleans; the mass shooting of children in

Newtown, Connecticut; and the terrorist bombing of the Boston Marathon, to name a few.

We are now up against the most profound changes the Earth has suffered since the Cretaceous extinctions 67 million years ago. There is an immediate, growing need for churches to be a training ground for resilience as they champion the common good. Many churches are already doing just that in conjunction with the Transition Towns movement.[3] Just as it is now clear that the unit of survival is the ecosphere taken as a whole, the unit of resilience will be the community in which we live. As churches focus on engaging this mission, town by town we will become a stronger people, more prepared for the profound changes we are facing together.

IT'S NOT JUST ABOUT ME: FROM PERSONAL TO COMMUNAL SALVATION

As I preach throughout the United Church of Christ, I often charge congregations to embrace God's call for us to become a "church for others." It's a provocative invitation. Initially, people respond by asking, "Aren't we that already?" But more often than not, after a while, they reluctantly acknowledge that in fact they are more a church for themselves than they are a church for others.

Jesus calls us to follow his lead by pouring ourselves out for others (Philippians 2:7). In promising that those who lose their life will gain it, Jesus is urging us to engage in a life of service (Matthew 10:39; Mark 8:35; Luke 9:24).

This supports the theme I explored in chapter 3—that God calls communities, not just individuals. In a repurposed church, individuals who might otherwise find their lives full of despair and grief will exchange that orientation for a life in and for community—a life that affirms our interdependence with other people and creatures the world over. It may have been Brian McLaren who first made a similar point by proclaiming that Jesus did not come with an evacuation plan. He came with a building plan—hoping to convince his followers to join him in building the Kingdom of Heaven on Earth, not by evacuating (whether by death or by spaceship) from the life-giving creation that God entrusted to our care.

STEP 1: CONFESS COMPLICITY;
STEP 2: CHANGE THE SYSTEM

Two weeks after the UCC became the first national body and the first religious denomination to vote to divest from fossil fuel companies, Yale Law School professor Stephen L. Carter pilloried the UCC, calling us hypocrites. Among other things, he cited the fact that the delegates who voted this resolution travelled to Synod using fossil fuel, and that our churches will continue to welcome worshippers who drive their cars to church. Professor Carter is a popular writer on such topics as civility, and occasionally writes syndicated op-ed pieces. Mindful of Jesus' attack on hypocrisy (John 8:7), he titled this one, "Casting the first stone . . . at Exxon?"[4]

Many pastors and church members are unable to get past this issue. They excuse themselves from engaging the challenge of climate change on the grounds that their lives—and any life they can imagine living— are dependent on fossil fuel. Not only are they allowing the perfect to be the enemy of the good, they are failing to understand that people enmeshed in a flawed system are not exempt from the struggle to transform that system. As Naomi Oreskes points out:

> Of course we [all use fossil fuels], and people in the North wore *clothes* made of cotton picked by slaves. But that did not make them hypocrites when they joined the abolition movement. It just meant that they were also part of the slave economy, and they knew it. That is why they acted to change the *system*, not just their clothes.[5]

Professor Carter is of course correct in at least one respect: reducing our personal carbon footprint is important. This has been the focus of many of the daily messages included in the worldwide annual Ecumenical Lenten Carbon Fast (http://www.macucc.org/carbonfast) that I and others initiated in 2011. Over the years, as part of the Ecumenical Lenten Carbon Fast, hundreds of churches have carried out environmental audits, many of which have resulted in churches reducing their carbon footprint by taking such measures as replacing boilers, improving energy conservation, and installing solar panels. Many churches hold "carbon free Sundays," where members bike or walk to church. In short, churches have long known that when engaging in social critique, the first place to look is at our own complicity. But it should never be the last.

Just as we must shift our preaching so that it focuses at least as much on communal salvation as on personal salvation, so the preponderance of our justice work should seek to expose and undo systemic injustice. Jesus himself was a powerful critic of the destructive systems of injustice within his own society. In our society, multinational corporations—especially the fossil fuel industry—wield incalculable power. To reverse this momentum, humanity must engage in profound structural change. Humanity needs to create a moral climate—rooted in science—that compels the most profitable industry the world has ever known to walk away from 80 percent of its assets. The oil, gas, and coal that nature took hundreds of millions of years to create are not the "property" of the fossil fuel industry.

A repurposed church will attend to God's call to speak truth to power. In late 2015, several state attorneys general initiated an investigation into whether Exxon was lying to its investors about the risks to all living things posed by Exxon's business plan.[6] In 2016 the Securities and Exchange Commission initiated a similar investigation. Several denominations have already voted to divest from the fossil fuel industry. A repurposed church would add to this witness by persistently addressing what in recent years has become a systemic evil masquerading as an industry that supplies what people want and need.

A repurposed church would summon all the gifts of the Spirit to courageously live with a clear understanding of what all people—including generations to come—truly need. As I discuss elsewhere, a repurposed church would take its lead from the early church (Acts 2:44) by organizing itself around a shared economy. A repurposed church would also support people as they transition to lives of meaning beyond the fulfillment of material wants.

We are in the midst of a moral, spiritual, economic, and cultural challenge as daunting as the challenge posed by slavery. I believe that the scale of the material and spiritual transformation required of us today is at least as great as what was required for the United States to move beyond a slave economy.

I also believe that within our lifetime, drilling for oil, blowing off mountain tops for coal, and fracking for gas and oil will all become as morally repugnant and as intolerable to us as it would be for us to own slaves. Yet this moral revolution will only become possible when repurposed churches, synagogues, mosques, and other houses of worship join in common cause with the worldwide climate movement. Our moral leadership is essential if we are to preserve a world worth saving.

EMBRACING SPIRITUAL PROGRESS IN PLACE OF MATERIAL PROGRESS

Imagine if faith leaders of all religious persuasions had recognized in 1989—when the first book about climate change for a general audience was published—that society needed to undertake numerous fundamental changes. Imagine if faith leaders had made it their business to ask which values humanity needs to alter and which values we must reclaim in order for us to avoid the cataclysms of a disrupted climate?

Such a communal soul-searching would absolutely include the necessity of reconsidering our sense of what counts as progress. One step in that direction might be to adopt the measure of Gross National Happiness[7] as a replacement for Gross National Product. Advocates for this and related notions are numerous. The fact that these proposals receive so little media coverage is an indication of the challenge they represent to the dominant values of contemporary society.

Similarly, what if religious leaders the world over had recognized the significance of the creation of the Intergovernmental Panel on Climate Change by the United Nations in November 1988? What if American religious leaders had realized in June 1988 that Dr. James Hansen's remarks to Congress[8] were intended not only for policy makers? His report—the first of its kind to Congress on global warming—constituted an alarm for anyone who recognizes God as Creator and creation as God's.

Imagine if tens of thousands of preachers had helped their congregations recognize that this unfolding reality required us to abandon our understanding of material growth as our most significant measure of progress. Imagine if they had said we needed to exchange material growth for spiritual growth. Imagine if churches, synagogues, mosques, and temples had all become laboratories of spiritual growth. Imagine if they had reflected from their pulpits on the work of economists who had been emphasizing indices of happiness.[9] If you are politely thinking that this is a pie-in-the-sky fantasy, imagine if leaders from all faith perspectives had engaged this campaign to the same extent and with the same gusto that a limited number of faith leaders engaged the antiabortion campaign, beginning in the late 1970s.

SACRIFICE AND SHARING AS GUIDING VIRTUES

In response to a climate crisis world, a repurposed church would boldly proclaim sacrifice and sharing as characteristic virtues promoted by the church. Imagine if churches throughout our land enthusiastically welcomed putting a fair and rising price on carbon. This could be accomplished as congregation after congregation affiliated with the Citizens Climate Lobby. Imagine coordinated efforts by a majority of faith communities focusing on two transitions: making certain that the true cost of carbon and the pollution it causes is reflected in its price, and making certain that the wealthy bear their fair share of the burden of this transition to a sustainable economy. Imagine church communities inspiring their adherents who have more than enough to rise up en masse in the public square and to insist that the burden of paying the true price of carbon must not fall on the poor.

EMBRACING MORAL INTERDEPENDENCE

In 1957 the UCC was founded after decades of negotiation. The scripture that best expressed the UCC's calling comes from the Gospel of John 17:21: "That they may all be one." How fanciful it must have seemed to others when the UCC forebears in the 1940s and 1950s (when denominationalism was at its zenith) looked beyond all the barriers that denominations and congregations had erected between themselves. How prescient, we now realize, of the UCC to see on the distant horizon a vision of unity without uniformity—a recognition that the God of many names calls all who would follow God to lead lives of interdependence. From its founding, the UCC affirmed our interdependence with God, our interdependence with current, past, and future generations, and our interdependence with all of creation.

This mark of the church was lived out in April 2013, twelve days after the Boston Marathon bombing. For the first time in history virtually all the Protestant bishop-level New England faith leaders gathered for a Climate Revival.[10] Hundreds of people from across New England and representing a dozen denominations filled the two large churches on downtown Boston's Copley Square. A month later, one of those bishops was speaking at the annual meeting of the Massachusetts Council of Churches—the oldest such council in America. He opened by saying how wonderful it was to have been included in such a profound witness as the Climate Revival, and then he said, "I can imagine in the not-too-distant future when the UCC and the Episcopal Church in Western Massachusetts will be one." You could have heard a pin drop!

I'd like to think that Diana Butler Bass is right when she talks about a Fourth Great Awakening: "a spiritual awakening, a period of sustained religious and political transformation during which our ways of seeing the world, understanding ourselves, and expressing faith are being (to borrow a phrase) 'born again.'" She goes on to say that we are in the midst of "a 'Great Turning' toward a global community based on shared human connection, dedicated to the care of our planet, committed to justice and equality, that seeks to raise hundreds of millions (of people) from poverty, violence and oppression."[11]

In his book *The Great Spiritual Migration: How the World's Largest Religion Is Seeking a Better Way to Be Christian*, Brian McLaren builds on Diana Butler Bass' point by suggesting that, going forward, churches will gather together people who share common values rather than people who share common beliefs.

A repurposed church that explicitly values continuity of creation could declare our moral interdependence with our billions of neighbors the world over as well as our countless yet-to-be-born neighbors. If the church persisted in its advocacy and prayer, in a decade or two the United States could modify its laws, strengthen our sustainable industries, and redirect our lives to effectively transition from a carbon-based economy.

GLOBAL WARMING INTENSIFIES ALL FORMS OF INJUSTICE

Many churches already manifest justice as a mark of the church. They understand that our world is full of an endless array of injustices, and that the church is called to oppose injustice wherever it may be found, whatever form it takes. But many churches are beginning to recognize that climate change is not just one moral issue among others. They understand that climate change is already intensifying these other concerns. Food insecurity is heightened as desertification and extreme weather events increase. Access to potable water becomes harder as draughts cause wells to fail. An increase in violence and social unrest is now linked to climate change. Climate refugees already number in the millions. As the Pentagon has often explained, climate change is a "threat multiplier." These and many more injustices will increase at an exponential rate if we don't respond immediately and effectively to the climate crisis.

CONFRONT THE POWERS AND PRINCIPALITIES

Science makes clear the urgent need to put an end to our business-as-usual practice of depending on fossil fuel. Making these changes will require moral confrontation with the powers that be.

Since people of faith and conscience can't possibly outspend the fossil fuel industry, we must seek a more hopeful future using a different kind of currency. Altogether, passion, prayer, persistence, our bodies, our love of creation, and our concern for eternity can offer a worthy witness to the myopic trajectory of market capitalism which operates with a time horizon measured in weeks and months rather than centuries and eons.

Churches often forget that we actually have the power to revoke the social license upon which the Exxons of this world depend in order to continue with business as usual. The church has a long history of confronting principalities and powers. Living as we do in a world disordered by climate change—a world in which unimaginable profits are concentrated in the hands of a few individuals and corporations (and of the politicians who benefit from their campaign donations)—a world in which creation itself is at stake—surely it's time to redirect the vocation of the church to confront the powers and principalities.

SHARING OUR FEARS AND HOPES: EMPOWERING ACTION

Churches seeking to live into these marks of the church must nurture among their members relationships that are based on love, respect for differences, curiosity, open minds, and open hearts. These qualities help establish a sense of safety that allows people to risk sharing divergent perspectives, along with our deepest concerns and callings, and our most profound despair and hope. I believe that one of the reasons the church has not yet responded to creation's cry is that the emotional and moral atmosphere of so many congregations does not invite this level of candor and vulnerability. Such an environment is hard won. As many congregations have discovered, the presence of one or two vocal members who embrace a more combative understanding of church can put any sense of safety out of reach.

But from the early church until today, congregations that learn to deal effectively with conflict, that welcome difference, and that worship a God who calls communities as well as individuals are the congregations that make a positive difference in the world.

TRUTH AND RECONCILIATION CONVERSATIONS IN EVERY HOUSE OF WORSHIP

In June 2014, I was keynoting the Annual Meeting of the UCC churches in Texas, Louisiana, and Mississippi. At a pastors-only breakfast, this was the first question:

> I serve a mid-sized church in downtown Houston where ExxonMobil is building its new world headquarters. Soon, I expect 80 percent or 90 percent of the checks in the offering plate to come from Exxon-Mobil. . . . Please comment.

A stunned silence fell upon the ninety or so pastors. I took a step back and closed my eyes, doing all I could to take this in. Then, after a long silence, I stepped forward and replied:

> Thank you for your profound question. I need to tell you: during that time of silence, Desmond Tutu came to me. If I may say so, I believe that God is calling us to initiate a Truth and Reconciliation Conversation in your congregation. Those people receiving their paychecks from Exxon are not bad people. Indeed—full disclosure—my father was one of the head chemical engineers of Mobil Oil. Bishop Tutu and President Mandela knew that South Africa could only begin to fulfill its hopes if the victims and perpetrators of apartheid could face together the pain, suffering and broken lives of those tragic and horrific decades.

I have shared this story many times; to the best of my knowledge, no church has initiated a Truth and Reconciliation movement. And while Pope Francis' Encyclical, *Laudato Si'*, represents a turning point in terms of the church's engagement of this issue, I believe that initiating Truth and Reconciliation Conversations could well be the most important contribution of the church to creating a world able to undergo the great transition we are now beginning. For many generations we have sought to conquer, dominate, and exploit nature. Now we must seek intergenerational and cross-species atonement. It seems to me that if the church, the synagogue, and the mosque are to offer meaningful hope in the years ahead, they must host such personal and communal, transparent and sacred conversations.

Imagine if we were to start a movement that inspired tens of thousands of congregations of all faith perspectives to make Truth and Reconciliation Conversations a normative expression of their life together, every bit as much as worship. Imagine people with conflicting ideological positions listening to one another with open hearts. While such candor is almost unheard of in our current political climate, I believe that faithful congregations can and must convene such sacred conversations.[12] As was the case in South Africa, houses of worship can initiate and lead such a healing and transformational process. And when we do, our generation's obligation to those unborn will motivate us to make the changes that science says we must.

CIVIL DISOBEDIENCE—THE CHURCH ACTS
ON ITS CONSCIENCE

From the beginning, faith communities have encouraged their members to express their conscience on important public issues. From the beginning, nonviolent civil disobedience has been one expression of faithful witness to the values of the church when those values are in conflict with the laws of the land. Many of us are aware that after Jesus' death, Peter and Paul spent more time in jail than they did as free men, because they acted in service of the church that was waiting to be born. In the next chapter I will discuss the need to make civil disobedience a normative expression of discipleship. In order for that to happen, the church must affirm its role of supporting those called by their conscience to engage in nonviolent civil disobedience.

A REPURPOSED CHURCH FOR A NEW MORAL ERA

As with any set of marks of the church, no single church can embrace all of these characteristics. The reason to gather them together is to make it clear not only that climate change represents a call to the church, but also that this is truly an opportunity for which the church was born. To meet this challenge will require the church to reclaim some ancient understandings of its calling and to understand its calling in some fundamentally new ways.

In a critically important article Bill McKibben makes the case for a World War II–type mobilization to fight climate change.[13] What I want to add to Bill's argument is that leadership and vision from a repurposed church are essential if our country is to make the transition that he outlines. Bill is right: we CAN do this—as long as we are guided by a moral compass that is oriented by the marks of a repurposed church.

QUESTIONS FOR GROUP DISCUSSION
AND FURTHER REFLECTION

1. While the subheadings of this chapter are not intended as a checklist for a faithful and vital church, it would be worthwhile

for your group to evaluate the extent to which your church is living into each of the marks named in the subheadings.

2. Share some examples of moral discontinuity. How might any of these relate to discontinuity of creation?

3. Review the justice work done by your congregation (some congregations refer to this as mission or outreach) and for each program, discuss the extent to which they focus on changing an unjust system (for example, ending homelessness in your city) versus remedying specific injustices (such as providing food, clothing, or shelter for a family in need).

4. How can it be that some of our most prominent religious leaders succeeded in the past several decades to make abortion widely illegal yet, over those same decades, their silence on climate change has resulted in the death of millions of climate refugees, not to mention so many others from illness and "natural" disasters amplified by climate change?

5. What's the relationship between civil disobedience and church? Share with your group any experience you may have with civil disobedience.

5

DISCIPLESHIP

Reorienting What We Prize

If the future is going to be different, we have to go far beyond these
little piecemeal gestures and begin to see the systems in which we're
embedded. . . . What would it take to shift the whole? . . . When all is
said and done, the only change that will make a difference is the
transformation of the human heart.
—Peter Senge[1]

If God is calling the church to take up a new vocation, it follows that
Christians must open themselves to a new understanding of discipleship. What does it mean to follow Jesus in a climate crisis world? What
values and virtues is God calling our generation to affirm and live out as
a faithful response to what we've done to God's creation? If Jesus'
supreme work is to reconcile us to God, to each other, and to all of
creation, how do we follow Jesus today, in the context of the climate
crisis?

I'm not suggesting that the climate crisis should overturn our centuries-old understanding of discipleship, but it must reshape it. Here's an
example of what I mean. The science is now clear that we must keep
the vast majority of known fossil fuel deposits in the ground. However,
since Edwin Drake pioneered modern oil drilling in 1859, each generation has claimed for itself as much of this limited resource as it could, in
order to fuel:

- our insatiable desire for material growth,
- our uncompromising insistence on convenience, and
- our relentless addiction to mobility.

Changing this pattern of behavior and expectation may be the greatest challenge civilization has ever faced. History shows that the support of religious leadership is essential for society to successfully navigate such fundamental transitions in values and behavior.

As followers of Jesus who are rooted in communities of faith, we have the power to redirect society's momentum. The last time I looked, material growth, convenience, and mobility were neither religious nor moral values. But what about preserving God's gift of creation for our children and grandchildren? Isn't that at the core of our covenant with God?

As we seek to partner with Jesus in his work of reconciliation, let us reorient what we prize:

- Let our behavior testify to a set of values that are in keeping with sustaining God's gift of creation.
- Let us join our voices—because we are followers of Jesus—with pathfinders like Diana Butler Bass, whose vision of a Great Turning offers a substantial way forward to redeeming all of creation.
- Let our discipleship come to be recognized in this climate crisis world by the courage and joy we demonstrate as we live into the following marks of discipleship.

RESILIENCE IN PLACE OF GROWTH

The extraction and use of fossil fuel over the past two centuries has enabled the industrial revolution to advance material growth on an unprecedented scale. Throughout the world, the length of human life has been extended, and many people have found that their quality of life has been enhanced. Access to relatively cheap power has built the modern world. But cheap power has also allowed industry, manufacturers, designers, inventors, engineers, and, most of all, consumers to tolerate waste and accept inefficiency. The vast majority of Westerners simply take cheap energy for granted. Because of this, the promise of material growth continues to have strong appeal, since the price we pay for fossil fuel does not reflect its true cost to human health or to the health of the planet's ecosystems.

Earlier I pointed out that with God there are no externalities. When the Rev. Dr. Martin Luther King Jr.'s lieutenants told him to stick to civil rights and to stop speaking out against poverty and war, King told them that he could not segregate his conscience. Similarly, as people of faith, we, too, cannot stand idly by as the human economy rolls along with "pathological indifference to the ecological costs."[2]

The notion that there are limits to growth began with Malthus over two hundred years ago. In the 1970s, when planet Earth carried about half the human population that it carries today, the Club of Rome published the bestselling environmental book of all time. Thirty million people bought *The Limits to Growth*,[3] but humanity's embrace of material growth remained undiminished. Historian J. R. McNeill, writing at the turn of the twenty-first century, rightly suggests that our "growth fetish" could best be understood in religious terms.

> Capitalists, nationalists—indeed almost everyone, communists included—worshiped at this same altar because economic growth disguised a multitude of sins. . . . Social, moral and ecological ills were sustained in the interest of economic growth; indeed, adherents to the faith proposed that only more growth could resolve such ills. . . . The overarching priority of economic growth was easily the most important idea of the twentieth century.[4]

Almost two decades later, the "religion" of material growth and the aspiration toward material prosperity have gained popular and political momentum. Adherents betray their ideological allegiance by making material growth the solution to almost every problem.

As followers of Jesus, we can no longer sacrifice the environment to economic growth. What's needed is moral leadership that motivates people to shift their aspiration from material growth to a resilience that builds sustainability. Popular examples of this shift include the trend towards farmers markets and various manifestations of localism.[5] When people experience shorter supply chains and increased self-sufficiency, they feel a sense of connection and satisfaction not usually associated with acquiring more things. Imagine, in the context of a world experiencing more and more catastrophic weather events, if we came away from those events focused on the incredible sacrifice, cooperation, and sharing displayed in the wake of disaster. What if we embraced our rebuilding as an opportunity to provide adequate material necessities, while focusing on amplifying cooperation in the context of a sustainable, shared economy? Make no mistake: this is a tall order. For centuries, the bulk of our behavioral shifts have been motivated by economic incentives. But not all of them.

Consider the abolition of slavery, which represented a shift not only in individual behavior but also in an entire economic system. Moral leadership—much of it from pulpits—motivated people to embrace economic sacrifice and the sacrifice of life and limb for the sake of universalizing our commitment to freedom and equality. Consider the ongoing LGBTQIA+ movement, which has codified marriage equality into law, opened the ranks of military service, and changed the practices of the IRS and of HR programs across the United States. Moral leadership—much of it from pulpits—has been essential to this transformation.

Invoking Golden Rule 2.0, religious leaders can counter the intoxicating attraction of material growth by offering the moral rewards that come with enhancing personal and communal resilience. People no longer have to live with the unspoken dread we feel because deep down we know that we contribute to the juggernaut of material growth that has already exceeded the carrying capacity of the planet. Churches can become communities where we gather to reorient our lives by amplifying our resilience and embracing the other values detailed below. As we do this, town by town we will become a stronger people, more prepared for the profound changes we must face.

COLLABORATION IN PLACE OF CONSUMPTION

Two days after 9/11, the church I served in Shaker Heights, Ohio, opened its doors for a service of prayer and healing. As was the case all over the country, our sanctuary was packed. Our country was ready for moral leadership. Two weeks later, after one of the biggest crashes in Wall Street history, President Bush encouraged every citizen to go out and buy something—perhaps a major appliance. Like many, I longed for visionary moral leadership in response to this crisis, and I was appalled by his suggestion. Nevertheless, the possible collapse of our economy seemed imminent, and for good or ill our present economy is built on material consumption. In my sermon a few days later, I supported President Bush's suggestion, but not without redirecting it. I encouraged anyone in my congregation who had the financial resources:

> To engage this needed consumption with a new end in mind. What if each of us began to embody the values of the "Make a Wish Foundation" in our personal lives? What if, motivated by our patriotism, the current economic circumstances, and the teachings of the One we call Lord, what if we were to get back to traveling (as our President has suggested), but not we ourselves. Rather, we could make it possible for a family who has never seen Disneyland to go and have a good time. What if we were to make a major purchase—like buying a new car with cash . . . And once you've bought that new car, give it to someone who needs it.

Many later told me that in the silence that followed, they were overwhelmed by all kinds of realizations: how blessed they were to have the resources to actually be able to do this; how shocked they were that I would suggest such a thing; how exposed they felt knowing that they could pull off a much needed win-win if only their generosity would allow them. It seemed that almost everyone recognized that this is what it might look like to follow Jesus and to address the immediate economic crisis.

In the mid-1980s shortly after I became pastor of a UCC church in Newton, Massachusetts, I naively asked my new congregation from the pulpit why each of the homes around the parsonage had their own lawnmowers. Sharing lawnmowers and other tools was one of many easy ways that our city could become an "Acts 2:44 community" (holding all things in common). Unfortunately, nothing came of that suggestion, apart from one very upset congregant suggesting to me privately that I was a Communist. In the intervening years, I've considered that encounter many times. For this person, concern about Communism overrode his commitment to generosity and sharing. For me, this encounter remains an enduring example of how difficult it can be to offer Good News when Gospel values challenge our immediate self-interest and our political or ideological point of view.

While many (perhaps most) churches support recycling, and a few do all they can to integrate sustainable practices into their common life, much bolder efforts lie ahead of us. For decades, Sojourners and other Christian communities have witnessed to Jesus' encouragement to love our neighbors as ourselves and to the early church's example of sharing all things in common. What if the church were to acknowledge the urgency of the climate crisis by elevating the practice of economic and environmental justice to the top of the list of ways that Christians live out our discipleship? Imagine tens of thousands of congregations engaged in an "Acts 2:44 Movement" consisting of a myriad of local experiments in democratized ownership and in pooling resources to leverage community engagement and economic revitalization. Here's an example that moved an entire congregation to tears.

As the economy plummeted late in 2008 and early in 2009, many churches hunkered down in survival mode, but others stepped up to the challenge. At the height of the crisis, at a Sunday morning worship service in January 2009, a pastor in a western Massachusetts church invited the congregation to express concerns or celebrations. An elderly woman stood. She was well known to the congregation, a widow, and not a person of means. With tremors in her voice, she asked for prayers. She could not make her next month's mortgage payment and she feared being tossed out on the street. Then she sat down.

The pastor knew in her bones what to do. She stood, and declared in a quiet but firm voice, "No one in our congregation will lose their home to foreclosure." She went on to say that if the promise of abundant life is true, then each congregation, as a community, must make it true. And then she sat down—still shaking. The only thing the pastor knew for sure was that she had no idea how this would work out.

Two weeks later during the time for celebrations and concerns, a different elderly widow who was known to have only her Social Security paycheck to live on raised her hand. She began by apologizing for taking a few weeks to do the math. Then she said, "I just wanted you all to know that I will cover the February mortgage payment." Few had ever experienced such a Spirit-filled moment. Truly, this was Good News. This congregation was beginning to live into a new story. Amidst their joyful tears, the relentless news of recession fell silent, and the miracle of abundance made everyone in that meeting house wealthy beyond measure. Two weeks later another person raised her hand and said simply, "I've got March."

What other opportunities for freedom, community, trust, safety, leadership, and transparency await us? These are the values and qualities our God wants for us as individuals and especially as a community of the faithful.

Just as congregational church polity paved the way for American democracy, local churches could become laboratories of collaboration, paving the way for the profound systemic change that is essential if humanity is to avoid catastrophe as we transition to a new way of living that puts people and planet at its core.[6]

WISDOM IN PLACE OF PROGRESS

I join Pope Francis in asserting that we who take Christ's name as our own are called to "leave behind the modern myth of material progress."[7] Pope Francis goes on to say:

> It is not enough to balance, in the medium term, the protection of nature with financial gain, or the preservation of the environment with progress. Halfway measures simply delay the inevitable disaster. *Put simply, it is a matter of redefining our notion of progress.* A technological and economic development which does not leave in its wake a better world and an integrally higher quality of life cannot be considered progress.[8]

It's not up to economists to redefine our notion of progress. This requires moral leadership. Reshaping our understanding of progress is a job for religious leaders. Imagine that next Sunday, priests and pastors from all over the country mount their pulpits to offer a ***moral critique*** of these appalling outcomes of our reckless pursuit of material progress:[9]

- Real wages for about 80 percent of American workers have not risen for at least three decades.
- The top 10 percent of Americans now own over 75 percent of our wealth.

- The richest 400 individuals in America, taken together, now possess more wealth than the bottom 186 million Americans combined.
- Poverty in American has increased from 11.1 percent in 1973 to 13.5 percent in 2015.
- Yet in 2015, the US economy produced the equivalent of $223,639 for every family of four in America.

Many pastors and laypeople avoid thinking about these realities. We tell ourselves, "That's the work of economists." But the moral implications of living as we do are enormous.

I will leave it to economists and politicians to identify what financial or other tangible incentives will encourage people to change their behavior and to do the right thing. My task here is to clarify the essential role that faith communities must play in transforming society: to proclaim the urgent moral call to stabilize the climate and to build a more just and sustainable society.

We are disciples of Jesus living amidst the realities of the twenty-first century. We have the responsibility to forge a wise and morally defensible path through the thicket of economic inequality, material aspiration, and corporate ascendency so that God's creation is not sacrificed on the altar of material growth. Pope Francis is right in declaring that, "Many people know that our current progress and the mere amassing of things and pleasures are not enough to give meaning and joy to the human heart."[10] As eco-theologian Sallie McFague puts it:

> The religious of the world, countercultural in their assumption that "to find one's life, one must lose it," are key players in understanding and promoting a movement [away] from a model of God, the world, and the self focused on individualistic, market-oriented accumulation by a few, to a model that sees self and planetary flourishing as interdependent. [11]

In fact, Sallie McFague's book, *Blessed are the Consumers: Climate Change and the Practice of Restraint*, stands out as a guide for Christians who recognize that God is calling us to a new understanding of discipleship.

BALANCE IN PLACE OF ADDICTION

The line most remembered from George W. Bush's eight State of the Union addresses came on January 31, 2006, when the former oil man from Texas declared "America is addicted to oil" and insisted that the United States "break this addiction."[12]

Four years later, I was preaching at Old South Church in downtown Boston for an ecumenical prayer vigil prompted by the Deepwater Horizon Gulf oil disaster. With George W. Bush's comment in mind, I told the congregation:

> I take no solace in pointing a finger at BP. I am reminded of G. K. Chesterton's response when he was asked what was most wrong with the world. He replied, "I am." My addiction to oil is one reason why BP was allowed to undertake the risky behavior of opening Pandora's Box. It is also why their risky behavior was rewarded with excessive profit and unbounded permission.

If Jesus is calling his followers to reconciliation and ultimately to freedom, then our discipleship must begin with candid, uncompromising confession. As an example of what not to do, BP's chief executive, Tony Hayward, referred to the Deepwater Horizon catastrophe as a "natural disaster."[13]

Accepting George W. Bush's diagnosis, what might we learn from the field of mental health? It turns out that the *Diagnostic and Statistical Manual of Mental Disorders*—the "mental-health bible"—has recently been revised after a decade of scrutiny. One of the newly revised sections of the *DSM-V* covers "substance-related and addictive disorders." For a disorder to qualify as severe, the patient must exhibit six or more of the following eleven criteria. In listing them, I've taken the liberty of substituting "fossil fuels" for "the substance." As science writer Dawn Stover points out in her column, "Addicted to Oil,"[14] this list should command our attention:

1. Taking fossil fuels in larger amounts or over a longer period than intended.
2. Wanting to cut down or regulate use of fossil fuels, with multiple unsuccessful efforts to do so.
3. Spending a great deal of time obtaining and using fossil fuels.

4. Craving fossil fuels.
5. Using fossil fuels so much that it interferes with obligations at work, home, or school.
6. Continuing to use fossil fuels even when it causes social or interpersonal problems.
7. Giving up or reducing important social, occupational, or recreational activities in order to use fossil fuels.
8. Continuing to use fossil fuels even when it is physically hazardous to do so.
9. Continuing to use fossil fuels despite already having a physical or psychological problem likely to have been caused by fossil fuels.
10. Requiring markedly increased amounts of fossil fuels as time goes on.
11. Developing withdrawal symptoms, such as agitation and irritability, when trying to quit.

In spite of the fact that the tax structure, the transportation system, and the infrastructure of our personal and work lives are all set up to favor our use of fossil fuels, people are beginning to rebalance the tipped scales. Take Texas, for example. When Professor Katharine Hayhoe tells people that her home state is America's chief supplier of wind energy, most people think she's kidding. But she's not—what she's saying is true. Might that be an indication of the system trying to rebalance? Imagine state-by-state coalitions of Christians lobbying their legislators to create and maintain regulations that generously reward all who install solar panels or wind generators. In April 2016 UCC churches all over the country (along with partners in other denominations) heard sermons focused on the need to keep the known reserves of fossil fuel in the ground.[15] As a result, many church members were moved to join one of the dozens of local protests across the country that focused on limiting oil, gas, and coal extraction and transportation, and on stopping the construction of new fossil fuel infrastructure.

MODERATION IN PLACE OF EXCESS

Reorienting what we prize describes the classic understanding of what it means to be on a spiritual journey. While our understanding of spiri-

tual journey usually applies to a personal quest, the reorientation described in this chapter is both personal and cultural. Support for each of
the shifts discussed here can be found in almost every religion. Can that
support be harnessed—not just to promote personal transformation but
to motivate cultural transformation, as well?

Can the church in America initiate an embrace of moderation in
place of excess?

The Pope's decision to take Saint Francis' name—along with the
Pope's relentless commitment to the poor and to our common home—
could be the beginning. In his stirring book, *Inspiring Progress*, Gary
Gardner offers this provocative perspective on St. Francis:

> The bishop of London, Richard Chartres, once noted that St. Fran-
> cis, the 13th century Tuscan advocate for the poor and a lover of
> nature, came from a wealthy family and was, by the standards of his
> day, a heavy consumer. A conversion experience convinced him to
> abandon the life of nobility and embrace a bare-bones lifestyle as a
> pathway to God. Chartres sees a lesson for people of faith. "We move
> toward God by subtraction, rather than accumulation."[16]

Not long ago I was preparing to preach in a well-to-do suburb.
Among other things, the service was celebrating Saint Francis Day with
a blessing of the animals. As I approached the church, I looked out my
car window to see what appeared to be a perfectly good, large home
built about forty years ago in the process of being knocked down. I
asked someone in the congregation if they knew the story behind this.
They replied, "Oh, this is happening everywhere. Young successful cou-
ples are buying McMansions and then knocking them down to replace
them with 'starter castles.'"

As a visiting preacher, I thought it best not to lift this up in my
sermon as an example of the excess we need to subtract. Confessing this
here attests to the fact that I'm still troubled by my silence. If John Hick
is right when he says that the function of mainstream religious traditions is "the transformation of human existence from self-centeredness
to Reality-centeredness,"[17] then communities of faith must find ways to
bridge the gap between belief and practice. When we muster the courage to face that gap, Jesus will gladly join us in building a repurposed
church filled with people who long for a community that supports them

in leading resilient lives of moderation, balance, wisdom, and collaboration.

VISION IN PLACE OF CONVENIENCE

It was not convenient for the Good Samaritan to stop and care for the
man who had been beaten (Luke 10:25–37). Unlike the priest and the
Levite who hurried past the victim, the inner moral compass of the
Good Samaritan would not let him pass. Compassion ruled his heart,
alerted his brain, and directed his body. The vision of goodness, mercy,
generosity, sacrifice, and trust inspired by this single story has shaped
millions of lives. It has become a moral standard used throughout the
world in every culture to prompt people not to settle for what their self-
centered instincts might suggest, but instead to aim higher.

Convenience is not the core enterprise of religion. While business
and the media both seek to make life more comfortable, convenience is
neither a religious nor a moral value. With this in mind, what if people
of faith were to examine the energy they currently pour into making life
more convenient and redirect it towards joining and building a movement? For example, I know many Christians who sacrifice convenience
in their personal lives in order to contribute in significant ways (through
their time or money) to the work and witness of a climate organization.
I also know many who ride their bikes and don't own a car. Here is
another example: carrying out acts of civil disobedience. Risking arrest
is never convenient. It requires a sacrifice of both time and freedom,
particularly if you go to jail. But people of faith are inspired by vision,
not convenience. Holding a clear vision before their eyes gives people
the motivation and energy to move beyond their immediate comfort
and convenience.

Discontinuity is the enemy of convenience. It interrupts our routines, disturbs our comfort, and puts a stop to the relative predictability
and ease of "normal" life. Every experience of discontinuity—flood,
fire, drought, extinction, disease—must be met with imagination and
vision in order for adaptation to proceed. For this reason, engaging the
imagination to nurture vision is how we extend the horizon of our hope.
Imagination and vision lead to hope. Faith is built on all three.

Climate communication expert George Marshall suggests that we would do well to frame our response to the challenge of climate change as a heroic quest in which the enemy may be our internal weaknesses rather than an outside group."[18] Among the characteristics that are universally present in heroes are vision and imagination. Heroes see possibilities and opportunities where others are inclined to accept their limitations and to capitulate to current conditions. For two thousand years, generations of churchgoers have been inspired by history's moral heroes—Mother Teresa, Mahatma Gandhi, Martin Luther King Jr., Antoinette Brown Blackwell, and so many others. Now it's up to our generation to make what may seem to be heroic behavior more commonplace. For this task, convenience is not our ally. But vision and imagination will carry us forward.

ACCOUNTABILITY IN PLACE OF DISREGARD

We are living amidst a great awakening. Just as climate change is the greatest moral challenge humanity has ever faced, the prospect of awakening carries with it as much promise as people have ever known. Nevertheless, to address the moral challenge and embrace the promise of a transition to renewable energy we must engage in both personal and systemic change. But most of us resist change.

A surefire way to hold change at bay is to avoid discussing the topic. George Marshall unpacks the complexity of our socially constructed silence around climate change in his chapter "Don't Even Think About It" in his book by the same title.[19] While some of his stories are shocking, each of us has had similar experiences of everyday climate denial. People prefer to talk about more "manageable" things. This explains people's receptivity to the public advertising campaigns to deny science that have been funded by Exxon and the Koch brothers. Believing those ads allows us to ignore climate change, continue with "business as usual," and delay facing a painful reality and the need to take action.

To me, the best way to make sense of this is to realize that our resistance as well as our awakening is fueled by fear and grief. To disregard the daily groaning of creation is becoming increasingly difficult. Gradually, many of us are beginning to realize that we've been wandering in a moral fog. Mary Evelyn Tucker describes this in her introduction to Kathleen Dean Moore's profound book, *Great Tide Rising*:[20]

> We are dwelling in a period of mass extinction and climate change. Loss is all around us. We are engulfed by it and at the same time we are nearly blind to it. Yet we feel in our bones some kind of unspeakable angst that will not leave us in the depths of night or even at daybreak when the birds greet the sunlight again. This crushing feeling of unstoppable destruction is holding us back from acknowledging our grief. Such loss of life demands not only mourning, but also recognition that we are in a huge historical whirlwind.

Later in that book, Kathleen Dean Moore brilliantly unpacks the oft-used comment from the Pogo cartoon that was published on the first Earth Day in April 1970, "We have met the enemy and he is us."[21] Yes—each of us is part of the problem. But accountability must not end with personal confession.

The Rev. Sally Bingham and Interfaith Power and Light have illuminated the path of accountability.[22] Along with their educational and organizing efforts, for decades they have invited congregations to take responsibility for making houses of worship more energy efficient and better equipped to conserve energy. And thanks be to God for those who initiated and developed sophisticated tools that enable us to track our personal carbon footprint and that give us responsible ways to offset it.[23]

However, in addition to these opportunities to own up to our personal choices and actions, we are awakening to new understandings of accountability.

In August 2011, 1,253 of us were arrested at the White House in the largest act of civil disobedience since the civil rights movement. We wanted the Keystone XL pipeline to become a household word, and we wanted to persuade the president to do what science was saying he must. Four-and-a-half years later, he did. President Obama became the first national leader in the world to cancel a fossil fuel project because of its impact on climate. This seemingly impossible achievement marked the beginning of a new chapter of accountability.

In June of 2013, the Synod of the United Church of Christ became the first national body to vote to divest from fossil fuel companies. At the time, the action was generally seen—and sometimes dismissed—as being merely symbolic. Yet by the time 400,000 people flooded the streets of New York City a little over a year later, close to 1,000 universities, cities, philanthropic foundations, and faith communities—including the Rockefeller Brothers Fund, whose assets came from Standard Oil—had joined the divestment movement. Altogether, their investments were worth over fifty billion dollars.[24] The world was paying attention.

Whereas earlier efforts at increasing accountability focused on reducing the demand for fossil fuels, both the movement to cancel the KXL pipeline and the movement to divest from fossil fuel companies focused on the supply side. One of the cries heard in rallies all over the country emphasized that we actually have the power to revoke the social license the Exxons of the world require in order to continue "business as usual" and to keep profiting from wrecking the Earth. This supply-side focus represented a new understanding of accountability.

Holding the most profitable industry in the history of the world accountable for its actions required research. In 2011 Carbon Tracker published a paper that identified the world's remaining carbon budget—that is, how much more fossil fuel we can burn and still have reason to think the planet will remain inhabitable.[25] These numbers could not be disregarded. A point of no return was on the horizon.

In the fall of 2015 the hashtag "#ExxonKnew" was created after *Inside Climate News* and the *Los Angeles Times* reported[26] that although ExxonMobil conducted research in 1977 affirming that climate change was caused by carbon emissions released from the burning of fossil fuels, the company nonetheless continued to fund politicians and organizations that denied climate science and continued to advocate against regulations that limited carbon emissions. Additional investigation and interviews have demonstrated that Exxon's duplicity is untenable. Their vigorous denial has been effectively countered in the court of public opinion by Naomi Oreskes and Geoffrey Supran on the "Op-Ed" page of the *New York Times*.[27]

Excellent reporting set the stage for legal accountability. In 2015 New York attorney general Eric Schneiderman launched an investigation into Exxon, and he was soon joined by other attorneys general.[28] At the time of this writing they are investigating whether Exxon—and perhaps other companies—committed fraud when it communicated to its shareholders (and the public at large) that climate change was not real. How could it not be fraud, since Exxon had funded scientific research in the 1970s and 1980s that concluded that climate change was real, dangerous, and caused by burning fossil fuel? On the heels of the investigation by the attorneys general, the Securities and Exchange Commission launched its own investigation as well. [29]

As followers of Jesus, living as we do in a time of climate crisis, we have an obligation to preserve and protect God's creation. Feigned obliviousness is not an option. Each of us is personally accountable for our habits and choices. Beyond that, each of us must also discern whether God is calling us to join the movement for systemic change. Like every other social change movement, we aim to make our personal behavior more informed and responsible. We also seek to change the system so that its laws, policies, and regulations promote a swift, just transition away from dirty energy and toward clean, safe, renewable sources of energy that are accessible to all, including the poor and the historically underserved.

SELF-GIVING LOVE IN PLACE OF SELF-CENTERED FEAR

Renowned religion scholar Karen Armstrong provides context for the idea that accountability is essential using the language of her discipline. "The truths of religion are accessible only when you are prepared to get rid of the selfishness, greed, and self-preoccupation that, perhaps inevitably, are ingrained in our thoughts and behavior but are also the source of so much of our pain. The Greeks would call this process *kenosis*, 'self-emptying.'" [30] "Get rid of" may be a bridge too far, but you get the point. Faithfulness calls us to reduce our investment, not only in selfish behaviors but in self-centered fear as well.

There's nothing easy about this shift. As many suggest, our brains are perpetually on alert to protect us from an immediate threat. Harvard psychology professor Daniel Gilbert points out that climate change is "a threat that our evolved brains are uniquely unsuited to do a damned thing about." [31] Confronted with a specific, proximate threat, we take action immediately. Looking at "hockey stick" shaped graphs showing climate change escalation, we yawn.

In a climate change world, faithful discipleship seeks to remedy this dysfunction. George Marshall argues that in communicating concern about climate change, we must appeal to both the rational and the emotional parts of the brain. Our perception of risk is located in the emotional brain. To get the attention of our emotional brains, our communication must emphasize proximity (climate change is not someone else's problem, it's here; it's now!). Explanations must draw from personal experience (let me share what it was like to go through Hurricane Sandy). Speakers and writers need to lift up images and stories that speak to shared values.[32]

There's nothing easy about this. George Marshall reports that every specialist he spoke with agreed that "we have still not found a way to effectively engage our emotional brains in climate change."[33] Later, in a chapter subtitled "What the Green Team Can Learn from the God Squad," Marshall focuses on the importance of conviction. He describes conviction as "the point at which the rational crosses into the emotional, the head into the heart, and we can say, 'I've heard enough, I've seen enough—now I am convinced.'"[34] He then suggests that the climate change movement could learn from religious practitioners to place conviction at the center of the movement.

Marshall is correct. People of faith know what it means to be convicted. That's what allows people of faith to set aside self-centered fear, freeing us for lives based on self-giving love. I agree with Marshall's focus on conviction. Over the ten years I have preached on climate change in UCC churches all over the country, I've seen people of faith becoming more and more convinced that if we are to be faithful to the One who created the Heavens and the Earth, we must allow our convictions to guide our actions and decisions.

CIVIL DISOBEDIENCE AND DISCIPLESHIP

I understand that for many Christians, including some of those already engaged in the climate change movement, civil disobedience is off the table. That was true, as well, in previous social change movements. First and foremost, civil disobedience is an act of personal conscience. God calls some, but not all, to consider this form of witness.

But as we enter the long emergency, it's time for the church to become more public in its recognition of civil disobedience as an appropriate expression of faithfulness to God. Put another way, it's time for the church to tell the truth about how industrial civilization is ending nature as humanity exercises hubris.[35] It's time for the church to testify to an understanding of God that endures despite our undoing of God's creation. Among other things, such testimony will create the conditions for the powerful witness of civil disobedience to become a normative expression of discipleship.

Throughout most of the nineteenth and much of the twentieth century, becoming a missionary was a normative expression of discipleship among Protestants in America. Likewise, at least among traditional "peace churches," in a time of war it is not unusual for a young member of the church to meet with the pastor for guidance regarding how to become a conscientious objector. Likewise, civil disobedience is a form of discipleship some have been called to, going as far back as the early church. Remember that Peter and Paul went to jail and thousands of Christians were martyred for defying Roman law.

Yes, for some, civil disobedience is out of bounds. But because we recognize God as Creator, we must not dodge the truth about environmental destruction so eloquently expressed by Wendell Berry in the conclusion of his 1979 essay, "The Gift of Good Land:"

> It is a contradiction to love your neighbour and despise the great inheritance on which his life depends. . . . It is possible—as our experience in this good land shows—to exile ourselves from Creation, and to ally ourselves with the principle of destruction. . . . If we are willing to pollute the air—to harm the elegant creature known as the atmosphere—by that token we are willing to harm all creatures that breathe, ourselves and our children among them. There is no begging off or "trading off. . . ." To live, we must daily break the body and shed the blood of Creation. When we do this knowingly, lovingly, skillfully, reverently, it is a sacrament. When we do it ignorantly, greedily, clumsily, destructively, it is a desecration. In such desecration we condemn ourselves to spiritual and moral loneliness, and others to want.

Soon, I believe, what will be clear to most of us is what Bill McKibben told Wen Stephenson in 2015: "I wish I'd figured out sooner what was going on, and started things like 350 long before. We needed a mass movement a long time ago."[36] As people of faith—convicted as we are about God as Creator and Jesus as Redeemer—we must face the horror of what we have done and are doing to God's creation. When we do, many of us will embrace the call of conscience to join others in nonviolent direct actions of civil disobedience.[37] Not only that, but we will also be transformed by Job's radical insistence that we are not the center of the world.[38] When that day finally comes, we will welcome Wendell Berry's wisdom in declaring that individualism is not the key to a good life—community is.

QUESTIONS FOR GROUP DISCUSSION AND FURTHER REFLECTION

1. Several examples of the shift from an emphasis on material growth to resilience are given in this chapter. What additional examples can you share—especially from your neighborhood or region? How might your church provide leadership to your community in this area?

2. Share your response to the story of the church that would not allow the mortgage of one of its elderly members to be foreclosed. What steps could your congregation take to become a place that is safe enough for someone in need to share as she did, and generous enough for another person to respond as she did?

3. Were you surprised that Pope Francis is calling for a redefinition of our understanding of progress? Consider approaching a local Catholic church to come together for a discussion of Pope Francis' Encyclical *Laudato Si'*.

4. Go to the Interfaith Power and Light website and find out when their next event (preach-in; Earth Day; etc.) is planned. Download the materials to plan how your congregation will participate.

5. Does your congregation have an endowment? If so, examine its assets. If you are holding any fossil fuel company stocks, learn more about the divestment movement and talk with the trustees (or whoever oversees your endowment).

6. Convene a discussion on civil disobedience. Invite testimony from someone who has done it—either from your congregation or from another congregation. Make sure it's a safe conversation where people can share whatever comments are in their hearts.

6

WORSHIP AS A PATHWAY TO FREEDOM

What happens in worship shapes how participants inhabit time.
—Willis Jenkins[1]

Theirs was the spirit of an anticipatory community that could give present form to a hoped-for future through a range of adaptable practices.
—Larry Rasmussen discussing the first Christians[2]

A few weeks after sixty-three of us spent three days and two nights in the central cell block of the jail in Washington, DC, Bill McKibben wrote a piece for the magazine *Christian Century* (October 3, 2011). This Methodist Sunday School teacher shared with the church-world that over the course of two weeks in August 2011, 1,253 people came from all over America to the front of the White House to be arrested. We were not a young group. Our average age was about the same as the average age of American churchgoers and, like the average American churchgoer, we were not radicals. Most of us had never been arrested before. Bill later wrote,[3] as difficult as jail was, it was not the end of the world. All 1,253 of us knew what the end of the world was—it was why we went to jail in the first place.

We came hoping for a miracle. Like many who come to church on Sunday morning, we were filled with what Bill described as "impatient love." If we were willing to incarnate our values by using our bodies to testify to our love for God's creation, might President Obama be willing to keep his word? ("It's time to end the tyranny of oil.") Might the largest nonviolent civil disobedience action America had seen in several decades convince President Obama to cancel plans to build the Keystone XL pipeline?

While this was not planned as a liturgical action, liturgy ("the work of the people") found its way into our collective experience. Mind you, the forty of us in the men's cell block represented a wide range of religious conviction and many of us were unaffiliated. But after an endless night, lying on cold slabs of stainless steel in the unforgiving wilderness of our jail cells, all of us were in need of some spiritual refreshment. As best we could figure, it was Sunday morning (our watches and phones had been taken, along with our belts, shoelaces, wedding rings, and wallets).

When Bill began singing the call and response spiritual "Certainly, Lord" it didn't take long for most of us to lift our voices. As people of conscience had done with countless spirituals throughout the civil rights movement, Bill adapted the words for the occasion. "Have you been to the jailhouse? / Certainly, Lord" and "Have you been in cuffs? / Certainly, Lord" and "Would you do it again? / Certainly, Lord. Certainly, Lord. Certainly, certainly, certainly Lord."

Then there was preaching. Once the chorus had quieted, Bill invited Gus Speth to offer a word. *Time Magazine* once described Gus as the "ultimate insider." He served as head of President Carter's Council on Environmental Quality, helped found the National Resources Defense Council, led the United Nations' largest program for international development, and served as dean of Yale's School of Forestry and Environmental Studies. I don't think I was the only person in the cell block who received as a sermon Gus' half-hour long comments on a book he was writing (*America the Possible*)—it was as inspirational as any sermon I had ever heard.

I first began to see this action through the lens of liturgy several hours after our arrest on August 19, 2011. Because the sidewalk in front of the White House is overseen by US National Park police, once we were crammed into a sweltering (over 105°F), cramped transport vehicle, we were driven to the US Park Police station in Anacostia. When we arrived, they had us sit on the grass (the tarmac was too hot). Our hands were still cuffed behind our backs. The heat and humidity were merciless.

After a couple of hours, two officers approached us. One was the size of a linebacker and was carrying in each hand a large 30-gallon garbage bag, filled with very heavy objects. Their gait was deliberate, and they were walking straight toward me. Baking in the sun, soaking every square inch of my clergy shirt with sweat, sitting cross-legged, my wrists and shoulders screaming with pain, I had no idea what to expect. The officer with the bags set them down a few feet from me. The other officer reached in one of the bags, pulled out a bottle of water, and said to me, "Father, give your flock something to drink."

Although I had been ordained for thirty-one years, I don't think I ever experienced a sacramental moment more moving than what transpired over the next half hour. The officer released me from pain by cutting off my handcuffs. Then it was my privilege to approach each of my courageous colleagues and to ask them if they wanted some water. I asked those who said yes to tilt their head back and open their mouth. With deliberate, slow, care-filled, ritualistic repetition, I went from person to person, offering each one the restorative gift that is essential to all living beings: water. Amidst the sweltering heat and the pain of the cuffs digging into their wrists, the gratitude these strangers expressed to me in this grace-infused moment was something I will never forget.

Bill McKibben concluded that *Christian Century* article with an invitation: come to Washington, DC, and join thousands of others in encircling the White House. Exactly one year before the 2012 election, we would ask President Obama to keep his word by cancelling the Keystone XL pipeline. The date for this action was November 6, 2011. It was a Sunday. So Bill added, "I'm not telling you to skip church to come to DC that day, but . . ."

After reading Bill's invitation, I emailed my own invitation to the 360 churches I oversee—but with a twist. I invited those that could to send a delegation to Washington, DC, and to convene worship in the streets surrounding the White House. Surely that action would be as holy as worship conducted in a pew.

HOW MUCH IS ENOUGH? CLIMATE TALK IN CHURCH

Many churchgoers and pastors who are reading this book will be sympathetic to its thrust. But a question that every congregation must negotiate is this: How much climate talk in the church is enough? Or, the more frequently asked question: How much climate talk in church is too much? In the next chapter, I will consider how to address that question in the area of preaching. Here, I will focus on worship.

How much prayer in church is enough? How much gratitude? How many tears are enough? How much joy? I've never heard anyone ask any of these questions. Yet I have led and also participated in many services in which the entire focus was prayer, or thanksgiving, or lament, or joy. All of these services were well-received because the gathered congregation experienced them as appropriate and fitting.

If we believe that God is the giver—the source—of all life, and if it is true—for now and for the indefinite future—that the foundation of life as we know it is in jeopardy, then wouldn't it be appropriate every time we connect with God to focus considerable attention on this crisis?

In African American churches in the South in the early 1960s, how frequently do you think worship or prayers or singing focused on civil rights? While each congregation and pastor had to discern what was appropriate—there were some who were early adapters while others followed later—by 1963, civil rights and the movement that bore that name were central to the worship experience of most African American churches in the South. Looking back, this seems natural, appropriate, and obvious.

How will our children look back at the church of today? How will they interpret the inattention of today's church to the greatest moral challenge humanity has ever faced? I highly recommend ethicist Willis Jenkins' response to this critical question as he attempts to speak to "the silence of theological ethics on intergenerational obligation."[4]

In what follows, I suggest a few innovative approaches to worship that are consistent with and expressive of the substance of this book. I also recommend numerous other sources of relevant worship ideas listed in this volume's bibliography.

THE FIRST ANNOUNCEMENT AT EVERY CHURCH SERVICE

What if the first announcement at every worship service in a church, synagogue, or mosque went something like this:

As we do every Sunday, I'd like to ask those who contacted their member of Congress or the White House this past week to advocate for new laws that will make our Earth sustainable to please rise as you are able and receive our applause. . . . Thank you, and I hope to see still more of you rise next week.[5]

If we accept the scientific realities of our day as well as the theological guides I noted in chapter 3, I find it unimaginable that congregations would not fully engage this weekly liturgical and spiritual practice. Now, you may be thinking, "This could never work in my congregation. People would see it as creating a partisan divide." How in God's name can advocating for the preservation of God's creation be understood as partisan? And why in God's name has the church allowed God's creation to be hijacked and reduced to just one more ideological dispute?

If we understand prayer to be a spiritual practice, then advocating for laws to preserve the common good—including protecting God's gift of creation—must also be understood as such. As Christians, we are called to proclaim the Good News—not by ignoring the fact that we have pillaged the Earth and privileged corporate profits—but by putting our bodies on the line. Once the spiritual practice of advocacy grows strong enough to exceed the influence of the fossil fuel lobby, the environmental policies of this country will change.

Yes—making this your congregation's first announcement would be political—but in no way would it be partisan. "Political" refers to the way government shapes a society; "partisan" means one-sided, focused on the values of one part of society. That's a distinction that every one of our congregations needs to understand, especially now, since climate change affects us all.

INVITE WEEKLY TESTIMONIES

For centuries, pastors have invited testimonies during worship around healing and the power of prayer. Imagine adding to your Sunday worship a 90-second testimony from someone who has recently taken an action to help sustain God's creation. Imagine cataloging these testimonies on your church website.

Imagine if the residents of flooded Houston, the citizens of the charred cities in Colorado, and the people in the parched farmland of west Texas had been prepared by their pastors to recognize that one day they could all become—we could all become—climate refugees. Imagine the victims of flood, fire, and drought immediately heading to Washington, DC, to engage in passionate and relentless legislative advocacy on behalf of unborn generations so that their grandchildren—our grandchildren—would face less catastrophic circumstances. This form of faithful Christian witness could rise up from congregations that had been prepared by weekly testimony.

I realize this is a "big ask." But when I read the Gospels, it seems that Jesus didn't shy away from "big asks." If, a week after the floods subsided or the crops were plowed under, congregations from various denominations were prepared to carry out political advocacy, imagine the power of such a transdenominational Christian witness. I'm thinking "revival." Rather than focusing on individual sin and salvation, such an ecumenical revival would inspire these climate refugees to transform their sorrow and despair into tireless Christian legislative advocacy on behalf of generations of children yet to come. Many of the courageous citizens of Newtown, Connecticut, have demonstrated this kind of commitment. They are a model of what discipleship requires.

TRANSFORM FAMILIAR LITURGIES AND CREATE NEW ONES

In the 1970s and 1980s the churches in South Africa played an essential role in ending apartheid. Many families chose to repurpose the funeral liturgies of their loved ones in order to declare the need for political change. Imagine what it took for these families to do this. They recognized that their personal suffering was part of a larger suffering. The same was true during the civil rights movement in the early 1960s. The recent PBS program *American Experience* focusing on "Freedom Summer" featured a portion of the sermon given at the funerals of the three voting rights activists who were murdered. Any personal grief that remained was channeled into an uncompromising and urgent call for political change.

Environmental racism, the sixth extinction, the war in Syria, "one-hundred-year floods" every five years, food shortages and starvation, sea level rise, the contamination of aquifers due to fracking, ocean acidification, ecocide, biocide—none of these injustices are part of the natural order. Because God calls the church to address injustice, God calls the church to address the injustice of climate change. And like apartheid in South Africa and the denial of civil rights and voting rights to African Americans in the United States, the church can and must transform its familiar liturgies to name these injustices, and to inspire people to take action together.

You and your congregation don't have to reinvent the wheel. Effective resources are available from the books and websites listed in the back of this book. Among the most inspiring are the liturgical resources created for the April 2016 "Keep It In The Ground" Sunday (http:// april2016.uccpages.org/). Toward the end of this eighteen-page collection, the pastors of Old South Church (UCC) in Boston provide this refreshing introduction for several "Blessings for Organizers":

> Political organizing is God-blessed and essential work, rooted in God's call to Moses to confront Pharaoh. In the face of a global crisis created by overuse of fossil fuels, organizing is one of the most effective, clear-eyed ways to witness to the hope proclaimed in the Gospels. These blessings are meant to lift up, honor and minister to Christians involved in organizing. The blessings are separated into a blessing for contacting voters or constituents through going door-to-door canvassing, a blessing for phonebanking, and a blessing for protest leaders. These blessings can be used after trainings, during general worship services, or at any other time your community sees fit to lift up the organizers among you.

Other excellent liturgical resources are available from Greenfaith (http:/ /www.greenfaith.org/), Interfaith Power and Light (http://www. interfaithpowerandlight.org/), and the Shalom Center (https:// theshalomcenter.org/prayer-service-because-earth-really-matters).

A relatively undeveloped theological resource from the Christian tradition is our understanding of the communion of saints or "cloud of witnesses" (Hebrews 12:1). What if every worship service acknowledged that the story that gives meaning to our lives was passed on to us by the saints and martyrs who rejected the temptations of power and dominion and testified instead to Christ's Lordship over all creation?[6] In this way, worship can heighten our consciousness of intergenerational interdependence and inspire us to take action.

ORGANIZE AND HOST A CLIMATE REVIVAL

Because climate change compels us to recognize that we're all in this together, it provides you and your congregation with an opportunity to come together with other churches in your town or region to make a common witness to your community. Not only have many churches conducted such interdenominational services, many houses of worship have come together for interfaith services as well.

In April of 2013 NEREM (New England Regional Environmental Ministries) convened a "Climate Revival"[7] in downtown Boston that brought together twenty-two denominational leaders in New England (Episcopal, Lutheran, UCC, Orthodox, American Baptist, Presbyterian) along with two national heads of communions. Over six hundred people attended the event, which also honored those who had been killed or injured in the Boston Marathon bombing which had taken place only twelve days before. This event provides a powerful model for the houses of worship in any town or city to lead on climate activism.

WORSHIP THAT INCLUDES ALL CREATURES

Living as we are amidst the sixth extinction, we would do well to recall that the covenant God makes after the flood is not only with Noah and his family, but with all creatures alive and yet to be born. And yet, as ethicist Willis Jenkins points out:

> In an era of biodiversity loss, the absence of nonhuman creatures from regular worship allows Christians to remain oblivious to what E. O. Wilson calls "the folly our descendants are least likely to forgive us." Amid biological disappearances, worshiping without other creatures makes congregants supine to the powers that disappear creatures.[8]

In *Ask the Beasts: Darwin and the God of Love*,[9] Elizabeth A. Johnson surveys and critiques the history of Christian theologians' arguments to exclude animals (and plants) from cosmic redemption. Because climate change harms all of creation, Christianity's historic anthropocentrism needs the kind of critique that Johnson and Paul Santmire[10] provide. All who worship on Sunday mornings would do well to ponder how our weekly indoor gatherings can help correct our anthropocentric focus, and whether worship services should be held more frequently outdoors.

ORDINATION VOWS AND NEW LIFE IN THE ANTHROPOCENE

I've already noted the silence of the church, along with the overwhelming majority of theologians and ethicists, on the topics of intergenerational obligation and how to nurture hope in the face of climate catastrophe. The church could remedy this oversight by updating its ordination vows.

What if denominations were to add this commitment to ordination vows: throughout the time the ordinand or his or her partner is awaiting the birth of a child, every sermon the ordinand preaches will at least touch upon God's covenant with all of creation and our obligations to future generations? A variation on this vow could be that whenever a child is born to a member of the congregation, the pastor's next sermon will be on intergenerational responsibilities. (In a sizable congregation whose average age is under forty, this could make intergenerational interdependence a regular topic in preaching. Not a bad idea!)

What if we added a monthly two-minute testimony to our worship services in which a member of the church who was pregnant—or their partner—would share a brief response to a question posed by ethicist Rachel Muers:

> In a world with a threatened future, "what does it mean that we can bear and raise children?"[11]

To prepare for this witness, churches can turn to resources like Dear Tomorrow[12]—a platform for people to create and share stories with their friends and family about why they care about climate change. Or a congregation could read *Coming of Age at the End of Nature: A Generation Faces Living on a Challenged Planet*[13]—a book of essays by millennials that all of us would do well to ponder.

IF EARTH WERE A SACRAMENT, HOW WOULD WE TREAT IT?[14]

Larry Rasmussen raises the provocative question in this section's title midway through his tour de force *Earth-Honoring Faith*. Archbishop Alex Brunett of Seattle began referring to the endangered Columbia River Watershed as a "sacramental commons" as early as the year 2000. Nine years earlier, in 1991, the US Conference of Catholic Bishops issued *Renewing the Earth: An Invitation to Reflection and Action in Light of Catholic Social Teaching*.[15] In it they said, "We need a change of heart to preserve and protect the planet for our children and for generations yet unborn." The bishops assert that the power to change our hearts lies "in the sacramental universe itself."

Rasmussen goes on to connect this "vision of a sacramental universe" to the teachings of Islam, Buddhism, Judaism, and the Orthodox Church—reminding us of a tradition more universal than most of us imagine. "In this tradition the drama of the liturgy is the ritual enactment or reenactment of cosmic community and the drama of creation's redemption."[16] I am reminded by my friend the Rev. Dr. Margaret Bullitt-Jonas that Anglican Archbishop William Temple shared this view and that the First Peoples have long recognized and have never forgotten the sacredness of the natural world.

I wonder if this discussion needs further exploration. Recognizing the distinct ways in which the world's religions honor the Earth, I wonder if it is not time to lift up a way in which any religious person—every religious person—might honor the Earth. A common ritual would testify that despite whatever may distinguish us (beliefs, practices, culture, national origin, age), we share a common concern, a common moral obligation, and common sacramental act. What if a daily ritual reminded us of the source of all life, and renewed our conviction to restore balance to God's creation? What if it included a vow that could be said in private, but could only be enacted in solidarity with others?

I began to develop these thoughts in the summer of 2014 after reading Rasmussen's book. In November 2014 when Rasmussen and I both spoke at Yale Divinity School's celebration of the one-hundredth anniversary of Thomas Berry's birth, we privately shared our common enthusiasm for such an initiative. Then in April 2016 my dear friend the Rev. Dr. Andrea Ayvazian (a Protestant UCC minister) preached an

Earth Day Sermon—"We Are Not Our Own"—in which she suggests, "maybe it's time to add a third sacrament to the two sacraments, baptism and communion, currently recognized by the United Church of Christ." Seeking to ritualize God's call to redeem creation, she proposes a Sacrament of Dirt—reminding us that dirt is holy, and that we are made of dirt and dust and will eventually return to that state. Such a sacrament would remind us that "we are first and foremost creatures of the earth [that] we are called to love, honor and protect."

At that same time, I was helping to roll out a national initiative for churches to focus a Sunday service on the theme, "Keep It In The Ground." In the midst of designing this initiative, I wondered if "keeping it in the ground" (that is, keeping coal, gas, and oil where they belong—underground) could come to be recognized by churches—and perhaps by other faith traditions—as a sacramental act. Keeping fossil fuel in the ground would be a physical representation of our commitment to honor the sacredness of all living things. Rituals for this sacrament would vary—just as there is variation in the current expression of Christian sacraments—but in this case, even more so. Possible "expressions" of this sacrament—or, to put it another way, expressions of the sacredness of creation—might include: installing a solar panel; walking in place of driving; blocking a coal train; etc. Each of these could be engaged by saying a ritualized prayer that recognized the essential unity of all these actions. Communities of faith could connect with these personal expressions of the ritual by having the worship leader ask: Which ones of us practiced the sacramental act of "Keeping It In The Ground" this past week? People could respond, one by one, and in response to each statement, the congregation could offer a powerful affirmation in unison.

While this is a provocative proposal, imagine if it gained traction! Imagine if such a personal and communal spiritual discipline could provide distinct congregations and diverse faiths with a unifying commitment to heal the Earth.

UNDOMESTICATING WORSHIP

Vincent Harding was worried about Congress creating a federal holiday in memory of the Rev. Dr. Martin Luther King Jr.; Professor Harding, a

social activist, impeccable scholar, and pacifist, was a close associate of
Dr. King's. In fact, Harding wrote one of Dr. King's most famous addresses—known variously as "Beyond Vietnam" and "A Time to Break
the Silence."[17] Dr. King shook America when he delivered this speech
on April 4, 1967, at Riverside Church. He also shook his most devoted
lieutenants. Most of them urged him to limit the focus of his witness to
civil rights. But as Dr. King famously said, "I cannot segregate my
conscience"—and in what would become his final years, Dr. King
argued that the struggles against "the giant triplets of racism, extreme
materialism, and militarism" were indivisible. Knowing that Harding
also saw these connections, Dr. King turned to Harding when he
wanted to ask America to undertake "a true revolution of values." Exactly one year after Dr. King delivered this call to conscience—while
visiting Memphis in support of a sanitation worker's strike—he was
killed.

Although millions of Americans fully supported making Dr. King's
birthday a federal holiday, Vincent Harding was unsettled. Twelve days
before President Reagan signed a bill creating the holiday, Harding
shared his concerns in an Atlanta speech:[18]

> There is a tremendous danger of our doing with Martin King pre-
> cisely what we have so often done to Jesus. That is, put him up on the
> wall and leave him there, to use his birthday as a holiday and an
> excuse for going wild over buying things, or domesticate him—taking
> him according to what we want, rather than what he is demanding of
> us.

I believe that love and truth are the most powerful forces on Earth. I
believe that religion—at its best—shows up in the world as people of
faith acting together to manifest love by testifying to truth in service of
creating a just world at peace. If we limit our experience of worship to a
particular building at a specific hour or two each week, we cannot fulfill
our vocation.

Building on Vincent Harding's concern, I worry that we are in danger of domesticating worship and thereby constraining its transforma-
tive power. I also believe that God has given us everything we need to
overcome the climate crisis—but in order to do so, we need to undo-
mesticate worship.

The Rev. Dr. William J. Barber II is leading the way. Since 2013, the Moral Monday Movement has declared that "the Holy Spirit has left the building" and entered the streets. Like the civil rights movement, the Moral Monday Movement is propelled by song, liturgy, ritual, movement, preaching, prayer, and celebration. And like the civil rights movement, the Moral Monday Movement embraces allies who share values, vision, conscience, conviction, and courage. In 2016–2017, Barber joined with three other prophetic religious leaders to initiate "The Revival: Time for a Moral Revolution of Values."[19] Their national tour was a collaborative project supported and endorsed by Repairers of the Breach, the Drum Major Institute, Healing of the Nations Ministries, Auburn Seminary, Kairos Center, the Samuel DeWitt Proctor Conference, Fight for $15, and the Middle Project, in coordination with local inviting groups.

Rev. Barber's witness—the brilliant way he has brought worship into the streets to become a light to the world, and a magnet for secular allies who share these values—is a model for how the church can respond to God's call to protect and restore creation.

TAKING LITURGY TO THE STREET, THE PIPELINE, AND THE TRACKS

The first time I participated in a public liturgy to block the expansion of fossil fuel infrastructure was May 25, 2016.[20] For months, local Boston residents and climate activists had been protesting Spectra Energy's construction of the West Roxbury Lateral pipeline. The morning began when one hundred people gathered not far from the construction site for what appeared to be a rally. The rally was led by a variety of interfaith clergy and included singing, call and response, reading from scriptures, preaching, and prayer. The congregation then marched to the construction site where fifteen other clergy and I sat down on the pavement, dangling our legs into the six-foot-deep trench that had been gouged in the middle of the street. We were a diverse group, including American Baptist, Buddhist, Episcopal, Hindu, Jewish, Presbyterian, United Church of Christ, and Unitarian Universalist. We continued singing, quoting scripture, preaching, and praying until one by one we were asked by the police officers to stand up and have our wrists cuffed behind our backs. After being packed into transport vehicles, we were driven to the police station where we were booked.

A month later, Karenna Gore, director of the Center for Earth Ethics at Union Theological Seminary and the daughter of former vice president Al Gore, joined twenty-two others in a similar street liturgy at the same site.[21] After arriving at the construction site, the twelve clergy led a mass grave funeral for climate change victims, featuring eulogies, prayers, and mourning. After the funeral, several clergy and other resisters lay down beside the trench, halting construction. Others climbed into the trench and lay down, as if in their coffins. Their arrests attracted considerable media attention.

This nonviolent action to evoke a mass grave was inspired by a Reuters' interview of a Pakistani grave digger a few weeks before.[22] He had just finished digging graves for three hundred people in anticipation of the next heat wave like the recent one in which more than 1,300 people perished.

Moved by this story, climate activist and Unitarian Universalist Tim DeChristopher helped to organize this "die-in." This was Tim's first act of civil disobedience since 2008 when he disrupted a government oil and gas lease auction by posing as a buyer in the sale. The story of Tim's courageous, prophetic witness is told in the film *Bidder 70*. He served twenty-one months in federal prison, after which he enrolled at Harvard Divinity School.

While the protest in metropolitan Boston was ongoing, the protest by the water protectors of Standing Rock was gathering momentum as they resisted the construction of the Dakota Access pipeline. In September 2014, Standing Rock Tribal Councilman Dave Archambault II had informed Dakota Access pipeline representatives that the tribe would not support this project. During the summer of 2016 the water protectors, representing scores of tribes, were joined by hundreds of others expressing solidarity with their witness. Their persistent, prayerful, nonviolent witness was met with water cannons, pepper spray, and attack dogs.

In early November 2016, over five hundred clergy from across the country assembled at Standing Rock to stand in solidarity with the water protectors.[23] Their worship included hymns, scripture, preaching, and prayer. Their confession took the form of burning copies of the Doctrine of Discovery, a series of religious documents from the fifteenth century that justified the colonization of the Americas and the oppression of its native people. The decrees, which were issued by popes, condoned the enslavement or killing of indigenous peoples who would not convert to Christianity.

Another call was issued for people of faith to gather at Standing Rock on December 4, 2016. Because the confrontation with private security forces was escalating, because of threats that the Standing Rock encampment might soon be forcibly evacuated, thousands of veterans indicated that they would also come that weekend wearing body armor and gas masks, ready to serve as "human shields." My friend and colleague the Rev. Dr. Margaret Bullitt-Jonas joined hundreds of other people of faith representing at least thirty faith traditions in a bitterly cold prayer service lasting hours. Her moving account of her experience offers profound testimony and insight that can serve as a guide for future worship services at other pipelines.[24]

No one responded when I invited hundreds of congregations to consider sending a delegation to Washington, DC, on November 6, 2011, to convene worship in the streets as part of a Keystone XL pipeline protest. Yet six years later, on July 3, 2017, the national Synod of the UCC passed a resolution that included a commitment "to resist all expansion of fossil fuel infrastructure and demand new sources of renewable energy that are accessible to all communities." Less than three weeks after that, on a street corner in Hingham, Massachusetts, two local UCC ministers and a Baptist pastor convened a prayer vigil as part of a weekly protest of Enbridge's plans to build a 7,700-horsepower fracked-gas compressor station in the adjacent town of North Weymouth.[25] (Enbridge is the new name of Spectra Energy.)

A few days earlier, a group of New England Quakers and fellow travelers concluded a 60-mile climate pilgrimage.[26] They began their walk at Schiller Station in Portsmouth, New Hampshire, one of the state's two coal-fired power plants. Along the way they slept on church floors, and were buoyed to learn of the national UCC resolution. When their pilgrimage reached the Merrimack coal-fired power station in Bow, New Hampshire, they held a worship service at the gates of the plant. Thirteen of them set up their tents on the tracks used by railroad cars to bring coal to the plant. After a beautiful night under the stars, they held a Sunday morning worship service. They were visited several times by Eversource officials (owners of the plant) and by railroad police, but they were never asked to leave, presumably so as not to cause a public stir.

A week before, on July 9, 2017, a group of nuns in Pennsylvania's rural Lancaster County consecrated a new chapel.[27] The chapel consists of an altar, a pulpit, and eight long pews set out in a field, on land that is owned by the nuns. That particular spot was chosen because it stands in the path of a projected natural gas pipeline called the Atlantic Sunrise project. These nuns are part of the Adorers of the Blood of Christ. In 2005, the order agreed to conduct their business transactions in keeping with principles of ecological justice that the sisters drafted in 2005. Their "land ethic" has prompted their chapters to protest hydroelectric power in Brazil and to work with Guatemalans opposed to gold mining. The Williams Company is now threatening to seize their land in Pennsylvania by eminent domain. Many observers have noted the parallels with the protests at Standing Rock. If the judge allows Williams to seize the land, the nuns are expected to appeal, and activists affiliated with Lancaster Against Pipelines are prepared to start a round-the-clock vigil at the site, with the aim of preventing Williams from destroying the chapel.

The good people of Nebraska have been resisting the proposed construction of the Keystone XL pipeline for years. An impressive coalition of farmers and environmentalists have bonded to form Bold Nebraska. Their newest strategy is to install solar panels on the ground along the proposed path that will be seized by eminent domain should the KXL pipeline be approved.[28] Several years ago I was the keynote speaker at the annual gathering of all the UCC churches in Nebraska. My host was unsure how my message on climate change would be received. Knowing that more than half in the audience were farmers, I opened my address by asking, "How many of you would call yourselves farmers?" And when about three-quarters of them raised their hands, I asked, "Do you mind if I think of you as scientists, because successful farmers draw upon science every day." They responded with applause, and we enjoyed a fine two days of conversation.

For many years, a growing number of denominations and congregations have participated in the Season of Creation that offers congregations a creation-based lectionary from September 1 through St. Francis of Assisi Day. The organizers have now expanded their vision to welcome congregations to engage in both liturgy and action. On their website[29] you'll find worship resources and statements from Ecumenical Patriarch Bartholomew and Pope Francis, along with a prayer service hosted by activist Bill McKibben. UCC eco-justice theologian Peter Sawtell has written a brief, helpful resource that will direct your congregation to both resources and suggested actions.[30] Peter's organization, Eco-Justice Ministries, is a partner of this new and more activist Season of Creation.

These examples make it clear that the church can play a critical role in revoking the social license that fossil fuel companies need in order to continue to wreck the Earth. Such prophetic witness is essential. Because fracking makes natural gas increasingly cheap and available, fossil fuel companies are claiming that new pipelines must be built, and hundreds of pipelines across the country are now in the works. At the same time, the cost of solar- and wind-generated energy continues to plummet, and in many places, now rivals the cost of natural gas. Adding new natural gas pipelines to America's pipeline network is as senseless as thinking that we need to run copper phone lines to every village in Tanzania, Kenya, Ghana, Senegal, Nigeria, and South Africa. (Newsflash: most people in these African nations already have cell phones![31]) But it's easy for a landowner or a rural town to fall for this ruse, and to sell access to a pipeline developer.

Churches can lead the needed intervention by raising consciousness and providing education through acts of public witness, making it difficult and expensive for gas companies to build new fossil fuel infrastructure. If we can multiply the above examples by a hundredfold, we can help assure the rapid transition to a clean energy economy that is essential for the flourishing of life on this planet.

CONCLUSION

At the beginning of this chapter, I pointed out that climate change activists—even those of us who engage in nonviolent direct action—are not radicals. As Bill McKibben points out, the real radicals are the oil, coal, and gas companies that are willing to wreck God's creation in order to make money for their current generation of shareholders. "No one has ever done anything more radical than that."[32]

But surely the acts of public liturgy, resistance, and peaceful civil disobedience described in this chapter are radical in the deep sense of that word. In each case, we invite the world to come with us back to the roots of our existence, for to be radical is to return to one's roots. In actions like these we incarnate our values by using our bodies to testify to our love of God's creation. I cannot imagine any action more faithful than this.

QUESTIONS FOR GROUP DISCUSSION AND FURTHER REFLECTION

1. Share a personal experience with your group illustrating your dependence on water for life.
2. What's your response to the suggestion that we consider convening worship in the streets? Have you ever participated in such a service for one or another cause?
3. Have each person in the group share how they would respond if your congregation introduced the suggestion regarding the first announcement in every church. Don't comment on how you think others would respond. Let each person speak for themselves.
4. Have someone in your group research the response of the Newtown, Connecticut, parents—particularly those who brought their grief to Washington, DC, to bear witness to Congress. How might your congregation prepare, as this chapter suggests, to bear witness following a hurricane, fire, or flood linked to climate change?
5. How might your congregation make use of the "Blessing for Organizers" reprinted here?
6. If you've had experience with including pets and perhaps other animals in worship, share it with your group. Is this a possibility for your congregation?
7. Look at the website for Dear Tomorrow and consider how your congregation might make their project part of your life together.
8. Together with your group, watch one of the many YouTube recordings of the Rev. Dr. William J. Barber II. What new possibilities for you and your congregation come to mind?

9. Have your discussion group host a church movie night to watch and talk about the movie *Bidder 70*.

10. Research whether there are any plans to build a fossil fuel pipeline within ten miles of your church. If so, follow up on the stories from this chapter, and reach out to others in your area who are concerned about the pipeline.

7

PROPHETIC PREACHING

Freeing the Pulpit from Fear

It is the vocation of the prophet to keep alive the ministry of the
imagination, to keep on conjuring and proposing futures alternative
to the single one the king wants to urge as the only thinkable one.
—Walter Brueggemann [1]

While this is a chapter for preachers on preaching, anyone interested
in how people of faith can communicate more effectively about climate
change will benefit from reading these pages.

CALLED TO PREACH ON CLIMATE CHANGE

Preaching matters! That was my first thought. Those were the first
words I scribbled when I was invited to write an Emergency Resolution
on climate change for the United Church of Christ's 2017 national
Synod. [2] Climate change is a moral issue, prophetic preaching matters,
and God is calling the church to engage.

Yes—preaching matters. Years of listening to sermons delivered by
William Sloane Coffin Jr., first at Yale University's Battell Chapel and
later at Riverside Church, exposed me to some of the best prophetic
preaching in the twentieth century. For several years I was Henri Nouwen's teaching assistant at Yale. Over our decades of friendship, I witnessed the healing and motivating effects of Henri's preaching on hun-

dreds of people. When we break open God's word for us today, it breaks open our hearts and invites us to engage new possibilities with wonder and courage.

One way I've tried to live into this truth over the past twelve years has been to encourage the 800+ United Church of Christ pastors in Massachusetts to preach about climate change. At various gatherings of pastors since 2006, I have asked how many of them preach regularly on climate change. In the first few years, I rarely saw a hand. In recent years, the response has been more encouraging. I follow up by saying that they should at least mention climate change in every third or fourth sermon. At this point, they generally look at me as if I have two heads and have forgotten everything I learned in seminary. Then I tell them that if we pastors don't provide this kind of leadership and motivation, in ten years, or at most fifteen, every single sermon will need to address grief—grief for the world that we abandoned.

After dozens of exchanges like this, I'm still astonished by the profound impact this statement has on pastors. As their awareness of climate change increases, pastors begin to realize the truth at the center of Pope Francis' encyclical *Laudato Si'* and the truth of what Ecumenical Patriarch Bartholomew has been saying for decades: climate change is the greatest moral challenge that humanity has ever faced.

That realization constitutes a calling. As leaders in their churches and their communities, pastors recognize that they have a crucial role to play in creating the moral conditions that will lead humanity to make the changes that science says we must make if we want to maintain a habitable and governable world. I find it impossible to imagine how humanity will accomplish this "Great Turning" unless religious leaders engage this moral, spiritual, economic, and cultural challenge at least as fully as preachers in earlier centuries advocated for the abolition of slavery.

WHY PREACHING ON CLIMATE CHANGE MATTERS

Preaching on climate change matters for two primary reasons that are in tension with one another. First, preaching on climate change matters because people don't want to hear about it. Second, preaching on climate change matters because people know they need to take action to address it.

There are many reasons people give for not wanting to hear about climate change, especially in church. Here are a few: Living day to day is already hard enough. Church is supposed to give me rest and refreshment and to recharge me for the next week. Climate change is not going to affect me; it's someone else's problem. The challenge is too enormous; there's nothing I can do about it, so why should I think about it? I come to church to be inspired, not to be depressed. Climate change is a political issue; politics doesn't belong in church.

Despite these complaints, at some level, most people recognize that something is terribly wrong with the world. Most parishioners recognize that human activity is primarily responsible for the catastrophe that is upon us, and that human beings have the responsibility to tackle it.

This tension is familiar to any pastor who has served a congregation whose history includes a significant, unseemly "secret" that everyone in the congregation knows and that no one wants to talk about. The "secret" could be about a current or former staff person, about church finances, an unresolved church "fight" that took place years ago, or about any number of other things. If such a congregation is to heal, the "secret" must be exposed, faced, and engaged. When this process is handled well, the congregation is blessed with renewed joy and freedom.

In a majority of churches, climate change is this kind of "secret."

Let me make this same point by citing some recent polling data. A 2015 poll conducted by Yale[3] revealed that two-thirds of American voters think that global warming is happening, yet two-thirds of Americans rarely or never discuss it.

If the work of the church is to make God's love and justice real, and since climate change amplifies every other social justice issue, it falls to the church to create the conditions in which people can face the reality of climate change and respond to God's call to take action to protect God's gift of creation. By preaching regularly on climate change, pastors give permission to the congregation to share with each other their fears, grief, dread, and feelings of impotence. Having named and shared those concerns, congregants can begin to offer each other the kind of solidarity that leads to courage and the capacity to act. If church is to provide hope for those who gather, it must be a safe enough place for people to share what is truly in their hearts—the fears and concerns that keep them up at night. Preaching that offers heartfelt, vulnerable testimony can play a crucial role in creating a safe place where congregants can listen and share their deepest fears and hopes.

Another reason why preaching on climate change matters emerges from a 2014 Survey on Religion, Values, and Climate Change.[4] It shows that people who have heard a sermon on climate change (even if only occasionally) are more likely to accept climate change as real. In addition, Americans who say their clergy leader speaks at least occasionally about climate change also score higher on the Climate Change Concern Index. More than six in ten Americans who report hearing about climate change from their clergy leader at least occasionally are either very (38 percent) or somewhat (24 percent) concerned about climate change.

That survey also revealed that for people worshiping in white mainline Protestant churches, only 10 percent of them report that their pastor speaks of climate change "often," and only 20 percent report that their pastor discusses climate change "sometimes." In African American Protestant and Hispanic Catholic congregations, people report that their pastor speaks about climate change much more frequently.

It is important to note that effective sermons provide congregants with a frame that allows them to understand and find meaning in a biblical passage or to be moved by and engage a social justice issue.[5] Often, what makes a sermon exceptional is that the sermon helps the listener to reframe a dilemma or an issue with which she or he has been struggling.

William Sloane Coffin Jr. did this for thousands of people on many occasions, although none had a greater impact than the sermon Bill gave following the death of his son Alex.[6] Bill's testimony that "God's heart was the first of all our hearts to break" when his beloved son died provided millions of people with a new frame through which to understand grief in their own lives. In the sermon, Bill explicitly rejected the platitudes that mourners often hear. "It was God's will" is one such phrase—as if a loving God would intend and plan the death of Bill's son. That this sermon immediately became the best known of all Bill's sermons is an indication of the profound longing among people of faith to have a new frame through which to understand loss and tragedy.

Given that every day it becomes more clear that life as we know it cannot be sustained, ordinary people need a new frame through which to understand the meaning of their own lives and the lives of their progeny. This reality represents both an existential threat and a call to social action. Preachers must be able to offer their congregations new perspectives that allow them to reframe how God might be calling them to redirect their individual lives, as well as their lives together as a congregation and as a community.

Take a moment to look at the material on http://www.climatewitness.org/. Pope Francis' Encyclical *Laudato Si'* "woke up" thousands of churches to the climate crisis and led to a new term: The Francis Effect. The Francis Effect prompted New England churches affiliated with NEREM (New England Regional Environmental Ministries) to pledge to preach on climate change in the fall of 2015. They called it a New Awakening. The website is filled with inspiring resources.

All of this leads us back to where I began: preaching matters. Clergy are trusted messengers whose testimony from the pulpit makes a difference in the attitudes and actions of their parishioners.

THE CHURCH WAS BORN FOR THIS

I can't count the number of times since my ordination in 1980 that I've thought with immense gratitude: "I get to do this!" Not only do pastors help to shape the individual lives of those who are part of their church communities, they also help give direction to the community where their congregation is located. Truly, this is a high calling.

In ordinary times that would be more than enough, but these are not ordinary times. Clergy today live out their calling at a time when the continuity of life itself is in jeopardy. There is no scientific debate on this. In 2014, the world's largest general scientific society, the American Association for the Advancement of Science, which includes over 121,000 members, published a paper, "What We Know."[7] This document makes clear that:

- Climate change is happening now.
- It's largely caused by humans.

- It has gotten worse in recent decades and it will keep getting worse at a faster and faster rate.
- Humanity is doing little to address it.

If all we do is continue to behave normally, carrying out our everyday actions without making a change, life as humans have always known it on this planet will come to an end.

Since 2007 I've put it this way: we are the first generation to foresee, and the final generation with an opportunity to forestall, the most devastating effects of climate change.

This is precisely why NOW is the time for every setting of the church—from small chapels to megachurches, from local congregations to national denominations, however varied their belief systems and historical traditions—to join the United Church of Christ in declaring that a new moral era has begun, and that our generation has a moral obligation to protect God's creation.

Truly, as Bill McKibben told me in 2007, this is an opportunity for which the church was born.

It's important to remember that religious leaders and their congregations have played a crucial role in nearly every social transformation:

- For millennia, it was normative to own slaves—until Samuel Sewall from Old South Church in Boston published the first antislavery pamphlet in 1701 and thus launched the Abolitionist Movement.
- For centuries, it was normative to allow only white men to interpret scripture from a pulpit—until the Congregational Church ordained Lemuel Haynes and Antoinette Brown (Blackwell).
- History will forever admire Dietrich Bonhoeffer for gathering a group of seminarians at Finkenwalde to prepare Christian leaders to oppose Hitler. Bonhoeffer's sermons, along with those of other courageous pastors whose voices Hitler could not silence, continue to inspire. [8]
- Martin Luther King Jr. helped to bend the moral arc of the universe toward justice by changing the aspirations of a nation.
- Archbishop Desmond Tutu inspired scores of clergy to work with him until the dignity and equality of all South Africans was written into the law.

The preaching of these religious leaders repurposed the church for their time and place. Their clarity—and the actions they took—were not immediately popular or successful. The majority of congregations kept doing what they had always done. Instead of offering a moral critique that could risk their status, their jobs, or perhaps even their lives, most pastors chose instead to attend to the immediate needs of their flocks. They continued to offer leadership that looked pretty much the same as it had for decades and perhaps centuries before.

But as we reflect on the history of the church and its centuries of witness, who do we hold up as an example of what it means to be a follower of Jesus? What does this say about our vocation—and our preaching—in today's world?

As the weight of climate injustice, environmental racism, the sixth extinction, and so much more now rests on our generation, it's time for the church to embrace its long history of prophetic witness. The fulfillment of our covenant and the continuity of life on Earth depend on it.

PASTORS MUST PREPARE THEIR HEARTS

If God is calling pastors to break the grip of society's dependence on fossil fuel, if pastors are being called (as Martin Luther King would say) to subpoena the conscience of America to take action on behalf of future generations, then we must first prepare our hearts. While pastors draw upon many effective approaches, I want to lift up two.

The first is to cultivate wonder. Perhaps the best way to do this is to embrace what both Emerson and Thoreau realized: "We are immersed in beauty." Again and again, nature's beauty has drawn out of me gratitude that words cannot express. How can it be that I have received the gift of consciousness, and not only that, now find myself surrounded by such unspeakable and diverse beauty that words are insufficient to express the gratitude that inhabits my heart? As Rachel Carson put it years ago, "Those who contemplate the beauty of the Earth find reserves of strength that will endure as long as life lasts."

If you're not already doing so, make a commitment today to cultivate wonder by appreciating and contemplating the beauty of creation—which is God's great gift to us. Precisely because it falls to our generation to take on the great challenge of climate change, we must persistently take in God's great gift of creation by appreciating and contemplating its beauty.

The second way we can prepare our hearts is to nurture our imagination. A good place to start is by reading poems by Mary Oliver, essays by Wendell Berry, or Walter Brueggemann's book, *The Prophetic Imagination*.

Our hearts do know what is possible:

- A more beautiful world—YES!
- A more balanced way of living—YES!
- A deeper connection with all things alive and yet to be born—YES!
- And imagination sufficient to accomplish what seems to be impossible—YES!

By engaging in these two disciplines—cultivating wonder and nurturing our imagination—not only do we prepare our hearts to faithfully proclaim God's prophetic word, but we accomplish something else that is essential to prophetic preaching: we expand our hope.

CULTIVATING COURAGE—"BE NOT AFRAID"

In preparing our hearts, we cultivate courage. I learned this from Br. David Steindl-Rast when he visited Henri Nouwen's class on spirituality in the 1970s. He reminded us that the English word "courage" comes from the old French word "cuer": heart.[9] The more we enlarge our hearts with love and gratitude for the gift of God's life-giving and life-preserving creation, the more our hearts will fill with the courage we need to overcome our fear.

The fear that most pastors experience as they hear God's call to offer a prophetic word is legitimate. Pastors understand "that for whatever reason, people tend to hear prophetic sermons louder than others. You can preach ten pastoral sermons and one prophetic sermon and the sermon that will be heard the loudest is the prophetic one."[10]

What does it take to overcome this fear? Wholehearted courage—rooted in love and gratitude. Jesus speaks to this dynamic. In fact, Jesus' most common instruction is "Fear not!" Henri Nouwen puts it this way:

Jesus invites us to move from the house of fear to the house of love. While Jesus totally understands our fear, he shows us that fear has no ultimate power. Only love endures.

My life's vocation has been to address humanity's greatest fear: that the continuity of our lives—the continuity of creation itself—is in jeopardy. In our years of working together, and in the scores of letters we exchanged, more than anyone else, Henri helped shape my vocation. Here are a few quotations from Henri's letters to me that pertain to this discussion of heartfelt courage. The first is from Henri to Cindy Shannon and me just after we became engaged.

> Love casts out fear and how powerful we are when we are free from fear! I can feel the growing freedom from fears in both of you and know that you are coming close to that love that can move mountains![11]

Describing how love overcomes fear and provides courage, Henri wrote this to me on October 30, 1982—six months before he visited Nicaragua and a year before his nationwide speaking tour opposing the war in Central America.

> I also discover that, only as a deep faithful lover of the church can I take risks on the level of peacemaking. You can only risk your life when you are in love.[12]

Exhausted, and at the conclusion of a six-month-long speaking tour across America to oppose the US war in Central America, Henri wrote to Cindy and me about the essential role of prayer, and how prayer, by connecting us to Christ, will make us brave.

> Be sure to make this inner peace your utmost priority. I say this to myself as much as to you! When we radiate the peace of Christ we are peacemakers and then our peace actions can witness to this inner peace. But without that inner peace our actions easily become instruments of the powers of war and destruction. . . . Prayer should be our first concern. Without prayer even our "good busyness" will lead to our destruction. If there is anything that I learned from my lecture/ preaching tour, it is this newfound insight that I want to share with you. . . . Never forget the words: "In the world you will have trouble; but be brave: I have overcome the world!"[13]

OFFER HOPE—WE ARE CALLED TO CHANGE THE STORY

Prophetic preaching must include a critique of the status quo. But if all the preacher does is rail against the principalities and powers, it's not enough. Prophetic preaching must offer hope.

Hope must be offered in a context of truth. Hope can never emerge from deception. We arrive at hope only after we have faced reality. Pastors are often reluctant to speak plainly from the pulpit about overwhelming realities that have no obvious solution. But Bill Coffin offers this perspective:

> Most people in the pews are far more prepared for painful truths than we give them credit for. What they want their preachers to do is to raise to a conscious level the knowledge inherent in their experience.[14]

On the way to hope, as pastors "raise to a conscious level the knowledge inherent in their (parishioners') experience," they would do well to be mindful of Kübler-Ross' five stages of grief—denial, anger, bargaining, depression, acceptance.

When it comes to climate change, we need to acknowledge our grief over the ongoing ruination of Creation. Only by doing so can we be receptive to a message of hope.

Prophetic preaching can and should be a powerful medicine for our souls at this time of climate crisis. Like many strong remedies and cures, it may leave us feeling unwell, exhausted and overwhelmed at first. But prophetic preaching is the bracing tonic that can buoy our spirits, leading us to discover hope.

To pull this together, all preaching helps people understand the story in which they are living their lives. Prophetic preaching invites people to critique the status quo and to examine their own lives. We need to name powers and principalities (for example, fossil fuel companies, the dismantling of the Environmental Protection Agency that began in 2017) and to confess our own complicity in the climate crisis (for example, flying, eating meat, owning stock in fossil fuel companies). Prophetic preaching taps righteous indignation and self-examination that seeks reconciliation. Prophetic preaching, by harnassing those two drives, prompts the individual to change his or her personal story and energizes the congregation to work together to change the story of how humanity relates to creation. Therein lies the Good News of the Gospel, resulting in lives of promise, possibility, and hope.

THE THEOLOGICAL FOUNDATION FOR PREACHING ON CLIMATE CHANGE

Any pastor newly convicted to preach on climate change can turn to numerous books that provide a thorough review of theological approaches to preaching on this topic. The bibliography in the back of this book is a good place to start.

Getting up to speed in an arena dominated by vehement ideological division can be intimidating. This is one reason why I find great value in staying focused on four theological cornerstones.

First, our covenant with God is an everlasting covenant. God does not care only for us; God covenants with all future generations and with every living creature (Genesis 9:12). All of scripture is a testimony to this truth.

Second, we must take seriously the most basic moral instruction of both the New Testament and Hebrew Scripture—a moral instruction found at the core of every world religion: We are called to love our neighbors as ourselves; and on this new E-a-a-r-t-h (as Bill McKibben calls it), we must recognize that future generations are no less our neighbors than those who live next door to us today. I refer to this as Golden Rule 2.0. You can find more on this in chapter 3.

Third, we must recognize that "the earth is the Lord's" (Psalm 24), and that we are stewards who hold the Earth in trust for future generations. Chapter 8 unpacks this important recognition.

Fourth, too much of our preaching focuses only on personal salvation. The reality is that scripture has much more to say about collective salvation than about individual salvation—and our preaching needs to reflect that. All of life—life not only with other humans but also with the rest of creation—is characterized by interdependence. The lives of all living things are woven together in a common destiny. The church needs to focus as much theological attention on collective salvation as it does on personal salvation. You can find more on this in chapter 3.

PREACHING ON CLIMATE CHANGE—
TEN CONSIDERATIONS

I want to offer ten considerations for approaching the climate crisis through preaching. Many of these considerations draw upon insights offered by George Marshall in his superb book: *Don't Even Think About It: Why Our Brains Are Wired To Ignore Climate Change.*[15] These considerations are also informed by ecoAmerica's *Let's Talk Faith and Climate: Communication Guidance for Faith Leaders* released in 2016.[16]

1. **Don't start with science, with fear, or with headlines.** Instead, begin by asking yourself: What is the collective story of your congregation? What is their social identity? What are their common, deeply held values? What do they care about most? And then: how do these values connect with the created order into which we were born . . . and how are these values challenged by the disorder and discontinuity brought by climate change? Research tells us that a compelling emotional story that speaks to people's core values has more impact than rational scientific data.

2. The second consideration may be counterintuitive: **It's good to acknowledge ambivalence.** Don't assume that everyone knows what you know, and even if they do know, don't assume that they care the same way you do. People have diverse priorities. A simple comment such as, "Some people are very concerned about climate change, and others are less so" will invite everyone in your congregation to go with you, wherever you may take them in the remainder of your sermon.

3. **Cite one fact, not a bunch of science.**[17] Be aware that too much emphasis on science can seriously backfire. It may not be helpful to explain what scientists mean when they report 2014, 2015, and 2016 as the hottest years in history. That's not to say that mentioning and citing facts should be avoided. With over 80 percent of Americans acknowledging that climate and weather are changing, to note, for example, that extreme weather events in New England have increased over 70 percent in recent years connects with people's experience. Try to share one powerful fact from a trusted messenger. Don't get all caught up in the details.

Stay on the mountaintop as a messenger while you give people a clear takeaway. Besides, what affects people most in listening to sermons are not data but values, moral narratives, and imagery.[18]

4. **Keep it simple.** For decades—perhaps centuries—preaching classes in seminaries have taught: tell them what you're going to tell them; tell them; tell them what you told them! Don't get drawn into the complexity of the climate science or ideological debates. As David Fenton of Fenton Communications says, "only simplicity works."[19]

5. **Do what the Golden Rule does.** (There's a reason why the Golden Rule is found at the core of every world religion!) In other words, **provide a narrative that invites people to recognize our *shared* humanity.** Tell a story that illustrates our mutual interests—for example, people and creatures all over the planet breathe the same air! When you discuss responses or solutions, be sure to emphasize cooperation. Regarding the challenge of climate change, no one has an alibi—we are literally all in this together.

6. **Embrace Jesus' most frequent admonition: "Fear not!"** At the moment, the prevailing narrative in our society regarding climate change encourages fear, denial, and unwillingness to accept our own responsibility. What insights can you call upon from how Jesus addressed the fear in the people around him? What encouragement can you take from the fact that living as he did in such a fearful time, Jesus nevertheless addressed those fears, and inspired endless courage, again and again and again? Go deep inside and ask yourself as a faith-leader: in the context of a world disordered by unchecked fear, greed, and growth, what is God's Good News? Preach on that.

7. **Lead your congregation to recognize that the time to act is NOW.** Of course, it's challenging to prompt action on an issue that may not seem to pose an immediate threat. As in most situations, when there is no deadline, people create their own timeline and delay action indefinitely. They may appreciate being informed, feel vaguely guilty for being unable to do very much, but take no further action. When it comes to climate change, as is shown elsewhere in this book, there are all kinds of actions your congregation can undertake right now. When extreme storms like

Hurricanes Harvey, Irma, or Maria hit, we can point out the connections to climate change[20] and urge immediate action, such as supporting disaster relief efforts and renewing our commitment to political advocacy for sane and sensible climate policies.

8. An eighth consideration concerns the wiring of our brains. In our sermons, we must speak of climate change in ways that **make it local, personal, immediate, and abrupt.** This is because people's brains are not suited to deal with threats that are distant or abstract. The best example of this I have ever seen is a Vimeo of the Rev. Ian Holland delivering a 2017 Earth Day sermon while wearing an orange life jacket over his robe.[21] Ian personalized the sermon by naming the roadways that will be flooded as the ocean rises. He asked people who live or commute on these roads to raise their hands. That made the future very real. Equally brilliant was his ability to make the congregation laugh by predicting that many in the congregation will just be stuck in place so they'd better enjoy one another.

9. **Claim your moral leadership as a member of the clergy**. For the most part, clergy are respected and trusted by their congregations, and research confirms that audiences are more receptive to messages from someone they respect and trust. Since we are clergy, it's essential to speak to our generation's moral obligation to take immediate action by embracing solutions already universally available.

10. Help your congregation to see how, in facing the reality of climate change, we can all **lead more faithful and hopeful lives.** Facing the climate crisis will not diminish the quality of our lives. Indeed, our lives will become more purposeful and faithful as we respond to the leading of the Spirit and seek to make our own lives—and the society in which we live—more just, loving, fair, and life-sustaining. Entrepreneurs are inventing new responses and solutions to climate change every day. As leaders of faith communities, it's up to us to offer new ways to live faithfully and hopefully in a world increasingly discontinuous with the world into which we were born.

Several of these considerations may come into play anytime we are called to preach prophetically. That being said, let me share with you an "elevator speech" offered by climate scientist and evangelical Christian Dr. Katharine Hayhoe.[22] Even though she's a climate scientist, Dr. Hayhoe doesn't start with science. She starts by affirming values that she and the person she is talking to hold in common. Then she says:

> Climate change will interfere with what we both care about. We know that climate change is caused by humans; we know it's going on here and all over the world; we know that it will affect what we both care about. And here are some of the things people are doing around here and all over the world to give ourselves a better future.

I hope that each of us, whether a preacher or not, can come up with our own "elevator speech," one which builds on shared values and names the positive actions we can take. If we want to be effective, we need to be inviting and supportive.

Let me conclude by sharing two things that I believe.

First: the church, the synagogue, the mosque, and the temple are a sleeping giant—and future generations are shaking us, trying to wake us up. To put it in Christian terms—although it applies to every faith perspective—we need to accept that we are not called to be a church for ourselves. We are called to be a church for others—*Koinonia*. And the most important "others" to whom we must give our lives are the vulnerable poor, who are those hit hardest by a changing world, and future generations.

Second: we really do have the power to bend the moral arc of the universe toward justice. If people of faith realize how decisive this moment is—if we realize that religion is actually a wholly owned subsidiary of creation—if we realize that we can affect not only the direction but also the pace of social transformation, then we will also realize that we can revoke the social license the fossil fuel industry requires in order to conduct "business as usual." Once we accomplish that, society will move at breakneck speed to engage opportunities to create a more life-sustaining way of life.

QUESTIONS FOR GROUP DISCUSSION
AND FURTHER REFLECTION

1. Discuss the suggestion that climate change is like a significant, unseemly "secret" that everyone in the congregation knows and that no one wants to talk about. In addition to reading and discussing this book, what else might your congregation do to address climate change directly?

2. Review the list of major historic social transformations in which the church played a significant role. In most cases, there were churches opposing these transformations as well. Discuss which side you want your church to be on when it comes to climate change.

3. Is Bill Coffin right when he says, "Most people in the pews are far more prepared for painful truths than we give them credit for"?

4. In addition to the four theological cornerstones that are offered for preaching on climate change, what others come to mind?

5. Review the ten considerations for preaching on climate change. Which ones surprised you? Are there others you would add?

8

WITNESSING TOGETHER

Communal Action Can Free Us from Fear

We are now faced with the fact that tomorrow is today. We are confronted with the fierce urgency of now. In this unfolding conundrum of life and history there is such a thing as being too late. . . . Over the bleached bones and jumbled residue of numerous civilizations are written the pathetic words: "Too late."
—Rev. Dr. Martin Luther King Jr. [1]

NOT THE VOCATION I STARTED WITH

In 2013 Jay O'Hara and Ken Ward piloted a lobster boat out near the Brayton Point power plant in Fall River, Massachusetts. The boat was named the *Henry David T*. They dropped anchor in just the right spot to block a gigantic freighter carrying 40,000 tons of coal. For a day or so, they prevented the tanker from reaching the Brayton Point coal-fired power plant. Eventually, they were arrested and charged with conspiracy, disturbing the peace, and a few other violations. Sixteen months later their trial was poised to begin. They insisted on a jury trial, and had prepared a necessity defense. Along with dozens of other supporters, I squeezed into the courtroom to hear opening testimony from world-renowned climate expert Jim Hansen.

The necessity defense, applied in this case, argued that the risk posed by climate change constitutes a greater harm than the criminal nonviolent action Jay and Ken had undertaken in the public interest. They planned to plead not guilty by reason of necessity, in order to draw attention to the failure of the law (as well as the enforcers of the law) to protect the citizenry. In a few other legal cases, the necessity defense resulted in acquittal of activists engaged in civil disobedience to draw attention to the risk and possible consequences posed by nuclear weapons. The O'Hara and Ward case was the first use of the necessity defense in a civil disobedience case centered on climate change.

As often happens, the start time for the O'Hara and Ward case was delayed. Then we began to hear rumors. When the judge entered the courtroom, the assistant district attorney asked to speak with him. Then the judge announced that:

- the conspiracy charge had been dropped,
- the other criminal charges had been downgraded to civil charges,
- the defendants had agreed to pay some reasonable court and police fees.

As the thunderous applause began to fade, word spread that the district attorney was going to hold an impromptu press conference in front of the courthouse in five minutes. No one knew what he would say.

Sam Sutter looked like the district attorney that he was. But he spoke like a father. He spoke like an activist. And under his arm was tucked a copy of the current issue of *Rolling Stone Magazine* featuring Bill McKibben's cover article, "The Fossil Fuel Resistance."[2] After assuring the citizens of Bristol County, Massachusetts, that the costs of the police would be covered by the defendants, he said that his decision was made with "the children of Bristol County and beyond in mind. Climate change is one of the gravest crises our planet has ever faced," he continued. "In my humble opinion, the political leadership on this issue has been gravely lacking." As the cheers erupted, he said one thing more.

> I am also extremely pleased that we were able to reach an agreement that symbolizes our commitment at the Bristol County District Attorney's Office to take a leadership role on this issue. . . . Climate change is one of the gravest crises the planet has ever faced. The

> evidence is overwhelming and it keeps getting worse. So we took a
> stand here today, [at] the Bristol County District Attorney's Office.[3]

As the crowd applauded and shouted, I wept. I waited until the
crush of the press subsided so that I could have a moment to speak with
DA Sutter. I told him that it seemed to me that he had invoked the
necessity defense for himself—that the horror of climate change was so
imminent, it necessitated new action and innovation on his part as a
district attorney. With a gleam in his eye, he responded, "Yes. Exactly."
I said that it seemed to me he was declaring that, in the context of a
climate crisis world, district attorneys must embrace a new vocation.
Again, he heartily agreed.

As he walked away, I thought of Martin Luther at the Diet of Worms
in 1521 invoking his understanding of necessity: "Here I stand; I can do
no other. God help me."

In 2006, when the Massachusetts Conference UCC Board of Directors concluded their interviews and offered me the position of Conference Minister and President, I said to them, "There's just one more
thing—I'll need your support for me to spend at least 10 percent of my
time on climate justice."

In the silence that followed, I imagined a few of them asking, "What
is it about overseeing almost 400 churches and over 800 clergy that this
guy doesn't understand? This is already a BIG JOB!!!" But in the conversation that followed, it became clear that they were not entirely
surprised. After all, climate change was my passion. But that was not
the point. I wasn't asking them to support my idiosyncratic interest or
passion. I was asking them to join me in acknowledging that the urgency and enormity of the climate crisis demands that all of us must consider making a significant adjustment in how we live out our calling. Once
we worked through all of that, they were 100 percent supportive, and
now I spend perhaps 25 percent of my time on climate, with the full
backing of my board.

Recently I was having dinner with several Ivy League business
school students; I wanted to run a question by them. Naively, I asked
how climate change figured into their studies, and into the overall mission of the school. They replied that the Technology and Operations
Management Program made use of a substantial case study focusing on
the implications for business posed by climate change. They agreed that

of all the "wicked problems" humanity has ever faced, climate change was the most challenging. While I was glad to see such serious engagement, I had been hoping for a deeper response. So I said this:

> You are among the best and brightest business school students in the world. If you aren't being groomed to provide systemic leadership in a climate crisis world, who will lead our economy in a new direction? What business leaders will help shift our economic system from rewarding current-generation investors to embracing multigenerational responsibilities? Who among the next generation of business moguls will help build an economy that values not only human flourishing but also the restoration of all of creation? If preparation for this challenge and these ideals are not, say, 25 percent of the Harvard Business School curriculum, how will our nation make the changes in its economic system that science says we need to make?

Using language more suited to the church, this was a conversation about the vocation of HBS. Each of us needs to ask ourselves similar questions, whatever our career or vocation. We must find ways to fulfil our calling that help those close to us and our community while also protecting future generations of human beings and preserving biodiversity. While leaders at the top of the most powerful human institutions must live out the answers to these questions, humanity will be able to adapt much more nimbly if we also crowd-source this challenge.

WHAT IS WITNESSING?

Witnesses tell the truth in a public setting about what they have seen and heard. Borrowing this notion from the court of law, the authors of both Hebrew Scripture and the New Testament charge the faithful to speak out and to live their lives as faithful witnesses. Isaiah suggests that God's people have been subpoenaed as witnesses to testify on behalf of God's authenticity (Isaiah 43:10). Jesus is referred to as "the faithful witness" to the Lord God (Revelation 1:5). Like Paul, who is told that he has been chosen to bear witness to what he has seen and heard (Acts 22:14–16), Peter and John were arrested for speaking about Jesus' resurrection. On trial the next day, they said, "We cannot keep from speaking about what we have seen and heard" (Acts 4:20).

In his excellent book on testimony, Tom Long has this to say about witnessing:

> Christians understand themselves to be in the biggest court case of all, the trial of the ages. What is being contested is the very nature of reality, and everything is at stake.[4]

Witnessing is usually done on behalf of a community, and it's often done alongside others. It includes not only the truth that we convey with our words (which is also called testimony), but also includes the truth that we bear with our bodies. In contemporary parlance, "showing up" is a form of witnessing. In addition to bearing witness with our words and our bodies, the way we use all the other gifts we have been given—from our time to our financial assets—also constitutes a witness.

What we do with the gifts we've been given—what we do with our assets—matters. Many pastors make this point by sharing the following story with their congregations: When we die and meet St. Peter at Heaven's gate, he will invite us to pull out both our checkbook and our appointment book, and then will ask us only one question: do these two records contain enough evidence to convict you as a Christian?

On April 22, 2017, tens of thousands of scientists used their words, bodies, time, and expertise to bear witness to the truth. This was necessary because an almost unlimited amount of financial and political resources have been marshalled over the past few decades to contest the truth of scientific findings on climate change. In a different political context, the strategies of the science deniers would be called propaganda. In the United States, people are allowed to distort the truth in order to advance their goal—bringing profit to current corporate shareholders. To protest the corruption of science and the promotion of climate denial, scientists gathered in over six hundred marches all over the world. They used their freedom to witness for the truth as they called for "Data—not dogma!" In a forthcoming book, Naomi Oreskes will argue that in a climate crisis world, scientists have a moral obligation to speak out publicly—to bear witness—to their values.

A final example of witnessing combines many of these elements. Since 2010, Joel Clement served as director of the Office of Policy Analysis at the US Interior Department. His work as a scientist and "policy wonk" focused on climate change. In 2013 he wrote a paper warning that the Arctic is warming faster than any other region on

Earth. In April 2016, confirming what Clements had warned, the island community of Shishmaref, Alaska, voted to relocate due to rising sea levels. In the first months of the Trump administration, Clement spoke out publicly about the dangers that climate change poses to Alaska Native communities. Then, on June 15, 2017, Clement was reassigned to an unrelated job in the accounting office of the US Interior Department. Among other duties, Clement found himself collecting royalty checks from fossil fuel companies. On July 19, 2017, Clement engaged a new form of witnessing. He filed a complaint and a disclosure of information with the US Office of Special Counsel. He claimed that his reassignment was retaliation against his disclosure of threats to the health and safety of American citizens. He also claimed that as a federal employee, he was protected from reprisal by the Whistleblower Protection Act and Whistleblower Protection Enhancement Act.[5]

MAKING CIVIL DISOBEDIENCE A NORMATIVE EXPRESSION OF CHRISTIAN DISCIPLESHIP

When I returned to my ministry among the UCC churches in Massachusetts after being released from the central cell block in the Washington, DC, jail in August 2011, I received a lot of positive feedback. Many people thanked me for my witness and told me they were proud of what I had done. Many also said they could not imagine doing anything like it. Too scary. Too intimidating. Too unthinkable—intentionally doing something illegal.

Later that fall, a men's group in one of my churches invited me to speak about my experience at their monthly gathering. They assured me that this would be an "off the record" conversation. They were not all in agreement with what I had done, but they all respected my conscience and courage. They wanted to hear the real story and to ask me some questions. It was a deeply moving conversation for all of us. What interested them most was how I could give up my freedom. Many of them could not imagine doing that. What most surprised them was my response, which I shared in the context of a brief quote from Paul's letter to the Christians in Galatia: "For freedom Christ has set us free" (Galatians 5:1). I told them: Never in my life had I felt freer than when I followed God's call and the call of my conscience to go to jail for a worthy cause. The freedom I experienced is that glorious feeling that results from making a decision and taking an action that is aligned with God's purposes. My next question for them was why more of them were not experiencing such a call, or why those who might have heard that call had not yet responded. Not only did this question stick with these reflective men, it stuck with me too.

That experience led me to begin to use the provocative expression: "Make Civil Disobedience a Normative Expression of Christian Discipleship." I cannot imagine society making the changes that science says we must unless thousands of people are willing to engage in the spiritual discipline of civil disobedience. Throughout history, significant social change has only happened when the conscience of America has been awakened and focused. In every case—ending slavery, women's suffrage, civil rights, voting rights, LGBTQIA+ rights—civil disobedience has played an essential role.

But "normative?" While many in our society and in our churches admire Henry David Thoreau, Mahatma Gandhi, Dorothy Day, Rabbi Abraham Joshua Heschel, the Rev. Dr. Martin Luther King Jr., Congressman John Lewis, and Father Dan Berrigan, we regard them and their repeated public acts of civil disobedience as exceptional. We admire their moral courage, but the vast majority of us also want to keep it at arm's length.

Or so I thought.

At the UCC national Synod on the fourth of July 2017, I put this to a test. The seven hundred delegates and a few thousand visitors were well aware that less than twenty-four hours earlier, 97 percent of the delegates voted for a resolution that called upon UCC congregations and members, among other things, to "resist all expansion of fossil fuel infrastructure." When I went to the microphone for a one minute "speak out" people expected me to say something about that resolution, and I did, but not exactly what they might have expected. I began by saying,

> It's time for the United Church of Christ to make civil disobedience a normative expression of Christian discipleship. If you are able, please stand if you have ever engaged in nonviolent civil disobedience. . . . Thank you! And please remain standing if you've participated in an action of nonviolent civil disobedience since our last Synod. . . . Thank you.

I'm sure that I wasn't the only person in the convention center who was shocked to see about 30 percent of the delegates stand, and at least half of them remain standing. As soon as I could catch my breath, I continued,

> Today is the fourth of July. Our country was birthed by actions of civil disobedience. Jesus' witness was nonviolent and the Empire regarded it as illegal. As John Dear says, the resurrection was totally outside of the law and its "principalities and powers." Gandhi described Jesus as "the most active resister known perhaps to history." In addition to Standing Rock, across the country there are scores of opportunities to resist the expansion of fossil fuel infrastructure. Is God calling you to make civil disobedience a normative expression of Christian discipleship?

I believe that the changes we must undertake are so substantial that it will take more than a limited number of people of conscience to bend the long moral arc of the universe toward justice. Our economic, corporate, and political systems, our lifestyles and aspirations, are tied to an unsustainable expectation of material growth. For two hundred years, this juggernaut has been powered by fossil fuel. If we are to untie this Gordian knot—if we are to overcome this inertia—ordinary people, motivated by faith and conscience, must regularly interrupt "business as usual" to draw attention to where we are headed, and to offer a better way.

DRIVEN BY LOVE AND GRATITUDE WITH FEAR AS A CATALYST

When considering civil disobedience and the other forms of witness, people have shared with me that love is their most powerful motivator—love of God; love of nature; love of beauty; love of their children; love of creatures and plants in all their diversity; love of the impossible way in which this planet provides all living things with everything we need to flourish. What I have seen time and time again is that when a person allows herself to love creation in these and other ways, and when a person also allows herself to face the extent to which humanity has compromised, extinguished, and threatened all that she loves, the courage emerges to respond to the call to bear witness.

Gratitude is another powerful motivating force among those who bear witness—gratitude for having been given life; gratitude for God's creation and all the ways it has nourished one's life; gratitude for the support that friends and loved ones have provided; gratitude for this particular moment, as well as the gift of time itself; gratitude for the dreams and aspirations that mysteriously arise from within.

As I am writing this chapter, an article in *New York* magazine has gone viral, igniting a firestorm of controversy. Only two weeks after publication, "The Uninhabitable Earth" has become the most-read article in the publication's history.[6] In just over 7,000 words, David Wallace-Wells describes what will happen if humanity fails to make the dramatic changes science says we must. It's a terrifying read. The fact that the article doesn't smooth over the horror is one of the reasons why millions of people have read it.

Many of the most prominent climate scientists quickly responded, indicating where Wallace-Wells misinterpreted the science. This is an important part of the controversy. Another criticism is best represented by the comments of Penn State climatologist Michael Mann. "The evidence that climate change is a serious challenge that we must tackle now is very clear. There is no need to overstate it, particularly when it feeds a paralyzing narrative of doom and hopelessness."[7]

Fear that what we love will be destroyed is a powerful catalyst for action. That fear is amplified if we learn that far-off consequences will soon be imminent. In an excellent analysis of both the article and the controversy, Jason Mark writes in *Sierra* magazine, "Wallace-Wells' essay is a calculated provocation designed to shake some people out of their complacency."[8] Mark reminds us that Rachel Carson opened her book Silent Spring with "A Fable for Tomorrow" that depicts a fictional town in which a dozen or so environmental calamities are suddenly concentrated. No one would dispute that the fear of a "silent spring" was a key motivation for the beginning of the environmental movement.

But a person needs more than fear to stay engaged and make long-term changes and enduring commitments. Fear can be an effective catalyst. But the most powerful motivators and sustainers of change are love and gratitude.

DIVESTMENT: REVOKING THE SOCIAL LICENSE TO WRECK CREATION

In August 2012, Bill McKibben opened up a new "front" in the fight to combat climate change. Up until then, the environmental movement was largely focused on impact from the consumer side. As a result, much of the emphasis was on recycling, reusing, and reducing our consumption.

When McKibben issued a call for institutions and individuals to divest from fossil fuel companies, he began focusing the world's attention on the supply side of climate change. The goal of the divestment movement was to increase public awareness of two realities. From a practical perspective, 80 percent of the known fossil fuel reserves (worth about $20 trillion) would need to be left in the ground. From a moral perspective, the divestment movement would revoke the moral license the fossil fuel companies need to continue their "business as usual" practices of making money for their investors by wrecking the Earth.

Bill envisioned a movement of institutions and individuals willing to be very public about the fact that what we do with our assets matters. Owning stocks is not just about making money. A core conviction of the American economic system is that ownership equals responsibility. By owning a stock, we are endorsing the actions of the company. A group of two hundred companies were identified as the ones chiefly responsible for extracting, transporting, refining, and selling fossil fuels.

Make no mistake: divestment is controversial. While many (including Nelson Mandela) believed that the movement to divest from companies doing business with South Africa was the strategic linchpin that succeeded in overthrowing that country's apartheid practices, some historians reject that claim.

Depending on the setting, the controversy showed up in a variety of ways. Those who are responsible for investing the financial assets of a church or other nonprofit institution would often say that their job was to invest in a way that yielded the most revenue for the church. However, most of these investors were already constrained by a number of guidelines for ethical investing (for example, no investments in guns, alcohol, tobacco, etc.). When the case was made that the church's ethical commitments should view fossil fuel companies in the same light, investors often said divestment from fossil fuel companies was simply not practical. Funds were not available that were free of fossil fuel companies. By 2015, that was changing and many major investment companies responded to the demand by offering fossil fuel–free funds. For example, in November 2014 the UCC's United Church Funds launched the Beyond Fossil Fuels Fund, which was available to any church institutional fund, regardless of denomination.

Another critique suggested that it was almost impossible to purge any portfolio entirely of fossil fuel holdings. When pressed in this way, I have always responded, "Don't let the perfect be the enemy of the good." As with most forms of witnessing, moral purity is not the goal. The goal is to create the conditions in our world where current "business as usual" will be regarded as immoral and unacceptable.

A final critique suggested that if you're trying to influence the company, you should try to change the company's policy as a shareholder advocate. The problem is that shareholder advocacy cannot change a company's core business. Shareholder advocacy can get Apple to institute more humane labor practices in China, but it can't get a coal company to stop mining for coal. Furthermore, on the issue of climate change, shareholder advocacy has no track record of success.

However, having said that, in May 2017 a shock reverberated throughout the fossil fuel industry. At ExxonMobil, 62.3 percent of shareholders voted to require the oil giant to include more detailed assessments of how climate policies impact its bottom line. Never had there been such a vote. It is thought to have been led by major shareholders, including BlackRock, Vanguard, and State Street.

One final note on divesting. Less than five years after the divestment movement was born, the *New York Times* reported that investment funds worth over $5,000,000,000,000 had dropped their fossil fuel stocks.[9] Five trillion dollars of invested funds that no longer include fossil fuel stocks is a good start—a sign that the divestment movement is making progress in its goal of revoking the moral license these companies need to carry out business as usual.

A NEW TAKE ON FIDUCIARY ACCOUNTABILITY

As people of faith, our forebears are responsible for introducing the notion of "fiduciary" and "fiduciary responsibility"—it has to do with keeping faith with the future. The popular understanding of fiduciary allows the directors of companies to claim the moral (and legal) high ground when all they do is maximize short-term monetary profit for their shareholders. For centuries, the church has ceded to the legal and investment world the exclusive right to interpret society's understanding of fiduciary responsibility. But it seems to me that it is both crazy and criminal to think that an investor has satisfied his or her fiduciary obligation by assuring maximum financial profit over the next quarter— while ignoring the fact that the investment will end up wrecking the home of the investor.

Imagine the impact if numerous faith leaders, along with lay leaders who serve in prominent positions in the financial world, drew attention to the inadequacy of the current laws governing fiduciary responsibility. Imagine what might change if these leaders decried the failure of fiduciary law to take into account the known intergenerational consequences if the fossil fuel industry continues its business-as-usual activity.

I was thrilled to hear former Securities and Exchange Commissioner Bevis Longstreth raise these and other significant questions about fiduciary responsibility on September 29, 2014, in a talk he gave to fiduciaries who gathered for the Boston Carbon Risk Forum at Harvard Law School.[10] The conclusion of his talk was similar to what he wrote in an article he posted on November 3, 2013.[11] In it, he made the legal argument for divestment from pension funds based solely on financial grounds. He explicitly left to others the responsibility "to advance arguments on the basis of global urgency, morality, chartered purpose or other worthy grounds."

In short, he concludes that while anticipatory divestment has unknown short-term consequences, "fossil fuel companies will prove to be bad investments over the long term and, therefore, with foresight that anticipates this result, should be removed from the long-term holdings of an endowment before the strengthening likelihood of this result becomes commonplace in the market."

To put this in my own words: if fossil fuel companies continue to succeed, our common home will no longer support life as we have known it. Because of this, fossil fuel companies will (sooner rather than later) become bad investments. Recognizing this, it is fiduciarily irresponsible to hold long-term investments in fossil fuel companies.

In conversations following the event, I was reminded of a possible legal precedent for raising this issue. In 1978, New York City was going bankrupt. The NYC Workers' Pension Fund invested about 33 percent of its assets in "junk bonds" to save the city from bankruptcy and thus restore the jobs of the city workers. When some fund participants sued the NYC Workers' Pension Fund for failing in their fiduciary responsibilities by making risky investments, their suit was denied. What seemed to some to be a risky investment at the time had the long-term consequence of saving New York City along with the jobs of NYC workers.

In chapter 3 I argued that the Golden Rule, as religions have understood it for thousands of years, is limited and needs to be updated. The "others" in "do unto others" needs to include future generations. In that same chapter, I highlighted the limits of market capitalism. When we focus only on immediate material gains, we sacrifice not only the beauty of creation but the capacity of creation to support life in the near-term future. Market capitalism dismisses these as "externalities." They are regarded as "external" to the ingredients market capitalism takes into account.

If fiduciary accountability requires us to keep faith with the future, then, like the Golden Rule, market capitalism needs to be updated. We must expand our understanding of fiduciary accountability to take into consideration the impact our investments have on the environment we are handing to our children. Anything short of this is irresponsibly delusional.

With this in mind, as people of faith, let us not limit the possible arenas in which we are called to bear witness on behalf of preserving God's great gift of creation.

A GLOBAL COMMONS—END THE OWNERSHIP OF NATURE

I couldn't resist. Upon hearing that dozens of climate activists were planning to spend the night in the oldest city park in the United States—the Boston Common—I told the organizers, "I'm in!" We were seeking to draw media attention to the ground-breaking climate legislation that was under consideration at the State House just yards away from our tents.

It was a chilly November night in 2009. The organizers were a ragtag group of student climate activists calling themselves Mass Power Shift. I had met them the year before when I spoke as part of the "Step It Up" campaign they helped organize. Later, they would become the Better Future Project and affiliate with the emerging (now world-renowned) 350.org.

The police stopped by around 3:00 a.m., requesting our IDs and informing us that what we were doing was illegal. When I popped my head out of my tent, I still had my clerical collar on. They seemed pleasantly surprised, and soon left us.

In the early morning, I thought about the hundreds of other nights I had spent outdoors, in a tent, under the stars, on a plot of land we humans had agreed would be held in common. My love affair with the commons began while hiking the John Muir Trail when I was sixteen. Three times, my wife and I took our sons on month-long camping trips to the national parks. Whatever issues I have with J. D. Rockefeller, I am grateful beyond words for his vision to use a portion of his wealth to preserve vast expanses of wild beauty for future generations. When funding for the National Park Service was in jeopardy in the late 1990s, it occurred to me there was something I could do. I wrote a letter to Bill Gates (then the richest man in the world) pleading with him to endow the National Park Service for the indefinite future. He could have done so at the time using less than 10 percent of his fortune. I then shared the letter as a sermon.

Countless preachers have drawn inspiration for their sermons from nature's beauty preserved in national, state, and local parks. Occasionally, you will hear in church mention of a local land trust and the benefit it provides the surrounding community. But rarely if ever is the peace-

ful time we seek in church on Sunday morning interrupted by a suggestion as radical as ending the ownership of nature.

Walter Brueggemann raises "the urgent questions of ownership,
control, and governance of the land and its embedded natural resources" in an arresting essay entitled, "To Whom Does the Land Belong?"[12] As always, Brueggemann offers strong biblical support for his
argument. His position—with which I agree—is astonishingly simple.

Only a misinterpretation of scripture justifies human domination
and control of the land. The Western world's understanding of land as
property which can absolutely be possessed is the result of modern
Enlightenment philosophy. Once the claim of a creator God had been
sidelined, instead of regarding land as creation, society began to regard
land as possession. Our consumer society only reinforces this, leading to
aggressive and absurd claims such as the oil found on God's Earth is
"our oil."

More than once in his brief essay, Brueggemann points to the risk
involved in preaching as a "witness and advocate for land as creation in
a society that is ideologically committed to land as possession." Risky?
Yes. Nevertheless, as I've already detailed, congregations that are located not far from proposed pipelines are actively protesting the exercise
of eminent domain.

A less risky recognition that the Earth is the Lord's (Psalm 24:1)
would be for churches to initiate a movement whereby the land currently owned by churches was turned into a land trust. It seems to me
that the implausibility of this suggestion confirms Brueggemann's point
that the church has forfeited one of the most elemental claims of
faith—that the Earth is the Lord's. Short of reversing society's insistence on owning nature, it's easy to imagine many churches embracing
the biblical command to be stewards of the land. A few pioneering
churches have already done so. These churches have turned much of
their land into community gardens—often organic or permaculture—
tended by both church members and community neighbors. This provides a public witness that invites the community to consider what for
many amounts to a new relationship to the land.

In July 2017, Quaker activist and writer Parker Palmer posted a
column on Krista Tippitt's blog, *On Being*, entitled, "We Are Owned by
the Wilderness." Mr. Palmer writes,[13]

The ownership of private property has long been a touchstone of the American dream—for better (when we're able to meet our basic needs) and for worse (when need becomes greed and overwhelms generosity and economic justice). But when "ownership" is applied wholesale to nature, there's no better, only worse. The arrogance that leads us to say "We own this patch of the planet" has also led us to foul our own nest and desacralize much of the earth.

I hope that the hints and suggestions made in this section inspire you to begin a pivot from focusing on ownership to celebrating a global commons.[14]

BUILDING THE KINGDOM OF GOD: SOCIETY BASED ON "THE COMMON GOOD"

Walter Brueggemann, in his essay "The Journey to the Common Good," identifies what Exodus can teach us as we move from a culture of anxiety and fear through an experience of abundance to a practice of neighborliness. He begins with these words,

> The great crisis among us is the crisis of "the common good," the sense of community solidarity that binds all in a common destiny— haves and have-nots, the rich and the poor. We face a crisis about the common good because there are powerful forces at work among us to resist the common good, to violate community solidarity, and to deny a common destiny.[15]

Brueggemann suggests that "an immense act of generosity is required in order to break the death grip of the system of fear, anxiety, and greed." The offer of the Eucharist, together with its unrestrained promises, is just such a generous act. The church is entrusted to extend that generous offer to all. Jesus calls faithful Christians to flee the kingdom of scarcity where our horizons are constrained by entitled consumerism. In its place, Jesus calls us to embrace a "covenantal commitment to the common good." Indeed, Brueggemann argues, the biblical narrative is a sustained appeal to welcome this alternative.

I join Brueggemann in his assertion that theological study can be (and must become) an enterprise of critical, outside-the-box reflection that propels the faithful to advance on this journey of freedom.

The religions of the world must challenge political leaders to govern in a way that assures the common good. When political leaders go astray, when they abrogate their responsibility, the religions of the world must remind the faithful of their obligation to call politicians and government to account. Living as we are amidst just such a crisis, God is calling us to bear witness to the promise of abundant life for all of creation as we use the gifts we have been given to celebrate the common good.

QUESTIONS FOR GROUP DISCUSSION AND FURTHER REFLECTION

1. Reread the brief description of the necessity defense at the beginning of this chapter and share your thoughts. Someone in your group may want to do some research on other situations in which the necessity defense has been tried.

2. Share a time when you responded to the call to bear witness—not in a courtroom before a jury—but rather a time when you told the truth in a public setting about what you had seen and heard.

3. Share your response to this idea: When we die and meet St. Peter at Heaven's gate, he will invite us to pull out both our checkbook and our appointment book, and then will ask us only one question: can you find in these two records enough evidence to convict you as a Christian?

4. An exercise familiar to many congregations is for each member to review her time, talent, and treasure, and identify how much she keeps for her own well-being, and how much she shares with the church or with other people in need. Once this is done, a variation would go on to ask the intergenerational question: how much of each of those gifts does she dedicate to supporting yet-to-be-born generations?

5. Discuss the case of Joel Clement, former director of the Office of Policy Analysis at the US Interior Department. Where does his case stand as you are reading this?

6. When it comes to climate change, is the conscience of America waking up? Have the public voices and witnesses succeeded in motivating Americans to turn our lifestyles and aspirations away from an unsustainable expectation of material growth? If not, what do you think about the proposal to "Make Civil Disobedience a Normative Expression of Christian Discipleship"?

7. How does fear that what you love may be destroyed affect you? Is it paralyzing or is it a powerful catalyst for action?

8. Discuss the assertion that what we do with our (personal) assets matters. Talking with friends (or even with family for that matter) about money or financial assets is challenging. Look back at chapter 4 and the discussion of Truth and Reconciliation Conversations. Can your group risk sharing with one another your response to the divestment movement?

9. Reflect on the final section of this chapter. Share with one another examples (in addition to the Eucharist) of how our society continues to celebrate and seek to extend the common good.

9

LIVING HOPE-FILLED LIVES IN A CLIMATE CRISIS WORLD

Our greatest intergenerational obligation, then, is to sustain love, for so we prepare future generations to judge us and, we hope, to forgive us.
—Willis Jenkins[1]

Since the mid-1980s, I have preached on climate change hundreds of times throughout the United States. No matter what the setting, every time I preach, I focus on hope. I continue to believe that the most important contribution people of faith can and must make as humanity confronts the climate crisis is to proclaim hope.

More often than not, when I meet with members of the congregation after worship to discuss the sermon, people are eager to share various examples of actions they have taken: changing light bulbs, installing solar panels, going from two cars to one, hanging their clothes out to dry, and so on. Less frequently, someone wants to go deeper into something I have said, such as "make civil disobedience a normative expression of discipleship" or "we all live at the same address, and at this moment every doorway has inscribed above it the number 408 (parts per million of carbon dioxide in the atmosphere)." Only rarely is someone willing to risk being vulnerable enough to express his or her despair, grief, or hopelessness. Those who do often ask me, "How can you know all these facts and still have hope?"

NOT OPTIMISM . . . BUT HOPE

Optimism is what many people mean when they are asked about hope. When our life is turned upside down by an accident, tragedy, or a natural disaster, we do our best to remain optimistic, and we admire those who persevere in their optimism. Not only is optimism a good thing, it's a necessary thing for personal survival under such conditions. In a time of crisis, it's essential to stay positive and focus on doing everything possible to find a way through the rubble that will lead to restoration.

But optimism is not hope. Optimism is all about the future and our expectation that things will turn out the way we want them to. Optimism is about attitude—not action—and because of that it carries neither cost nor risk. By taking a positive view amidst a challenging situation, an optimist may inspire others in ways that make an actual difference. But holding an optimistic view in a difficult situation changes nothing in and of itself. Thus, Cornel West says that the optimist "adopts the role of the spectator"[2] and Rabbi Jonathan Sacks adds that "Optimism is a passive virtue, hope an active one."[3]

Optimism, while helpful, is not nearly enough given all that is at stake during this time of global climate crisis. Life in a time of catastrophe and profound discontinuity demands an "accept no substitutes" mindset. Deep-seated hope is what we need, and what God intends for us. "'For surely I know the plans I have for you,' says the Lord, 'plans for your welfare and not for harm, to give you a future with hope'" (Jeremiah 29:11). But what is this hope, and how do we embrace it?

FACING REALITY—A PRECONDITION OF HOPE

"How can you know all these facts and still have hope?" When I'm pressed by this question, before I get to hope, I invite the person to share with me their emotional response to what I said. When it comes to climate change, what do they find most disturbing? Invariably, this invitation is welcomed.

Often, they share a small detail—a particular animal that is now extinct; a relative who was forced to move because of extreme drought; a neighborhood that will be under water in fifteen years; the fact that

Glacier National Park will soon have no glaciers. It helps to share one's worry and pain with someone willing to listen empathetically. It is welcomed. When the courage to express an overwhelming concern is received with an affirming, understanding response, the paralyzing bonds of fear are loosened.

One of the most consequential outcomes of the politicization of the issue of climate change is that the obvious experiences and concerns of ordinary people are self-censored. An October 2015 report from the Yale Program on Climate Change Communication points out that two in three Americans (67 percent) think global warming is happening—yet most Americans rarely or never discuss it (65 percent).[4] I think there are two reasons for this. First, people care deeply about many of the things threatened by climate change. Because they care deeply about these things, they are unwilling to enter into what will inevitably become a politicized conversation that is likely to dismiss their deeply held concern. Second, many people believe that sharing these deeply held concerns will do nothing more than amplify their own fear and depression and bring other people down. To put it another way, they believe that communicating these deeply held concerns—saying them out loud to another person—will erode their hope.

These fears are based on a thin and misguided understanding of hope. However grim, reality cannot undermine or cancel the hope God offers us. Indeed, Dr. Jerome Groopman says it well, "Hope, unlike optimism, is rooted in unalloyed reality."[5] He says later, "To hope under the most extreme circumstances is an act of defiance."[6] Jesus said it even more clearly, "The truth will set you free."

Hope is the most important contribution people of faith can and must make as humanity confronts the climate crisis. To become people of hope we must be willing to stare reality in the face. We must be willing to face not only the scientific reality of a rapidly warming world but also the political reality that there are individuals, groups, and entire industries devoted to spreading misinformation and lies about the climate crisis. If hope is essential to Christians, then exposing the lies perpetuated by the powers and principalities that deny climate change must become a first-order priority. Christians cannot stand idly by and allow the greatest moral challenge humanity has ever faced to be framed as an ideological issue by people with unlimited financial resources acquired by the abuse of God's creation. Part of staring reality in the face means exposing the lies being spread by those who seek to fan the flames of doubt and promote an ideological divide. In its commitment to speak truth to power, the climate justice movement has much in common with other social movements.

Not surprisingly, any pastor or congregation that responds to this call will experience a good bit of resistance. This is why prophetic witness must always be informed by pastoral sensitivity. My suggestion (detailed in chapter 4) to convene Truth and Reconciliation Conversations on Climate Change is intended to address the resistance while allowing everyone in the congregation to experience enough safety to go beyond optimism and actually take in the grim reality of climate change.

EXPRESSING GRIEF—A PRECONDITION OF HOPE

A Truth and Reconciliation Conversation on Climate Change can also provide a safe context in which people can share not only their grief, but also their deep love for God's creation. The smoke of grief and the fire of love are inseparable. For anyone who loves life, loves their children, or delights in the natural world, recognizing the realities of climate change will trigger grief. However, more often than not, social norms restrict the expression of such grief.

It is difficult even to talk about grief. There are taboos in normal conversation that block the discussion of anything considered too depressing. When we feel dread about what may lie ahead, outrage at what is happening to our planet, or sadness about what has already been lost, it is likely that we have nowhere to take these feelings. As a result, we tend to keep them to ourselves; we suffer in isolation.[7]

Walter Brueggemann expands this observation in his book *Reality—Grief—Hope: Three Urgent Prophetic Tasks*. Brueggemann draws from the response of the prophets to the destruction of Jerusalem as a guide to understanding post–9/11 America and the witness we are called to bear. Much of what he says can serve as a guide for repurposing the church as we respond to climate change.

> Given that state of legitimate sadness that is kept numb and unvoiced, the prophetic task, I propose, is to encourage, permit, and engage the practice of public grief over a world that is gone. This is, I have shown, what the prophets did as they anticipated the coming

destruction. . . . The alternative toward health and new life is the shared, out loud, honest work of grief. Such voiced grief is an alternative to violence. Such grief, moreover, turns loss to energy for newness. . . . There is no shortcut. The task requires trust that does not blush and history that does not blink. It is as though, embracing our loss, we offer a requiem for a lost world, willing to let it rest in the embrace of honest words.[8]

Bill McKibben has devoted his entire adult life to this prophetic task. While still in his twenties, in 1989 he wrote the first book on climate change, *The End of Nature*. In addition to summarizing the already well-developed science, in that groundbreaking book, McKibben reflected on what it means that human activity has curtailed nature's wild independence. No longer did our crushing footprint land only here or there upon an otherwise untrampled landscape. No longer did humans live alongside primitive forests and wild streams unaffected by our so-called progress. By changing the planet's climate and other life-systems, the totality of our impact has made "every spot on earth man-made and artificial." Thus, we have ended nature—spoiling its most pristine places and robbing nature of its wildness by subjugating it to our needs. For millions of years, human beings both battled against and benefitted from nature. But as McKibben points out, now that we have become sufficiently powerful to dominate nature, "there is nothing but us."

Grief—while not explicitly discussed—is threaded through the pages of *The End of Nature*. Grief became more prevalent over the next two decades during which most of humanity ignored reality, too many politicians lined their pockets with the bribes from companies that were busy raping the earth, and the 2009 United Nations Climate Change Conference in Copenhagen dashed humanity's hope. McKibben's 2010 book *Eaarth* helped guide the emerging climate movement through grief. (The title is intentionally misspelled to draw attention to the fact that we no longer live on the same earth most of us were born on.) In his excellent narrative on the climate movement, *What We're Fighting for Now is Each Other: Dispatches from the Front Lines of Climate Justice*, Wen Stephenson rightly refers to McKibben as a "modern-day Jeremiah." McKibben, in his humility, refuses to call himself a prophet. Nevertheless, since 1989 Bill McKibben has been the lead voice insisting that the world face the reality of climate devastation. He has done so in a way that helps to legitimize our grief—grief for the world our generation has wasted. Like Jeremiah and the other biblical prophets, Bill has created the conditions for, and has manifested in his own life, an authentic, active, and determined hope.

ACKNOWLEDGING THE EXISTENTIAL THREAT OF CLIMATE CHANGE

If we are to embrace a hope that can sustain us, we need to acknowledge that global climate change presents us with more than "just" political, economic, and technological challenges. Climate change threatens us on many levels. It gives rise to a well-founded, gnawing fear that we can't protect ourselves, we can't protect our family and community, and we can't protect our world.

The horror of that personal threat can be seen in the faces of Puerto Ricans whose lives were turned upside down in 2017 and in the faces of Houston families made homeless for the third time in three years by a so-called five-hundred-year flood. Perhaps we know someone whose asthma has grown worse, or someone with Zika. Much as we don't want to think so, it's becoming more and more clear that few of us can insulate ourselves from the onslaught of personal threats that climate change has amplified. We realize, "that could be me" and we are shaken. We feel exposed. We feel vulnerable. We are unsettled by the discontinuity.

On a relational level, many of us know someone whose days and nights are now spent contending with some dramatic change in their health or their living circumstances because something unexpected happened—a massive forest fire, a drought, a foreclosure on their flooded home, loss of job due to an algae bloom or lack of snow in the mountains, and so on. Suddenly we realize that we can't protect our immediate family and those we love from such catastrophe.

We are shaken at the broadest existential level when we read Elizabeth Kolbert's *New York Times* best seller, *The Sixth Extinction*—or we read a Reuters interview of the grave digger in Karachi, Pakistan, who is proud to have already dug graves for 300 people in anticipation of another summer heat wave like the one that just killed more than 1,300 people[9]—or we learn that for decades the US military has been concerned about the dramatic impacts of climate change on national secur-ity[10]—or we ponder the mounting evidence that as temperatures rise, people perform dramatically less well.[11] Any of these can trigger dread—and dread will cancel optimism.

THE CONVICTION OF THINGS NOT SEEABLE

What might hope look like in the face of such utter catastrophe? Plenty Coups, the great chief of the Native American Crow tribe, offers a glimpse of what hope in the face of extinction looks like. His tragic tale is recounted by Jonathan Lear in his book, *Radical Hope: Ethics in the Face of Cultural Devastation.*[12]

In the late 1920s, thirty years after the Crow tribe was pressured by the US government to give up their hunting way of life and enter a reservation, Plenty Coups uttered these words, reminiscent of ancient Israel's lament by the rivers of Babylon (Psalm 137:1):

> When the buffalo went away the hearts of my people fell to the ground, and they could not lift them up again. *After this nothing happened.*[13] [emphasis mine]

All that mattered in life to the Crow nation had been taken. Even though many survived for decades, their days and years were as noth-ing. Everything familiar and reliable had ended, and, as Plenty Coups testified, they were required "to live a life I do not understand."

For Lear, Plenty Coups' perseverance, when everything but life it-self had been taken from his people, is a manifestation of radical hope. Plenty Coups shared his hope through a dream that was received, pro-cessed, and interpreted by the tribal elders. As you read how Lear recounts the dream, picture how it applies to our own lives now as well as in the years ahead:

> Our traditional way of life is coming to an end . . . that life is about to disappear;
> We must do what we can to open our imaginations up to a radically different set of future possibilities;
> I need to recognize the discontinuity that is upon me . . . I need to preserve some integrity across that discontinuity;

I do have reason to hope for a dignified passage across this abyss,
because God—Ah-dabt-dadt-deah—is good;
We shall get the good back, though at the moment we have no more
than a glimmer of what that might mean.[14]

And so—as Lear puts it—"radical hope anticipates a good for which
those who have the hope as yet lack the appropriate concepts with
which to understand it."[15] To this, Willis Jenkins adds, "Industrial civilization has not yet collapsed and it is likely to keep inventing ever more
destructive instrumentalities to sustain its powers."[16]

In a time such as this, we must embrace the testimony of Chief
Plenty Coups by acknowledging that the continuity of creation upon
which thousands of generations of humans have sought moral progress
is over. And one thing more. We must recognize that the existential
dread we experience can serve as a precondition of hope. When we
have a safe context in which we can share our dread with trusted
friends, by the grace of God, the Holy Spirit will ignite in us a tenacious
and defiant hope.

THE CONVICTION OF THINGS NOT SEEN—TELLING A NEW STORY OF HOPE

"How can you know all these facts and still have hope?" For me, faith
and hope are rooted in the conviction that, regardless of how bad things
may be, a new story is waiting to take hold—something we have not yet
seen or felt or experienced. We are not called to sustain or extend our
current way of life. Rather, we must ask God and the Earth itself to
teach us what projects and activism we are called to engage—new possibilities for loving neighbors, doing justice, and walking humbly with
God. God is calling us—as individuals and congregations—to work with
God and others to champion that new story.

For the vast majority in our society, that new story remains unseen.
Wresting our future from the grip of fossil fuel seems impossible—our
addiction is too strong, affordable options are too few, and the powers
that defend the status quo are mighty, indeed. But what once served to
elevate living standards and build the modern world has become an
increasingly heavy millstone that is sinking the prospects of all of creation. We cannot be freed by chipping away at this millstone. We must

begin to live into a new story by changing the human prospect and restoring creation's viability.

That's what the Water Protectors of Standing Rock have done. Their courageous, unflinching discipline inspired thousands to join them and millions to imagine with them the new world that is waiting to be born. They prepared themselves through prayer and ritual to face down sheriffs, paramilitary contractors, attack dogs, rubber bullets, pepper spray, and high-pressure water cannons in subzero temperatures. They were fueled by hope, hope for a revolution rooted in love—love for God's great gift of creation.

Telling stories of hope—and throwing our lives into the struggle to make those stories real—is nothing new. William Wilberforce and Thomas Clarkson worked tirelessly for more than two decades before England passed laws to abolish slavery. In America, Frederick Douglass and William Lloyd Garrison worked even longer before their efforts met with success. The same is true for the women's suffrage movement and the civil rights movement. Although the Rev. Dr. Martin Luther King Jr. was jailed twenty-nine times, he continued to hold onto an expansive dream of civil rights, economic equality, and the end of war. Mother Teresa was driven by the hope that she and the order she founded could be the face of God for the poor. She held on to this hope despite decades during which her requests to found such an order were denied by the church. She held on to hope despite her painful sense in prayer that God had abandoned her. Today she is recognized as a saint and her order is flourishing. Nelson Mandela, imprisoned for twenty-seven years before he would be voted president of South Africa, believed that the old story of apartheid was a relic and that a new story of freedom and equality was waiting to be born. When Mahatma Gandhi envisioned an India free of British rule, he didn't weigh the chances of success. He relied on his convictions and he challenged the conscience of those rulers, mindful of an expression often attributed to him: "First they ignore you, then they ridicule you, then they fight you, and then you win."

This is how we write the future. This is how we shape history: we envision new possibilities and we act on them as if they were inevitable.[17]

LIVING A NEW STORY OF HOPE

In every state, in every country, in thousands of towns the world over, a new story of hope is emerging. Imaginative people, filled with hope, are entering uncharted territory. Having jettisoned their powerlessness as individuals, they are uniting with others and discovering a new kind of power. I have seen this firsthand in congregations when we discuss the possibility of divesting from fossil fuel companies. For some, expressing hope by redirecting their assets is a first step on the path of freedom. I have heard scores of parishioners who had never gone to a "protest march" share with their home congregation their exhilaration and re-newed commitment to represent their values in the public square. More than one person over seventy years of age has shared with me their gradual realization that with age comes a kind of freedom and clarity about the things you love. These friends had never imagined that they would engage in the spiritual discipline of civil disobedience. But after a great deal of prayer and discernment, we found ourselves in jail together, with an increased commitment to redirect the gifts God has given us to protect creation.

I could go on and on: the nuns who built a chapel on the exact spot a pipeline construction company was about to claim by eminent domain; the millennials living in a "tiny house"; the family moving to one car that's electric and powered by new solar panels; the retired business-woman who writes a letter each day to her elected officials and has lunch each week with influential people to recruit them in common cause; the pastor who is finding a way to invite and challenge her con-gregation to stand up for God's creation.

We can't accept God's invitation to help create a new story unless we are willing to take action. We become partners with God when we act in unfamiliar, untested ways. Those new actions will be guided by a pre-ferred future that embraces:

- resilience in place of growth
- collaboration in place of consumption
- wisdom in place of progress
- balance in place of addiction
- moderation in place of excess
- vision in place of convenience

- accountability in place of disregard
- self-giving love in place of self-centered fear

SPIRITUAL PRACTICES FOR CULTIVATING HOPE

Hope is connected with a new story that has not yet been made clear. For Christians, Advent reminds us of this when we anticipate the birth of the One who will bring a New Story of redemption and reconciliation. The story of Jesus' life and death portray a courageous testimony to a new understanding of truth. The story of Christ's resurrection reveals that death is not victorious. The Book of Acts continues the new story by describing how the power of the Holy Spirit overturns the expectations of the disciples and empowers them to live into a new story. Years later, sharing the Good News with the troubled believers in the pagan city of Corinth, Paul tells the Corinthians that they themselves are his letter of recommendation; they are the best evidence that his ministry has not been in vain (II Corinthians 3:1–6). This is Paul's way of trusting that even the Corinthians can live into a new story.

Living into a new story requires a departure from the old story—a break with business as usual. Such a radical shift needs to be fueled by courage. In challenging Caesar, Pontius Pilate, and the Empire they represented, Jesus showed extraordinary courage. Likewise, it took courage for the Rockefeller Brothers Fund to divest from their holdings in fossil fuel companies. It took courage for Attorneys General Eric Schneiderman and Maura Healy to launch an investigation into how ExxonMobil committed fraud by lying to their investors about what the company knew regarding the risk of climate change.[18] It takes courage to engage in civil disobedience and hand your freedom over to the authorities—if only for a little while. After we engage reality, encounter grief, and experience dread over the consequences of climate change, we may know in our minds and hearts that business as usual is no longer acceptable. However, it still takes courage to live into a new story.

I don't know how to live into a new story without practicing both trust and gratitude. It takes trust to believe that God is calling humanity to relinquish the old story. That's not easy for a third-generation coal miner or for someone commuting 100 miles a day in a ten-year-old car to work two jobs to make ends meet. If making God's love and justice real is the work of the church, then local churches are just the place where this transition can begin. Courageous communities willing to embark on an "Acts 2:44 Movement" can become a showcase for the world by manifesting a new kind of "life together" that is faithful to Gospel values (see chapter 5).

A memorable example of this emerged in 1981 when President Reagan announced that the Department of Defense would be building a neutron bomb—a "clean" nuclear weapon designed to destroy people rather than property. Opposing this initiative was a broad coalition of religious leaders who had been gaining considerable momentum under the banner of the "New Abolitionist Covenant." Seeking a consistent pro-life ethic, they argued for the abolition of all nuclear weapons. The idea of a neutron bomb was particularly alarming since it preserved property while extinguishing life.

For the 2,400 people in Amarillo, Texas, who worked at the Pantex assembly plant, this moral issue was personal. Pantex was where the triggers for all the US nuclear weapons were made. For many of them, the moral issue came to a head when the Bishop of the Roman Catholic Diocese of Amarillo, Leroy Matthiesen, urged those in his congregation who worked at Pantex to consider resigning their jobs.[19] However, he didn't stop there. He promised that the church would provide for those who resigned from Pantex. The church would make sure those folks had adequate food, clothing, and shelter until they found other employment. Bishop Matthiesen believed that as a religious leader, God was calling him and the diocese he led to make a new story real.

God has given us everything we need to embrace a new story regarding climate change. Humanity has all the technology it needs to immediately transition to a fossil fuel–free economy. But to relinquish our dependence on fossil fuel requires deep trust that there is another way—trust that technology is indeed available and trust that humanity can actually make such a transition happen. So-called early adopters lead the way, but more often than not they are ridiculed (or worse) by those with vested interests in maintaining the old story. Trust allows us to adopt a "can-do attitude"—something that is as American as apple pie.

Gratitude is just as important as trust. Creation is a gift. Life is a gift. The opposite of gratitude is taking life for granted—living our lives oblivious to the reality that we did nothing to deserve to be here. Cultivating a life of gratitude leads to adopting a particular set of attitudes, values, and behaviors. I find that gratitude and wonder are almost inseparable. My gratitude for the gift of life readies me to respond with wonder to the intricacies and mysteries of life. Gratitude leads to generosity and sharing. When we experience life as a gift, we are less likely to clutch what is ours and instead can learn to relate to others "with open hands."[20] A life of gratitude prepares a person to make sacrifices. This is because when we are full of gratitude, our focus is on God the creator—God the giver of life. When we root our lives in God, the creator and giver of life, it becomes easier to set aside our own needs, agendas, even our own lives, for God, God's children, and for creation itself.

I don't know how we can live into a new story without recognizing and embracing interdependence.[21] Creation is an interdependent web whose life comes from its ancestors and prepares a way for its descendants. No part of creation is independent and self-sufficient. As Bill McKibben puts it, the most important thing an individual can do about climate change is to stop being an individual. This is tough advice in a culture that worships rugged individualism. This perspective also challenges what many churches now regard as fundamental to their identity: that each congregation is autonomous in relation to other congregations and to the denomination with which they are affiliated.

The Rev. Dr. Martin Luther King Jr., who so memorably proclaimed hope in his "I have a dream" speech, made affirming our interdependence a platform of the civil rights movement. "Injustice anywhere is a threat to justice everywhere. We are caught in an inescapable network of mutuality, tied in a single garment of destiny. Whatever affects one directly, affects all indirectly."[22]

The reality of environmental and planetary interdependence made the front pages of America's newspapers in the 1970s and 1980s. Acid rain became a buzzword—and for good reason. Scientists showed that the loss of biodiversity in thousands of lakes and streams in the Northeast was caused by pollution from industrial plants in the faraway Midwest. Suddenly, people realized that Midwest manufacturing was killing forests and fish in the Adirondacks. This recognition resulted in new laws that included a cap-and-trade program, which succeeded in significantly reducing the airborne pollution ahead of schedule and for about half the projected cost.[23]

If lakes and forests in the Northeast were going to survive, a new story needed to be written, one that honored interdependence and mutual regard. That new story had to be shaped not only by New Englanders but also by captains of industry in the Midwest and by politicians across the country. These primary actors had to work together; they also had to believe in the possibility that together they could find a just solution. For a religious person, such a belief amounts to aligning our efforts with our understanding of God's intentions. Honoring interdependence is a practice that builds hope and points us toward a more just and stable future.

Finally, for hope to take hold, the church must cultivate moral imagination. The life that awaits us in the new story we are called to champion is very different from the life most of us have been conditioned to value and prize. For most of us in the developed nations, the immediate effects of climate change are incremental. Since we are not directly experiencing the discontinuity and havoc climate change is already causing, we continue our business-as-usual approach to life. This will remain true—at least for a while—even once we have ended the denial of climate change.

To cross the abyss between our current story and the story that God calls us to champion requires nurturing moral imagination. That is how we can preserve integrity during this time of discontinuity. When churchgoers and pastors ask what they can do, I invite them to cultivate their moral imaginations. We need to believe that the transition to a world free of fossil fuel is possible, and that our generation is called to lead that transition. If I'm carrying a copy of *The Green Bible*, I'll read to them the conclusion of Archbishop Desmond Tutu's foreword:

> [Jesus'] supreme work is to reconcile us to God and to one another and, indeed, to reconcile us to all of God's creation. It is possible to have a new kind of world, a world where there will be more compassion, more gentleness, more caring, more laughter, more joy for all of God's creation, because that is God's dream. And God says, "Help me, help me, help me realize my dream."[24]

God is calling all of us to unleash our imaginations, unmuzzle our mouths, unbind our hands, unshackle our feet, and open our wallets. Each of us must use our unique God-given gifts to hasten the day when each human heart is governed not by grief but by hope, not by constraint but by generosity, not by selfishness but by sharing.

Yes—God still has a dream. As broken-hearted as God must be over what we have done to the gift of creation, God still has a dream. However much we rebel, however much we ignore God's instructions, however much we abuse God's gift of creation, we cannot diminish the power of God's dream. It is a dream anchored in love, not exploitation. It is a dream in which every living thing is a reflection of God, vibrantly alive with grateful, joyful hearts. In God's dream, everyone has enough and all are beneficiaries of God's abundance. God dreams that humans seek spiritual rather than material progress. God's dream envisions a just world at peace because gratitude has dissolved anxiety and generosity has eclipsed greed. God dreams of a time when love and mutual respect will bind humanity together, and the profound beauty of creation will be treasured. Let us embrace God's dream as our own. Suddenly, the horizon of our hope comes nearer. As we live into God's dream, we will rediscover who we truly are and all of creation will be singing.

QUESTIONS FOR GROUP DISCUSSION AND FURTHER REFLECTION

1. Share examples from everyday life of how we subjugate nature to serve our needs.
2. Optimism is not hope. Is there a challenging circumstance in your life where you initially met the challenge by being optimistic, and then, after taking in the reality/enormity of the challenge, you shifted from optimism to hope?
3. Share with another person or in your group a feeling or experience of dread associated with climate change on a personal level, a relational level, or on an existential level.
4. Think of the people and towns in Kentucky, southern Ohio, or Wyoming where coal continues to be everything. Imagine yourself as the governor or mayor. What is your responsibility to the next generation? Can you come up with a "new story" that would shape your leadership as you helped people migrate from a career that will abruptly end soon to something more promising?

5. This chapter makes clear that God is calling humanity to champion a new story. In fact, God invites us to coauthor this new story. Who is God for you? With your group, or with one other person, talk about the God who occupies your soul. How is your experience of hope enlarged by or limited by your understanding of and experience of God?

6. Read together the next to last paragraph of this chapter which focuses on God's dream. Then go back, sentence by sentence, and try to identify some specific action you can take in your life to shift toward the values and attitudes that are part of God's dream.

EPILOGUE

The year is 2100. You're sitting in a hot arena with about five thousand others. The air conditioners, powered by solar energy, have reduced the outside temperature by 25°F to the standard setting of 88°F. Like everyone, you travelled to this event in an electric vehicle charged by solar or wind power. While travelling long distances is rare, you were willing to sacrifice to attend this gathering convened by the World Council of Churches. Millions of others from all over the Earth are participating in the conference electronically. It promises to be a wonderful celebration of the enormous progress made over the past eighty years. The opening speaker is a teenage girl.

IMAGINE: A MESSAGE TO THE CHURCH—PRESENTED BY A TEENAGER IN 2100

Thank you. . . . My name is Evergreen Suzuki. Over one hundred years ago, my great-great-grandmother, Severn Cullis-Suzuki, addressed the 1992 Rio de Janeiro Earth Summit. I know I'm young, but she was only twelve. For six minutes, the 172 governmental representatives sat in silence, listening intently. She spoke on behalf of generations to come. She spoke on behalf of countless animals dying across the planet. She spoke of extinction. She reminded the adults of their limits—and reminded them that they had to follow the same rules they had taught their children for generations: not to hurt other creatures, to share and not be greedy.

For six minutes those leaders were attentive and remorseful. When she finished, their gathering seemed to generate momentum. In decades past, when world leaders gathered at Kyoto, Copenhagen, and then Paris, they struggled to come to terms with the most obvious realities: the sacrifice of creation at the altar of material progress, our unchecked greed, our resistance to change, and our refusal to share.

Fortunately, enough people knew what needed to be done and took action. Our forebears in the faith crafted the Earth Charter.[1] Rooted in "global interdependence and universal responsibility," it offered a set of sixteen principles that together required a "change of mind and heart."

I don't have to tell you that change is hard—and revolutionary change is much harder.

But somehow, after Hurricanes Katrina, Sandy, Harvey, Irma, and Maria, people were ready for change. They were beginning to connect the dots between unprecedented catastrophe and climate change. When Houston, America's fourth largest city, flooded, they glimpsed what the horrific future would involve: tens of millions of climate refugees worldwide. Of course, that was only the beginning.

A tipping point was when scientists, activists, and children sought justice from the courts. They demanded justice for unborn generations, for marginalized communities of color, for indigenous communities, and for poor white communities. Not only did the attorneys general of several states go after fossil fuel companies, but Our Children's Trust captured the attention of the country and the world. It was when kids—like me—faced down the most powerful and well-funded forces in the world that hope began to emerge. Once the highest court in the land recognized that children had a right to grow up on an Earth not wrecked by the grownups who lived before them, momentum grew. These kids made America realize that our country had been sleeping through a revolution—as Martin Luther King Jr. warned—and that it was time to wake up. Can we recognize their courage with applause?

We could name so many others whose voices and vision helped America reimagine new possibilities. Not a kid grows up in America today who doesn't learn about the contributions made by James Hansen, Naomi Oreskes, Wangari Muta Maathai, Lennox Yearwood, Rachel Carson, Elon Musk, Pope Francis, Ecumenical Patriarch Bartholomew, Katharine Hayhoe, and Bill McKibben.

The church finally woke up at the end of the second decade of the twenty-first century—and that's why I'm here today. Just when fewer and fewer people were going to church, and the prospects for God's creation were growing dim, something happened. Our forebears in the faith realized that if they loved God, they had to protect creation. They put their bodies on the line. While we don't know their individual names, we know them as legion. Once a few thousand of them courageously resisted the powers and principalities, many more followed.

After a while, America began to catch the dream that motivated these people of faith. A new kind of candor crept into our personal and national conversations. Some churches began to practice a new sacramental act that made use of the ground as the principle element. Sometimes, the ritual helped people connect with the Earth. Other times, it empowered people to muster the courage to bear witness to the need to keep fossil fuels in the ground. Some newly called ministers insisted that their ordination vows include an additional vow that if they or their partner became pregnant, during those nine months, each of their sermons would speak of God's covenant with all of creation and our obligations to future generations. These younger pastors often attracted numerous younger people who heard about these sermons. Gradually, churchgoers came to be seen throughout the community as creation protectors. They actually borrowed that phrase from the courageous witness of thousands of native peoples in 2016 at Standing Rock, South Dakota; those brave and intrepid visionaries called themselves water protectors.

In 2010, Bill and Melinda Gates and Warren Buffett initiated The Giving Pledge, challenging the richest people in the world to commit to give away at least 50 percent of their wealth to good causes before they died. When this initiative began, it puzzled many who thought "the person who dies with the most toys wins." But in the third decade of the twenty-first century, after over one thousand billionaires had made the pledge, these billionaires made a collective decision to set aside half of their collective philanthropic funds to endow all the national parks of fifty-three countries. As a result of their action, humanity began to embrace a new attitude toward nature. The Parliament of the World's Religions played an important role in extending the impact of this commitment. For years, the Parliament had been developing materials helping people of every faith perspective to realize that every religion embraces the Golden Rule, and that each religion needed to extend the Golden Rule to include all future generations and all creatures as our neighbors. Endowing the world's national parks inspired the next several generations to embrace a new understanding of life's meaning—one that was both interdependent and intergenerational.

By the third decade of the twenty-first century, humanity began to speak with a single voice, recognizing that this was the only Earth, our only home. Those who promoted the colonization of other planets as a way to assure humanity's survival were sidelined. Also silenced were those who "transcended" Earth's problems by assuming "human consciousness" could continue eternally in the form of ones and zeros (the singularity). At about that same time, the church amplified Jesus' call to build the Kingdom of God on Earth, reminding us that Jesus offered us a building plan, not an evacuation plan. By and large, the church abandoned the idea that life's purpose and reward was to get into a future Heaven. People embraced Jesus' Good News: Heaven is right here, right now, everywhere and always.

People also began to see that narcissism and self-dealing was a bankrupt way of living. Believers of the so-called prosperity gospel realized that its "God" was nothing more than a creation of self-promoting pastors. In contrast, new leaders emerged, leaders who manifested generosity, generativity, and a willingness to accept boundaries and limits. These leaders showed us that we could be satisfied with enough, and still be full of gratitude and joy. People listened to those leaders.

It certainly wasn't easy. In fact it was devastating when over a billion people had to relocate. Generations later, we continue to mourn the hundreds of millions who died as climate refugees. India, Pakistan, and Bangladesh were hit especially hard. However, Muslim and Hindu leaders were able to make major improvements by helping people to realize that their religious perspectives were not in conflict with one another, and that they could honor and support one another.

In these and many other ways, the twenty-first century underwent a moral revolution that birthed a new moral era. Thought leaders like Thomas Berry, Joanna Macy, Ta-Nehisi Coates, Diana Butler Bass, Brian McLaren, and David Korten set the stage by imagining a way forward. Tens of thousands of people risked their freedom to protect the Earth, inspired by Tim DeChristopher, the Valve Turners, and the courageous actions of those who led the 1982 Warren County Civil Disobedience Campaign (523 of whom were arrested for exposing environmental racism).

Today, this planet—our home—is so much less hospitable to human life than was the Earth on which my great-great-grandmother Severn was born. The dream of that Earth has long since faded. But a new dream has emerged. Thanks to your religious witness, our political, corporate, and cultural leaders are now acting in morally accountable ways. Over the past fifty years, our common crisis has brought humanity together. There are so many ways in which we are now beginning to bend the moral arc of the universe toward justice.

Let us thank our forebears in the faith for rising above their despair to imagine that another world was possible. And let us praise the high resolve, courage, and ingenuity they persistently tapped to demonstrate their love of God, and the wondrous gift we have been given.

QUESTIONS FOR GROUP DISCUSSION AND FURTHER REFLECTION

1. Let those who are familiar with the writings of some of the people mentioned in this speech share with others in the group why their writings and witness may be viewed as "historic" in the year 2100.
2. After reading this book, is the account represented in this speech from the year 2100 imaginable for you? Evergreen Suzuki speaks of humanity's moral pivot. Does your experience allow you to say "yes"—are you able to "see" that possibility?
3. Of the various key ingredients Suzuki mentions as crucial, were there any that surprised you? Are there any that—for you—are not morally compelling? Are there any missing? In other words, are there some additional "conversions" or "pivots" that she doesn't mention that you think are essential?

APPENDIX

PREACHING SUGGESTIONS FOR A CLIMATE CRISIS WORLD

Introduction

The UCC resolution included in the introduction calls for the church to embrace a new vocation. What this vocation might look like is developed in chapter 3. It is so important, for our congregants and for our own integrity as religious leaders, that we pastors preach on the vocation of today's church. The stage can be set by reviewing how the vocation of the church has changed in response to huge societal challenges throughout history. Then offer your version of the case made in this book as to why climate change calls for the church to embrace a new vocation. Ideas for how to do so are given below, organized by chapter.

Chapter I

Reread the quotation from Gus Speth at the head of the chapter. The themes of selfishness, greed, pride, and spiritual transformation can be found throughout the chapter. Consider shaping a sermon—or better yet, a sermon series—on the need for a personal and societal spiritual transformation that results in society reorienting what we prize. See the transformations described in chapter 5.

Reflect on the fact that one reason churches have bells in tall steeples is to warn the community of emergency. How would church life be different if congregations were to embrace this calling?

Consider a sermon linking your congregation's traditional social justice concerns with climate change. Chapter 1 only makes such a link with the issue of hunger; many more justice issues can be linked to the climate crisis.

Chapter 1 invites every preacher to reflect on what we pay attention to and what we ignore, postpone, or deny. Can we understand scripture as an invitation to pay attention to crises and concerns that, however painful, must be addressed?

Remind and inspire your congregation by using the story of the Montreal Protocol. Help them realize that "we can do this!" The same is true regarding Mark Jacobson's research—many will be surprised and motivated to learn this.

You could devote an entire sermon to Bill McKibben's suggestion that the single most important thing a person can do in response to climate change is to "stop being an individual."

Many congregations would welcome a sermon on the Gospels' account of the feeding of the enormous crowd that challenges the notion of scarcity and proclaims the liberating reality of abundance.

Chapter 2

Invite your congregation to contribute photographs of their favorite place on Earth, following the illustration in chapter 2. Then preach a sermon on the impact of the bulletin collage as a testimony to your congregation's relations to one another and to the Earth.

Most congregations would appreciate (and many might be surprised) to hear a sermon that cites scriptural passages from diverse faith traditions, all of which proclaim that each generation has a responsibility to assure that future generations can flourish.

Review the brief joint statement issued by Pope Francis and Ecumenical Patriarch Bartholomew on September 1, 2017, marking the World Day of Prayer for the Care of Creation. Archdeacon John Chryssavgis, Bartholomew's theological advisor on environmental issues, provides an excellent commentary here: Commentary by Archdeacon Chryssavgis, https://cruxnow.com/commentary/2017/09/01/pope-patriarch-common-declaration-shared-world/. Prepare a sermon emphasizing the environmental principles common to Catholic, Orthodox, and Protestant Christians.

Prepare a sermon on "the miracle of faithfulness amidst discontinuity." Draw from diverse experiences of discontinuity, times when the world seemed upside down. Share your understanding of the following from chapter 2: "God does not abandon us in our despair. Quite the contrary. The more deeply we take in the lifelessness of drought and clearcutting, the choking exhaustion of heat waves, the helplessness of rising waters, the loneliness of extinction, the more receptive we are to miracle. Nothing we have done—nothing we can do—will extinguish the Holy Spirit who breathes into us renewed conviction and unfamiliar courage that cannot be taken away."

Shape a sermon on what it means for a person of faith to obey her conscience. Gather illustrations from diverse circumstances. Ask how these kinds of courageous actions—so common in scripture—might inspire us to take action on climate change.

Chapter 3

Any sermon addressing the three questions posed at the beginning of this chapter will be worthwhile. Invite your congregation, as they consider these important questions, to consider how they can proclaim God's love for creation while they work to stop humanity from running Genesis in reverse.

Bill McKibben sees climate change as an opportunity for which the church was born. Your sermon on this could help many in your congregation to reframe their thinking on climate change.

Consider using the commentary on Dietrich Bonhoeffer, Rabbi Heschel, and Konrad Adenauer to offer a sermon on the relationship between the state and the church—especially in times of moral crisis.

Nearly every pastor has encountered a parishioner who somehow believes that he or she can hide his or her most harmful behavior from God. A sermon pointing out that "with God there are no externalities" could be both humorous and serious, thereby helping people think in new ways about our relationship to the Earth.

When was the last time you preached on communal salvation? The text offers several useful approaches to this underemphasized cornerstone of scripture.

A sermon on covenant, rooted in Genesis 9, could be offered each year.

What would be your insight into expanding the Golden Rule to include all creatures and future generations as well?

What teenager in your congregation could you invite to preach a sermon on Our Children's Trust?

Many if not most preachers mention catastrophic "natural" disasters that are dominating the front page of the Sunday newspaper in their sermons. When the next major hurricane (or once-in-500-years flood, or local rain bomb) occurs, focus your congregation's moral attention on climate change by recounting personal stories related to the disaster. Stories leave strong images in the hearts and the minds of the listeners.

If religion has a responsibility to teach humanity to value nature, prepare a sermon that offers your assessment of the extent to which the church has done so. Does humanity need a moral intervention? Does the church need a wake-up call?

Chapter 4

Preach a sermon exploring the connection between the discontinuity of creation and the moral discontinuity humanity has experienced in recent times.

Reread the brief section on valuing spiritual progress over material progress. What scriptures support this? Whose life journey has followed this path? Outline a sermon rooted in scripture that will provoke those who have "ears to hear" to make some adjustments.

This chapter suggests that congregations responsive to God's call today will focus on developing common values among their members, such as relationships based on love, respect for differences, curiosity, open minds, and open hearts. Read Brian McLaren's book, *The Great Spiritual Migration: How the World's Largest Religion Is Seeking a*

Better Way to Be Christian. Consider preaching a sermon or sermon series on this profound ecclesial shift.

Consider initiating a Truth and Reconciliation Conversation about climate change in your congregation. If your congregation is like most, before you suggest such a program, you'll need to help your flock rework its understanding of what church (in a time such as this) is for. Can church provide a safe enough place for people to listen to one another with openness to change? If so, church may offer a way for our society to emerge from the current ideological divide.

What if congregations were unified around values and conscience rather than commonly held beliefs and rituals? Responding to this question alone could shape several sermons.

Chapter 5

Preach on the abundant examples in scripture of community resilience.

In a sermon on a recent hurricane or similar catastrophe, encourage a response such as that suggested in the chapter. Invite your congregation to continue their offerings of time, talent, and money into the recovery phase. Remind them that we find ultimate satisfaction in sharing, not material acquisition.

Criticizing consumerism from the pulpit may be risky. Be on the lookout for an illustration in the news that you could use to initiate a more in-depth discussion.

The income inequality statistics cited in this chapter are disturbing. Can you find a way to share them in a sermon? The goal is to offer a wise and morally defensible path through the thicket of economic inequality, material aspiration, and corporate ascendency?

Consider offering a sermon on keeping fossil fuels in the ground. Ample resources are available at http://april2016.uccpages.org/.

Over the next year, as you write your sermons, prompt yourself to expand your imagination so that you can offer vision that extends the horizon of our hope.

Chapter 6

Contained within this chapter itself are suggestions on how to preach about worship. As a preacher, ask yourself what guides how a particular service balances the various parts of worship? How would worship be different if it were to acknowledge that creation itself is in jeopardy?

If you haven't recently preached a sermon that helps your congregation understand the distinction between partisan and political, consider doing so. Cite the many times Jesus spoke politically, and the many ways he rejected partisanship, both by his words and deeds (dining with sinners, healing on the Sabbath, etc.). Apply those examples of how Jesus lived to the need for the church to address climate change.

Inventory your sermons over the past year. How frequently do you mention or deal with issues of intergenerational responsibility? How might you increase that frequency going forward?

If you have thoughts about how a sacramental experience of the Earth might motivate your congregation to engage the issue of climate change, preach a sermon on it.

Chapter 7

Pick one of the major historic social transformations in which the church played a significant role that are listed in this chapter. Do a little research to familiarize yourself with the role of the church on both sides (perhaps all sides) of the discussion. Craft a sermon in which you offer this historic account as guidance for your congregation on how it might respond to climate change.

Consider a sermon on wonder. Prepare by having several one-on-one conversations with parishioners and ask them about their relationship to wonder—and how it has evolved over the span of their lives. Take a risk and share your own experiences of wonder with your congregation.

How does wholehearted courage overcome fear? Share examples from scripture and from your life and from the lives of people in your congregation.

Share with your congregation the changes you would like to make in the story of how humanity relates to creation.

Watch the Vimeo of Rev. Ian Holland's 2017 Earth Day sermon. How might your next climate change sermon benefit from what you learned from his?

Chapter 8

What is the relationship between career and vocation? Bill Coffin once pointed out to a church full of Yale undergraduates that the root of the word career is "race"; then he drew a contrast between a "rat race" and a calling from God. That may be a bit much, but one of your sermons could point out that our whole lives (not just Sunday morning) are in God's hands. Therefore, it behooves us to bring into our work the values and vision God calls us to live out.

At the end of chapter 4, I mentioned an article by Bill McKibben comparing our current climate crisis to WWII.[1] During that war, Americans redirected their lives in response to the threat. They understood that they were fighting for their future. Can you and your congregation think and pray together about how God might be calling you—as a community or calling individuals within your community—to redirect your plans and focus your gifts in response to the challenge of climate change?

Paul's letter to the Galatians begins with these profound words: "For freedom Christ has set us free." Preach a sermon on freedom and climate change. If, in twenty years, 20 percent of Americans and 30 percent of people worldwide are spending half their lives dealing with the discontinuity of climate disruption, are any of us (except the most wealthy who can insulate themselves from such problems) truly free?

Preach a sermon in which you give examples from scripture and from your own life of when fear has been an effective catalyst to take action. Provide examples in which the core motivation to change was rooted in love and gratitude. What conclusion do you want to offer?

There may be people in your congregation you could convene to discuss fiduciary responsibility. After reading chapter 8, invite them to share their views. Such a conversation would likely provide plenty of material for an engaging sermon.

Read Walter Brueggemann's essay, "To Whom Does the Land Belong?"[2] Prepare a sermon based on Brueggemann's interpretation of scripture. Consider including your own commentary on land trusts and publicly owned parks, as well as your thoughts on whether or not the church has forfeited one of the most elemental claims of faith—that the Earth is the Lord's.

Chapter 9

This chapter suggests that authentic hope can emerge once we have named and confronted dread. It suggests that dread associated with climate change is present on a personal level, a relational level, and an existential level. What examples come to mind—from scripture, from your personal life, from your congregation, or from our culture—that illustrate the emergence of authentic hope from paralyzing dread?

The chapter suggests that God is calling us to champion a new story. How about shaping a sermon that begins by inviting people to understand all the ways in which Jesus offered humanity a new story? Then suggest that God is now calling us to join others in offering the world a new story.

Few people know that Iowa depends upon wind power for a huge percentage of its electricity. By 2020, it could be 40 percent. Why doesn't every American know this story? Consider writing a sermon on how moral aspirations—illustrated by sharing stories like this—could accelerate our adoption of sustainable energy.

How should a faithful Christian determine what to do with their God-given freedom? Share your thoughts on this question. What examples from scripture, from history, or from current culture would you hold up as exemplary?

Epilogue

Write your own version of the letter in the epilogue. Offering "good news" from a possible future provides your congregation with a powerful testimony of your hope. Stand before your congregation and suggest specific changes that they could embrace today which might contribute to a new trajectory for humanity's tomorrow. The fiftieth anniversary of Earth Day is in 2020. Perhaps that is the time to preach such a sermon.

NOTES

INTRODUCTION

1. Lynn Townsend White Jr., "The Historical Roots of Our Ecological Crisis," *Science* 155 (March 10, 1967).

2. See Brian McLaren, *The Great Spiritual Migration: How the World's Largest Religion Is Seeking a Better Way to Be Christian* (New York: Convergent Books, 2016).

3. Ta-Nehisi Coates, *Between the World and Me* (New York: Random House, 2015), p. 150.

4. ecoAmerica, "American Climate Perspectives August 2017," accessed September 1, 2017. http://ecoamerica.org/wp-content/uploads/2017/08/ecoamerica-american-climate-perspectives-august-2017-impacts.pdf. My comments, included in the report, are as follows: "When people of faith led the civil rights movement in the 60s, it wasn't the case that every churchgoer in America was supportive of the cause. In fact, many clergy who spoke their conscience from their pulpit quickly learned that not all their parishioners agreed. But they also found that by speaking out, they were able to awaken the conscience of many. As this survey shows, our pews are filled with churchgoers who still need to be convinced that God's creation—our common home—is in jeopardy. When church is faithful, it is speaking truth and awakening conscience. Science is doing its part—there is no scientific debate about the reality of human caused climate change. While many church leaders are witnessing to this truth, this survey makes clear that God's creation is crying out for additional effective witnesses. Pope Francis, Ecumenical Patriarch Bartholomew and many Protestant denominational leaders have provided outspoken leadership. It's time to bring this message to every congregation."

5. National Caucus of Environmental Legislators, accessed September 1, 2017. http://ncel.net/climate-action/.

6. Charles Lee, "Toxic Wastes and Race in the United States—A National Report on the Racial and Socio-Economic Characteristics of Communities with Hazardous Waste Sites," Commission for Racial Justice UCC (1987), accessed September 10, 2017, http://d3n8a8pro7vhmx.cloudfront.net/unitedchurchofchrist/legacy_url/13567/toxwrace87.pdf?1418439935; see also Robert D. Bullard, Paul Mohai, Robin Saha, and Beverly Wright, "Toxic Waste and Race at Twenty: 1987–2007," Justice & Witness Ministries UCC (March 2007), accessed September 10, 2017, http://d3n8a8pro7vhmx.cloudfront.net/unitedchurchofchrist/legacy_url/491/toxic-wastes-and-race-at-twenty-1987-2007.pdf?1418423933; see also Dr. Robert Bullard's website http://drrobertbullard.com/; Peter Sawtell, "Race, Toxic Waste, and Church," *Eco-Justice Notes* (April 27, 2007), accessed September 10, 2017, http://www.eco-justice.org/E-070427.asp.

7. John Dorhauer, "Commentary: The Three Great Loves," *United Church of Christ News* (April 27, 2017), accessed September 10, 2017, http://www.ucc.org/commentary_three_great_loves_04272017.

1. THE SITUATION IN WHICH
WE FIND OURSELVES

1. Gus Speth tells me that he said something like this in 2007 at a gathering of scientists and evangelicals who were uniting to protect creation: https://www-tc.pbs.org/now/shows/343/letter.pdf. Rev. Ken Wilson, pastor of Vineyard Church in Ann Arbor, Michigan, quoted Gus to the *Miami Herald* in an article entitled "Religion Rejuvenates Environmentalism," published February 18, 2010. That article is reproduced here: http://fore.yale.edu/files/2010_UNEP_emails.pdf, page 44. This same quote appears in ecoAmerica's *Blessed Tomorrow* (2016), "Let's Talk Faith and Climate: Communication Guidance for Faith Leaders," accessed September 1, 2017, https://ecoamerica.org/wp-content/uploads/2017/03/ea-lets-talk-faith-and-climate-web-2.pdf.

2. For an excellent article on the history of accelerating atmospheric CO_2 levels, see Barry Saxifrage, "Atmospheric CO_2 Levels Accelerate Upwards, Smashing Records," *National Observer* (April 10, 2017), accessed September 8, and September 10, 2017, http://www.nationalobserver.com/2017/04/10/opinion/atmospheric-co2-levels-accelerate-upwards-smashing-records.

3. "Invitation to 'Blow the Trumpet' on Climate Change," Massachusetts Conference UCC, accessed September 8, 2017, http://www.macucc.org/blogdetail/92909.

4. Nadja Popovitch, "Mapping 50 Years of Melting Ice in Glacier National Park," *New York Times*, May 24, 2017, accessed September 8, 2017, https://www.nytimes.com/interactive/2017/05/24/climate/mapping-50-years-of-ice-loss-in-glacier-national-park.html.

5. John Vidal, "'Extraordinarily Hot' Arctic Temperatures Alarm Scientists," *The Guardian*, November 22, 2016, accessed September 8, 2017, https://www.theguardian.com/environment/2016/nov/22/extraordinarily-hot-arctic-temperatures-alarm-scientists.

6. David Wallace-Wells, "The Uninhabitable Earth," *New York Magazine* (July 9, 2017). See also Justin Gillis and Henry Fountain, "Global Warming Cited as Wildfires Increase in Fragile Boreal Forest," *New York Times*, May 10, 2016, accessed September 8, 2017, https://www.nytimes.com/2016/05/11/science/global-warming-cited-as-wildfires-increase-in-fragile-boreal-forest.html.

7. Samuel Osborn, "World's Oceans Are Warming 13% Faster than Previously Thought, Scientists Warn," *Independent*, March 12, 2017.

8. B. Hönisch, et al., "The Geological Record of Ocean Acidification," *Science* 335 (March 2, 2012): 1058–63.

9. Andrea Thompson, "West Coast Waters on Acid Trip; Fishing Industry in Peril," *Climate Central* (June 6, 2017), accessed September 10, 2017, http://www.climatecentral.org/news/ocean-acidification-hotspots-west-coast-21517.

10. Lorraine Chow, "Louisiana Faces Faster Levels of Sea-Level Rise Than Any Other Land on Earth," *EcoWatch* (January 4, 2017), accessed September 10, 2017, https://www.ecowatch.com/louisiana-sea-level-rise-2178631264.html.

11. Jeff Goodell, "Will We Miss Our Last Chance to Save the World From Climate Change?" *Rolling Stone* (December 22, 2016), accessed September 14, 2017, http://www.rollingstone.com/politics/features/will-we-miss-our-last-chance-to-survive-climate-change-w456917.

12. David Wallace-Wells, "The Uninhabitable Earth," *New York Magazine* (July 9, 2017), accessed September 14, 2017, http://nymag.com/daily/intelligencer/2017/07/climate-change-earth-too-hot-for-humans.html.

13. Union of Concerned Scientists, "When Rising Seas Hit Home: Hard Choices Ahead for Hundreds of US Coastal Communities (2017)," accessed September 14, 2017, http://www.ucsusa.org/global-warming/global-warming-impacts/when-rising-seas-hit-home-chronic-inundation-from-sea-level-rise#.WWf78IqQzox.

14. Michael T. Klare, "Climate Change as Genocide: Inaction Equals Annihilation," *TomDispatch*, April 20, 2017, http://www.tomdispatch.com/post/176269/tomgram%3A_michael_klare%2C_do_african_famines_presage_global_climate-change_catastrophe/.

15. Nicholas Casey, "Loss of Fertile Land Fuels 'Looming Crisis' Across Africa," *New York Times*, July 30, 2017, accessed September 14, 2017, https://www.nytimes.com/2017/07/29/world/africa/africa-climate-change-kenya-land-disputes.html?_r=0.

16. Tatiana Schlossberg, "Era of 'Biological Annihilation' Is Underway, Scientists Warn," *New York Times*, July 11, 2017, accessed September 14, 2017, https://www.nytimes.com/2017/07/11/climate/mass-extinction-animal-species.html?mcubz=1.

17. Bill McKibben, *Eaarth—Making a Life on a Tough New Planet* (New York: Times Books, 2010).

18. David Ray Griffin, *Unprecedented—Can Civilization Survive the CO_2 Crisis?* (Atlanta: Clarity Press, 2015).

19. Noami Oreskes, "The Scientific Consensus on Climate Change," *Science* 306 (5702) (December 3, 2004): 1686.

20. World Bank on impact of climate change on poverty, accessed September 14, 2017, http://www.worldbank.org/en/topic/climatechange; see also, Naomi Oreskes, "The Hoax of Climate Denial," *TomDispatch*, June 16, 2015, accessed September 14, 2017, http://www.tomdispatch.com/post/176011/tomgram%3A_naomi_oreskes%2C_why_climate_deniers_are_their_own_worst_nightmares/#more.

21. Holly Richmond, "This Chart Makes It Painfully Obvious that Climate Deniers Are Ridiculous," *Grist* (January 14, 2014), accessed September 14, 2017, http://grist.org/climate-energy/this-chart-makes-it-painfully-obvious-that-climate-deniers-are-ridiculous/.

22. Damian Carrington, "The Anthropocene Epoch: Scientists Declare Dawn of Human-Influenced Age," *The Guardian*, August 29, 2016, accessed September 14, 2017, https://www.theguardian.com/environment/2016/aug/29/declare-anthropocene-epoch-experts-urge-geological-congress-human-impact-earth. Original paper: Colin N. Waters; Jan Zalasiewicz; Colin Summerhayes; Anthony D. Barnosky; Clément Poirier; Agnieszka Gałuszka; Alejandro Cearreta; Matt Edgeworth; Erle C. Ellis, "The Anthropocene is Functionally and Stratigraphically Distinct from the Holocene," *Science* 351 (6269) (January 8, 2016), accessed September 14, 2017. See also, the Indiana University Consortium for the Study of Religion, Ethics, and Society (CSRES), Forum Spring 2016: Special Issue on the Anthropocene, https://csres.iu.edu/pages/forum-folder/index.php.

23. Wallace-Wells, "The Uninhabitable Earth."

24. "John Tyndall," http://en.wikipedia.org/wiki/John_Tyndall.

25. "Guy Stewart Callendar," http://en.wikipedia.org/wiki/Guy_Stewart_Callendar.

26. Dana Nuccitelli, "Scientists Warned the US President about Global Warming 50 Years Ago Today," *The Guardian*, November 5, 2015, accessed September 14, 2017, https://www.theguardian.com/environment/climate-consensus-97-per-cent/2015/nov/05/scientists-warned-the-president-about-global-warming-50-years-ago-today.

27. Wallace S. Broecker, "Climatic Change: Are We on the Brink of a Pronounced Global Warming?" *Science* 189 (4201) (August 8, 1975): 460–63, accessed September 14, 2017, http://science.sciencemag.org/content/189/4201/460.

28. Nicholas D. Kristof, "When Our Brains Short-Circuit," *New York Times*, July 2, 2009. "If you come across a garter snake, nearly all of your brain will light up with activity as you process the 'threat.' Yet if somebody tells you that carbon emissions will eventually destroy Earth as we know it, only the small part of the brain that focuses on the future—a portion of the prefrontal cortex—will glimmer . . . The objects of our phobias, and the things that are actually dangerous to us, are almost unrelated in the modern world, but they were related in our ancient environment," Mr. Haidt said. "We have no 'preparedness' to fear a gradual rise in the Earth's temperature."

29. "Teilhard de Chardin's 'Planetary Mind' and Our Spiritual Evolution," *On Being* (January 23, 2014), accessed September 14, 2017, https://onbeing.org/programs/ursula-king-andrew-revkin-and-david-sloan-wilson-teilhard-de-chardins-planetary-mind-and-our-spiritual-evolution/.

30. Per Espen Stoknes, *What We Think About When We Try Not to Think About Global Warming* (White River Junction, VT: Chelsea Green, 2015).

31. George Marshall, *Don't Even Think About It: Why Our Brains Are Wired To Ignore Climate Change* (Bloomsbury: New York, 2014), pp. 228–29.

32. The Yale Program on Climate Change Communication reports that more than half of those who are interested in global warming or think the issue is important "rarely" or "never" talk about it with family and friends (57 percent and 54 percent respectively), http://climatecommunication.yale.edu/publications/climate-spiral-silence-america/.

33. The Rev. John H. Thomas, "A New Voice Arising: A Pastoral Letter on Faith Engaging Science and Technology," United Church of Christ, January 2008, accessed September 14, 2017, http://d3n8a8pro7vhmx.cloudfront.net/unitedchurchofchrist/legacy_url/1489/pastoral-letter.pdf?1418424941.

34. In 2015, the global emissions of CO_2 from fossil fuels were estimated to be 36 billion metric tons. It is estimated that the annual cost to society of the harmful environmental and health effects of fossil fuels is $5.3 trillion. Currently, the fossil fuel industry pays none of these costs. Were the fossil fuel industry to pay for the Social Cost of Carbon (SCC), the cost would be nearly $150 per metric ton of CO_2! See chapter 3 for a more complete discussion.

35. Oreskes, "The Hoax of Climate Denial."

36. Dino Grandoni, "The Energy 202: What Would Be the Point of Pruitt's 'Red Team-Blue Team' Climate Exercise?" *Washington Post*, July 3, 2017, accessed September 14, 2017, https://www.washingtonpost.com/news/powerpost/paloma/the-energy-202/2017/07/03/the-energy-202-what-would-be-the-point-of-pruitt-s-red-team-blue-team-climate-exercise/5959a234e9b69b7071abca32/?utm_term=.6cf3e804b9e7.

37. Brad Johnson, "Inhofe: God Says Global Warming Is a Hoax," *ThinkProgress* (March 9, 2012), accessed September 14, 2017, http://thinkprogress.org/climate/2012/03/09/441515/inhofe-god-says-global-warming-is-a-hoax/.

38. Jack Jenkins, "Limbaugh: 'If You Believe In God, Then Intellectually You Cannot Believe In Manmade Global Warming'," *ThinkProgress* (August 14, 2013), accessed September 14, 2017, http://thinkprogress.org/climate/2013/08/14/2469341/limbaugh-christians-global-warming/.

39. See Tom Engelhardt, "Ending the World the Human Way—Climate Change as the Anti-News," *TomDispatch*, February 2, 2014, accessed September 14, 2017, http://www.tomdispatch.com/blog/175801/.

40. Jill Fitzsimmons, "STUDY: Warmest Year On Record Received Cool Climate Coverage," *MediaMatters* (January 8, 2013), accessed September 14, 2017, http://mediamatters.org/research/2013/01/08/study-warmest-year-on-record-received-cool-clim/192079.

41. Again, see Engelhardt, "Ending the World the Human Way—Climate Change as the Anti-News."

42. Rebecca Leber and Jeremy Schulman, "Yes, the Mainstream Media Does Publish Fake News—A Timeline of Global Warming Denial in the Media," *Mother Jones* (July 5, 2017, accessed September 14, 2017, http://www.motherjones.com/environment/2017/07/timeline-climate-denial-news/.

43. Derek Duncan, "Commentary: Tuvalu Tells Us, Ignoring Climate Change Won't Make the Problem Go Away," United Church of Christ, July 6, 2017, accessed September 14, 2017, http://www.ucc.org/commentary_tuvalu_tells_us_ignoring_climate_change_won_t_make_the_problem_go_away_07062017.

44. CNA Military Advisory Board, "National Security and the Accelerating Risks of Climate Change," Center for Naval Analyses (May 2014), accessed September 14, 2017, https://www.cna.org/CNA_files/pdf/MAB_5-8-14.pdf.

45. "A Movement Is Born: Environmental Justice and the UCC," United Church of Christ, accessed September 14, 2017, http://www.ucc.org/a_movement_is_born_environmental_justice_and_the_ucc.

46. See also James Gustave Speth and J. Phillip Thompson III, "A Radical Alliance of Black and Green Could Save the World," *The Nation* (April 14, 2016), accessed September 14, 2017, https://www.thenation.com/article/a-

radical-alliance-of-black-and-green-could-save-the-world/ showing the systemic connection between the issues of race and class.

47. Adam Smith, *The Theory of Moral Sentiments* (1759). https://en.wikiquote.org/wiki/Adam_Smith.

48. Brian Greene, "Reimagining the Cosmos," *On Being*, KTPP, June 1, 2017, accessed September 14, 2017, https://onbeing.org/programs/brian-greene-reimagining-the-cosmos-jun2017/.

49. John Chryssavgis, "Pope and Patriarch: A Common Declaration for a Shared World," *Crux* (September 1, 2017), accessed November 12, 2017, https://cruxnow.com/commentary/2017/09/01/pope-patriarch-common-declaration-shared-world/.

50. "Montreal Protocol," Wikipedia, accessed September 14, 2017, https://en.wikipedia.org/wiki/Montreal_Protocol#Chlorofluorocarbons_.28CFCs.29_Phase-out_Management_Plan.

51. "We Are Still In!" accessed September 14, 2017, http://wearestillin.com/.

52. See Peter Sawtell, "Stop Being an Individual," *Eco-Justice Notes* (May 20, 2016), accessed September 14, 2017, http://www.eco-justice.org/E-160520.asp.

53. Walter Brueggemann, "The Liturgy of Abundance, The Myth of Scarcity," in *Deep Memory, Exuberant Hope: Contested Truth in a Post-Christian World*, ed. Patrick D. Miller (Minneapolis: Fortress, 2000), pp. 69–75.

54. Rev. Debra Williams, "A Green Haven at Trinity United Church of Christ," *Faith in Place* (March 9, 2017), accessed September 14, 2017, https://www.faithinplace.org/news/green-haven-trinity-united-church-christ.

55. The Solutions Project, accessed September 14, 2017, http://thesolutionsproject.org/.

56. Quora, "We Could Power The Entire World By Harnessing Solar Energy From 1% Of The Sahara," *Forbes Magazine* (September 22, 2016), accessed September 14, 2017, https://www.forbes.com/sites/quora/2016/09/22/we-could-power-the-entire-world-by-harnessing-solar-energy-from-1-of-the-sahara/#739582f8d440.

2. A LOVING GOD FOR A BROKEN WORLD

1. Diana Butler Bass, *Grounded: Finding God in the World—A Spiritual Revolution* (New York: HarperOne, 2015), p. 26.

2. Pope Francis, *Laudato Si': On Care for Our Common Home* (Huntington, IN: Our Sunday Visitor Publishing Division, 2015), paragraph 9 quoting Ecumenical Patriarch Bartholomew, "Lecture at Monastery of Utstein, Nor-

way" (June 23, 2003). See also the joint statement issued by Pope Francis and Ecumenical Patriarch Bartholomew on September 1, 2017, marking the World Day of Prayer for the Care of Creation. Archdeacon John Chryssavgis, Ecumenical Patriarch Bartholomew's theological advisor on environmental issues, provides an excellent commentary here: https://cruxnow.com/commentary/2017/09/01/pope-patriarch-common-declaration-shared-world/.

3. Pope Francis, *Laudato Si'*, paragraphs 11 and 58.

4. A version of this story first appeared February 15, 2013, in *Sojourners Magazine*, accessed September 24, 2017, https://sojo.net/articles/dust-you-shall-return-meantime-acting-gratitude-and-conviction.

5. This parable draws upon four sources. (1) National Public Radio program *RadioLab*, "Even the Worst Laid Plans?" found in season 8, episode 1: "Oops," accessed September 8, 2017, http://www.radiolab.org/story/91724-even-the-worst-laid-plans/. (2) Sermon by the Rev. Quinn G. Caldwell, May 11, 2014, accessed September 24, 2017, http://www.oldsouth.org/sermon/2014-05-11. (3) Edwin Dobb, "New Life in a Death Trap," *Discover Magazine* (December 1, 2000), accessed September 24, 2017, http://discovermagazine.com/2000/dec/featnewlife. (4) *PitWatch—Berkeley Pit News & Info*, update, accessed September 8, 2017, http://www.pitwatch.org/.

6. Jim Robbins, "Hordes of Geese Die on a Toxic Lake in Montana," *New York Times*, December 12, 2016, accessed September 24, 2017, https://www.nytimes.com/2016/12/12/science/snow-geese-deaths-montana.html.

7. For an excellent reflection on generativity and hope, see Julianne Lutz Warren, "Toward Generativity: An Uneasy Word of Hope," Association for the Study of Literature and Environment (ASLE) website, accessed September 24, 2017, https://www.asle.org/features/julianne-lutz-warren-senior-scholar-center-humans-nature/.

INTERLUDE

1. Attributed to Gandhi, as cited in Leonardo Boff, *Cry of the Earth, Cry of the Poor* (Maryknoll, NY: Orbis, 1997), p. 2.

2. "Historic Paris Agreement on Climate Change," United Nations Framework Convention on Climate Change (December 12, 2015), accessed September 14, 2017, http://newsroom.unfccc.int/unfccc-newsroom/finale-cop21/.

3. Andrea Thompson, "First Half of 2016 Blows Away Temp Records," *Climate Central* (July 19, 2016), accessed September 14, 2017, http://www.climatecentral.org/news/first-half-of-2016-record-hot-by-far-20540.

4. The inspiration for writing such a letter comes from my friend Naomi Oreskes. In 2014 Naomi and coauthor Erik Conway wrote *The Collapse of*

Western Civilization: A View from the Future (New York: Columbia University Press, 2014)—a brilliant work of science-based fiction that awakens in the reader acute anticipatory grief for the world we are destroying. The letter's theological approach is informed by Walter Brueggemann's writings on the prophet Jeremiah, especially "Only Grief Permits Newness," *Hopeful Imagination: Prophetic Voices in Exile* (Philadelphia: Fortress, 1986), and *Reality, Grief, Hope: Three Urgent Prophetic Tasks* (Grand Rapids: Eerdmans, 2014).

5. "World Population Prospects 2017," United Nations Population Division, accessed September 14, 2017, https://esa.un.org/unpd/wpp/Graphs/Probabilistic/POP/TOT/.

6. Paddy Manning, "Too Hot to Handle: Can We Afford a 4-Degree Rise?" *Sydney Morning Herald*, July 9, 2011, accessed September 14, 2017, http://www.smh.com.au/environment/too-hot-to-handle-can-we-afford-a-4degree-rise-20110708-1h7hh.html; and Robert Engelman, "Revisiting Population Growth: The Impact of Ecological Limits," *YaleEnvironment360* (October 13, 2011), accessed September 14, 2017, http://e360.yale.edu/feature/how_environmental_limits_may_rein_in_soaring_populations/2453/.

7. See Brueggemann, "Only Grief Permits Newness."

3. THE CHURCH'S VOCATION TODAY

1. Larry Rasmussen, *Earth-Honoring Faith: Religious Ethics in a New Key* (New York: Oxford University Press, 2013), p. 358.

2. See Angie Thurston and Casper ter Kuile, "How We Gather," accessed September 8, 2017, http://howwegather.org/.

3. For example, see Molly Phinney Baskette, *Real Good Church* (Cleveland: Pilgrim Press, 2014).

4. Seth Bornenstein, "It's not just Alberta: Warming-Fueled Fires Are Increasing," Associated Press, May 10, 2016, accessed September 17, 2017, https://apnews.com/8942f3f94b6643aab1108a74139af9f1/its-not-just-alberta-warming-fueled-fires-are-increasing. Justin Gillis and Henry Fountain, "Global Warming Cited as Wildfires Increase in Fragile Boreal Forest," *New York Times*, May 10, 2016, accessed September 17, 2017, https://www.nytimes.com/2016/05/11/science/global-warming-cited-as-wildfires-increase-in-fragile-boreal-forest.html.

5. Sr. Joan Chittister, preface to *Listening to the Earth: An Environmental Audit for Benedictine Communities* by Benedictine Sisters of Erie, Pennsylvania, at Lake Erie-Allegheny Earth Force (London: Earthforce, 2006), accessed September 8, 2017, http://www.arcworld.org/projects.asp?projectID=297.

6. Charles Marsh, *Strange Glory: A Life of Dietrich Bonhoeffer* (New York: Vintage Books, 2015), p. 239.

7. Marsh, *Strange Glory*, p. 232.

8. Marsh, *Strange Glory*, p. 247.

9. Nahum Norbert Glatzer, ed., *The Judaic Tradition: Texts* (Springfield, NJ: Behrman House, 1982), p. 614.

10. Prof. Tim Gorringe, "Climate Change: A Confessional Issue for the Churches?" (Annual Lecture presented to Operation Noah, 2011).

11. Klaus Scholder, "Political Resistance or Self-Assertion," in *A Requiem for Hitler* (London: SCM, 1989), p. 139.

12. Pope Francis, *Laudato Si'*, paragraph 21.

13. James Gustave Speth, *The Bridge at the Edge of the World: Capitalism, the Environment, and Crossing from Crisis to Stability* (New Haven, CT: Yale University Press, 2008), p. 54.

14. Wallace E. Oates, "An Economic Perspective on Environmental and Resource Policy," in Wallace E. Oates, ed., *The RFF Reader in Environmental and Resource Management* (Washington, DC: Resources for the Future, 1999), p. xiv, as quoted in Speth, *The Bridge at the Edge of the World*, p. 53.

15. Paul Ekins, *Economic Growth and Environmental Sustainability* (London: Routledge, 2000), pp. 316–17, as quoted in Speth, *The Bridge at the Edge of the World*, p. 50.

16. Gregg Muttitt, "The Sky's Limit: Why the Paris Climate Goals Require a Managed Decline of Fossil Fuel Production," Oil Change International report (September 22, 2016), http://priceofoil.org/2016/09/22/the-skys-limit-report/.

17. See Citizens Climate Lobby website, https://citizensclimatelobby.org/.

18. See CO_2-Earth website, https://www.co2.earth/.

19. Richard Rood, "If We Stopped Emitting Greenhouse Gases Right Now, Would We Stop Climate Change?" *The Conversation* (July 4, 2017), accessed September 17, 2017, http://theconversation.com/if-we-stopped-emitting-greenhouse-gases-right-now-would-we-stop-climate-change-78882.

20. See Bill McKibben's interview of Jacqueline Patterson, "Climate Justice Is Racial Justice Is Gender Justice," *YES! Magazine* (August 18, 2017), accessed September 1, 2017, http://www.yesmagazine.org/issues/just-transition/climate-justice-is-racial-justice-is-gender-justice-20170818.

21. Larry Rasmussen, *Earth-Honoring Faith: Religious Ethics in a New Key* (Oxford: Oxford University Press, 2013), see especially 111–14, where he quotes extensively from Václav Havel, "Address of the President of the Czech Republic, His Excellency Václav Havel, on the Occasion of the Liberty Medal Ceremony," Philadelphia, July 4, 1994.

22. Andrew Revkin, "Do Humans Need a Golden Rule 2.0?" *Dot Earth New York Times Blog*, May 25, 2010, http://dotearth.blogs.nytimes.com/2010/05/25/do-humans-need-a-golden-rule-2-0/?partner=rss&emc=rss. In this blog, Andrew Revkin tells of the 2010 PEN World Voices Conference, which had a session on global warming. The show was stolen by novelist Jostein Gaarder, the Norwegian author of *Sophie's World,* who spoke of intergenerational responsibility.

23. James Hansen, "Why I Must Speak Out About Climate Change," TED Talk, February 2012, https://www.ted.com/talks/james_hansen_why_i_must_speak_out_about_climate_change. Hansen gave this talk a year before we were arrested together in front of the White House protesting the KXL pipeline.

24. Joe Romm, "Earth's Rate Of Global Warming Is 400,000 Hiroshima Bombs A Day," *ThinkProgress Blog* (December 22, 2013), https://thinkprogress.org/earths-rate-of-global-warming-is-400-000-hiroshima-bombs-a-day-44689384fef9#.gvwznjyc3. Romm discusses the importance of using this and other metaphors to help people understand the impact of climate change.

25. Martin Luther King Jr., "Letter from a Birmingham City Jail," in *A Testament of Hope: The Essential Writings of Martin Luther King, Jr.*, ed. James M. Washington (San Francisco: Harper & Row, 1986). See also Pope Francis, *Laudato Si'*, paragraph 92.

26. *"Juliana v. U.S.* Climate Lawsuit," Our Children's Trust, last accessed September 17, 2017, https://www.ourchildrenstrust.org/us/federal-lawsuit/.

27. In December 2017 the United Church of Christ issued a "Call for More Than a Thousand Sermons in Solidarity with the Youth Awakening a Nation to Climate Action." http://www.eachgeneration.org.

28. Joanna Rogers Macy, *Despair and Personal Power in the Nuclear Age* (Philadelphia: New Society Publishers, 1983).

29. It must be said that for Hiroshima, Nagasaki, thousands of Pacific Islanders dislocated for nuclear testing, and thousands of "downwinders" in and around Utah, nuclear weapons certainly inflicted death, destruction, and discontinuity.

30. Valerie Ziegler, "Do We Have a Story to Tell?: Reflections on Barbara Rossing's The Rapture Exposed," review of *The Rapture Exposed,* by Barbara Rossing, *Reflections* (2005), Yale University.

31. George Marshall, *Don't Even Think About It: Why Our Brains Are Wired to Ignore Climate Change* (New York: Bloomsbury, 2014), p. 49.

32. Marshall, *Don't Even Think About It*, p. 50.

33. Larry Rasmussen, "The Baptized Life," in *Holy Ground*, Lyndsay Moseley, ed. (San Francisco: Sierra Club Books, 2008), 182ff. While these ideas are all Rasmussen's, he borrows the first quotation from Thomas Berry.

34. Rasmussen, *Earth-Honoring Faith,* p. 111. He quotes Holmes Ralston III, "Saving Creation: Faith Shaping Environmental Policy," *Harvard Law and Policy Review* 4 (2010): 121.

35. Rasmussen, *Earth-Honoring Faith,* p. 358.

4. THE MARKS OF THE CHURCH
IN A CLIMATE CRISIS WORLD

1. Diana Butler Bass, *Christianity After Religion: The End of Church and the Birth of a New Spiritual Awakening* (New York: HarperOne, 2012), p. 251.

2. "A Greener Bush: George Bush Deserves Praise for His Recent Environmental Moves—But He Could Be Bolder Still," *The Economist* (February 13, 2003), accessed September 17, 2017, http://www.economist.com/node/1576767.

3. See http://www.transitionus.org/transition-towns.

4. Stephen L. Carter, "Casting the First Stone . . . at Exxon?" *The Day*, July 15, 2013, accessed September 17, 2017, http://www.theday.com/article/20130715/OP03/307159998/0/SEARCH.

5. Naomi Oreskes quoted in interview by Wen Stephenson, "Is the Carbon-Divestment Movement Reaching a Tipping Point?" *The Nation,* April 22, 2015, accessed September 17, 2017, https://www.thenation.com/article/carbon-divestment-movement-reaching-tipping-point/. See also excellent article by K. C. Golden, "We Have Met the Wrong Enemy," *Climate Solutions*, May 22, 2015, accessed September 17, 2017, http://www.climatesolutions.org/article/1432250679-we-have-met-wrong-enemy.

6. See chapter 5 for a more detailed discussion.

7. See Gross National Happiness website, http://www.grossnationalhappiness.com/; see also Jody Rosen, "Bhutan: A Higher State of Being," *New York Times*, October 30, 2014, accessed September 17, 2017, http://www.nytimes.com/2014/10/30/t-magazine/bhutan-bicycle-gross-national-happiness.html?_r=0.

8. As reported by Philip Shabecoff, "Global Warming Has Begun, Expert Tells Senate," *New York Times*, June 24, 1988, accessed September 17, 2017, http://www.nytimes.com/1988/06/24/us/global-warming-has-begun-expert-tells-senate.html.

9. Justin Fox, "The Economics of Well-Being," *Harvard Business Review* (January–February 2012), accessed September 17, 2017, https://hbr.org/2012/01/the-economics-of-well-being.

10. "Climate Revival—Denominational Leaders Sign Shared Statement," accessed September 17, 2017, http://www.macucc.org/climaterevival

denominationalleaderssignsharedstatement.

11. Bass, *Christianity After Religion*, pp. 5–7 and elsewhere.

12. Resources to support Truth and Reconciliation Conversations on Climate Change are currently being developed. Find updates on their availability here: http://www.macucc.org/environment.

13. Bill McKibben, "A World at War," *The New Republic* (August 15, 2016), accessed September 17, 2017, https://newrepublic.com/article/135684/declare-war-climate-change-mobilize-wwii. "We're under attack from climate change—and our only hope is to mobilize like we did in WWII."

5. DISCIPLESHIP

1. Peter Senge, et al., *Presence: Human Purpose and the Field of the Future* (New York: Doubleday, 2005), p. 26.

2. Rasmussen, *Earth-Honoring Faith,* quoting Heather Eaton, "Reflections on Water," unpublished paper, n.p., made available to Rasmussen by Eaton.

3. Donella H. Meadows, Dennis L. Meadows, Jorgen Randers, and William W. Behrens III, *The Limits to Growth* (New York: Universe Books, 1972).

4. J. R. McNeill, *Something New Under the Sun: An Environmental History of the Twentieth-Century World* (New York: W. W. Norton, 2000), pp. 334–36.

5. Richard Heinberg, *Afterburn: Society Beyond Fossil Fuels* (Gabriola Island, BC, Canada: New Society Publishers, 2015), pp. 133, 161.

6. See various projects and papers found at http://www.thenextsystem.org and http://democracycollaborative.org/. See also Rachel Botsman and Roo Rogers, *What's Mine Is Yours: How Collaborative Consumption is Changing the Way We Live* (New York: Harper Business, 2010). The book documents the increasing popularity of the collaborative consumption model and the ways that expanding it would fundamentally change the workings of our economy.

7. Pope Francis, *Laudato Si'*, paragraph 78.

8. Pope Francis, *Laudato Si'*, paragraph 194. Emphasis mine.

9. Gar Alperovitz, James Gustave Speth, Ted Howard, and Joe Guinan, "Systemic Crisis and Systemic Change in the United States in the 21st Century," Democracy Collaborative, September 2016 (paper prepared for the "After Fossil Fuels: The Next Economy" Conference in Oberlin, Ohio, October 6–8, 2016).

10. Pope Francis, *Laudato Si'*, paragraph 209.

11. Sallie McFague, *Blessed are the Consumers: Climate Change and the Practice of Restraint* (Minneapolis: Fortress Press, 2013), p. xii.

12. George W. Bush, "Address Before a Joint Session of the Congress on the State of the Union," January 31, 2006, accessed September 17, 2017, http://www.presidency.ucsb.edu/ws/index.php?pid=65090.

13. Bob Herbert, "An Unnatural Disaster," *New York Times*, May 29, 2010.

14. Dawn Stover, "Addicted to Oil," *Bulletin of the Atomic Scientists* (May 18, 2014), accessed September 17, 2017, http://thebulletin.org/addicted-oil7174.

15. See "Keep It In the Ground" website, accessed September 17, 2017, http://april2016.uccpages.org/. See also "Climate Witness" website, September 17, 2017, http://www.climatewitness.org/.

16. Gary Gardner, *Inspiring Progress: Religions' Contribution to Sustainable Development* (Washington, DC: Worldwatch Institute, 2006), p. 123, quoted in McFague, *Blessed are the Consumers*, p. 33.

17. John Hick, *An Interpretation of Religion* (New Haven: Yale University Press, 1989), p. 300, quoted in McFague, *Blessed are the Consumers*, p. 19.

18. Marshall, *Don't Even Think About It*, p. 234.

19. Marshall, *Don't Even Think About It*, p. 81.

20. Kathleen Dean Moore, *Great Tide Rising: Towards Clarity and Moral Courage in a Time of Planetary Change* (Berkeley: Counterpoint, 2016), p. 2.

21. Moore, *Great Tide Rising*, p. 281. Her analysis parallels my response in chapter 4 to Yale law professor Steven L. Carter's criticism of the UCC's resolution to divest from fossil fuel companies.

22. See Interfaith Power and Light website, http://www.interfaith powerandlight.org/.

23. As of this writing, the EPA makes a carbon footprint calculator available on its website, https://www3.epa.gov/carbon-footprint-calculator/. There is a range of opinion about the efficacy of purchasing carbon offset. It's important to look closely at whether the projects in question are certified, where they are, and what tangible results are occurring or will occur. You can learn more about approaches and options from the Stockholm Environment Institute's Carbon Offset Research & Education website, http://www.co2offsetresearch.org/consumer/index.html.

24. John Schwartz, "Rockefellers, Heirs to an Oil Fortune, Will Divest Charity of Fossil Fuels," *New York Times*, September 21, 2014, accessed September 18, 2017, https://www.nytimes.com/2014/09/22/us/heirs-to-an-oil-fortune-join-the-divestment-drive.html.

25. Carbon Tracker, "Unburnable Carbon: Are the World's Financial Markets Carrying a Carbon Bubble?" (July 13, 2011), accessed November 12, 2017, https://www.carbontracker.org/reports/carbon-bubble/.

26. See Neela Banerjee, Lisa Song, and David Hasemyer, "Exxon: The Road Not Taken," *Inside Climate News* (September 16, 2015), accessed September 18, 2017, https://insideclimatenews.org/content/Exxon-The-Road-Not-Taken; and Sara Jerving, Katie Jennings, Masako Melissa Hirsch, and Susanne Rust, "What Exxon Knew About the Earth's Melting Arctic," *Los Angeles Times*, October 9, 2015, accessed September 18, 2017, http://graphics.latimes.com/exxon-arctic/.

27. In support of the work of the attorneys general, see Naomi Oreskes and Geoffrey Supran, "What Exxon Mobil Didn't Say About Climate Change," *New York Times*, August 22, 2017, accessed September 18, 2017, https://www.nytimes.com/2017/08/22/opinion/exxon-climate-change-.html?mcubz=1.

28. David Hasemyer and Sabrina Shankman, "Climate Fraud Investigation of Exxon Draws Attention of 17 Attorneys General," *Inside Climate News* (March 30, 2016), accessed September 18, 2017, https://insideclimatenews.org/news/30032016/climate-change-fraud-investigation-exxon-eric-shneiderman-18-attorneys-general.

29. John H. Cushman Jr., "SEC Involvement Sharpens #ExxonKnew Focus on What Its Accountants Knew," *Inside Climate News* (September 21, 2016), accessed September 18, 2017, https://insideclimatenews.org/news/21092016/exxon-sec-questions-financial-risks-climate-change-eric-schneiderman-ny.

30. Karen Armstrong, *The Case for God* (New York: Alfred A. Knopf, 2009), p. 20, as quoted in McFague, *Blessed are the Consumers,* p. 35.

31. Marshall, *Don't Even Think About It,* p. 46.

32. Marshall, *Don't Even Think About It,* p. 49.

33. Marshall, *Don't Even Think About It,* p. 50.

34. Marshall, *Don't Even Think About It,* p. 225.

35. This is how Bill McKibben puts it in *The End of Nature* (New York: Anchor, 1989)—the first book on climate change for the general reader. See the excellent discussion of Bill McKibben and other prophets in chapter 2 of Wen Stephenson's compelling book, *What We're Fighting for Now is Each Other* (Boston: Beacon Press, 2015).

36. Stephenson, *What We're Fighting for Now is Each Other,* p. 71. McKibben is referring to the organization of climate activists 350.org which he founded in 2008.

37. See Climate Disobedience Center website, http://www.climatedisobedience.org/.

38. Stephenson, *What We're Fighting for Now is Each Other,* p. 71.

6. WORSHIP AS A PATHWAY TO FREEDOM

1. Willis Jenkins, *The Future of Ethics: Sustainability, Social Justice, and Religious Creativity* (Washington, DC: Georgetown Press, 2013), p. 311.

2. Larry Rasmussen discusses the first Christians in his chapter "Shaping Communities" found in *Practicing Our Faith,* Dorothy C. Bass, ed. (San Francisco: Jossey-Bass, 1997), p. 130.

3. Bill McKibben, *Oil and Honey: The Education of an Unlikely Activist* (New York: Times Books, 2013), p. 34.

4. Jenkins, *The Future of Ethics*, p. 316.

5. Note: I suspect many evangelicals would support this. See the 2010 post by Dr. Russell Moore, Dean of the School of Theology at Southern Baptist Theological Seminary, "An Evangelical Crusade To Go Green With God," Forum on Religion and Ecology, June 27, 2010, accessed September 18, 2017, http://fore.research.yale.edu/news/item/an-evangelical-crusade-to-go-green-with-god/.

6. See Jenkins, *The Future of Ethics*, p. 298.

7. Video appearances by Archbishop Desmond Tutu and Bill McKibben, along with a video of Katharine Jefferts Schori, the Presiding Bishop of the Episcopal Church, preaching at Trinity Church in Copley Square, can be viewed at http://www.macucc.org/climaterevivaldenominationalleaderssign sharedstatement. There you will also find a statement titled "Lazarus, Come Out: A Shared Statement of Hope in the Face of Climate Change" signed by over twenty denominational leaders.

8. Jenkins, *The Future of Ethics*, 313.

9. Elizabeth A. Johnson, *Ask the Beasts: Darwin and the God of Love* (London: Bloomsbury, 2014), p. 228.

10. Paul Santmire, *The Travail of Nature: The Ambiguous Promise of Christian Theology* (Minneapolis: Fortress, 1985).

11. Rachel Muers, "Pushing the Limit: Theology and Responsibility to Future Generations," *Studies in Christian Ethics* 16(2) (2003). Jenkins cites other articles from Muers in *The Future of Ethics*, footnote 66 on p. 320.

12. See Dear Tomorrow website, http://www.deartomorrow.org/en/home/.

13. Julie Dunlap and Susan A. Cohen, eds., *Coming of Age at the End of Nature: A Generation Faces Living on a Challenged Planet* (San Antonio: Trinity University Press, 2016).

14. Rasmussen, *Earth-Honoring Faith*, p. 257.

15. US Catholic Bishops, *Renewing the Earth: An Invitation to Reflection and Action in Light of Catholic Social Teaching* (Washington, DC: US Conference of Catholic Bishops, November 14, 1991).

16. Rasmussen, *Earth-Honoring Faith*, p. 263.

17. Martin Luther King Jr., "Beyond Vietnam—A Time to Break the Silence" (sermon delivered at Riverside Church, New York City, April 4, 1967), accessed September 18, 2017, http://www.americanrhetoric.com/speeches/mlkatimetobreaksilence.htm.

18. Harding delivered his speech on October 23, 1983, at a conference titled "The Black Church, the Third World, and Peace," in Atlanta, Georgia. Excerpts from the speech were reprinted in "Struggle and Transformation," *Sojourners Magazine* (October 1984), accessed September 1, 2017, https://sojo.net/magazine/october-1984/struggle-and-transformation.

19. See "The Revival: Time for a Moral Revolution of Values" website: http://www.moralrevival.org/.

20. Alexis Sachdev, "Religious Leaders Arrested in Protest of Controversial Natural Gas Pipeline," *Metro USA*, May 25, 2016, accessed September 18, 2017, http://www.metro.us/boston/religious-leaders-arrested-in-protest-of-controversial-natural-gas-pipeline/zsJpey---DZ7s2dnUYimns; Tiffany Vail, "Antal Among 16 Clergy Arrested at Pipeline Protest," Massachusetts Conference UCC, May 25, 2016, accessed September 18, 2017, http://www.macucc.org/newsdetail/antal-among-16-clergy-arrested-at-pipeline-protest-4882568; see also Clergy Climate Action website, http://www.clergyclimateaction.org/.

21. "Al Gore's daughter Karenna arrested in Boston," *New York Times Women in the World*, June 30, 2016, accessed September 18, 2017, http://nytlive.nytimes.com/womenintheworld/2016/06/30/al-gores-daughter-karenna-arrested-in-boston/.

22. Yiming Woo, "Pakistan Digs Mass Graves as Heat Wave Looms," Reuters Video, May 20, 2016, accessed September 9, 2017, http://www.reuters.com/video/2016/05/20/pakistan-digs-mass-graves-as-heat-wave-l?videoId=368574166. "Thank God, we are better prepared this year. God forbid that it happens again but we have already dug graves to accommodate 300 bodies." "Hospitals and morgues in the Pakistani port city were overwhelmed last year as temperatures soared to 44 degrees Celsius."

23. Carol Kuruvilla, "Standing Rock Protestors Burn Document That Justified Indigenous Oppression," *Huffington Post*, November 4, 2016, accessed September 18, 2017, http://www.huffingtonpost.com/entry/interfaith-clergy-dapl-doctrine-of-discovery_us_581cb86ae4b0aac62483d92f .

24. Margaret Bullitt-Jonas, "Standing Rock: Good Tidings of Great Joy—Faith and Fear Duke It Out," *Reviving Creation*, December 13, 2016, accessed September 18, 2017, http://revivingcreation.org/standing-rock-good-tidings-of-great-joy/.

25. Tiffany Vail, "Prayer: The Missing Ingredient in a Fight for the Environment," Massachusetts Conference UCC, July 19, 2017, accessed September

18, 2017, http://www.macucc.org/newsdetail/prayer-the-missing-ingredient-in-a-fight-for-the-environment-8794043.

26. Jay O'Hara, "Quakers Blockading Bow Coal Plant Break Camp After 24 Hours," Climate Pilgrimage website, July 16, 2017, accessed September 18, 2017, https://climatepilgrimage.org/press-release-quakers-blockading-bow-coal-plant-break-camp-after-24-hours/.

27. Julie Zauzmer, "Catholic Nuns in Pa. Build a Chapel to Bock the Path of a Gas Pipeline Planned for Their Property," *Washington Post*, July 16, 2017, accessed September 18, 2017, https://www.washingtonpost.com/local/social-issues/catholic-nuns-in-pa-build-a-chapel-to-block-the-path-of-a-proposed-gas-pipeline/2017/07/16/0096e7ce-6a3c-11e7-96ab-5f38140b38cc_story.html?tid=ss_mail&utm_term=.0c2b3525ecc0.

28. Mark Hefflinger, "SOLAR XL: Resisting Keystone XL by Building Clean Energy in the Pipeline's Path," Bold Nebraska website, July 6, 2017, accessed September 18, 2017, http://boldnebraska.org/solarxl.

29. Season of Creation website, http://seasonofcreation.org/.

30. Peter Sawtell, "Act and Pray in the Season of Creation," *Eco-Justice Notes*, July 28, 2017, accessed September 18, 2017, http://www.eco-justice.org/E-170728.asp.

31. Damon Beres, "In Parts Of Africa, Cell Phones Are Everywhere And Landlines Barely Exist," *Huffington Post*, April 20, 2015, accessed September 18, 2017, http://www.huffingtonpost.com/2015/04/20/africa-phone-study_n_7081868.html.

32. McKibben, *Oil and Honey*, p. 44.

7. PROPHETIC PREACHING

1. Walter Brueggemann, *The Prophetic Imagination* (Minneapolis, MN: Fortress Press, 1978), p. 40.

2. The introduction of this book provides the Resolution and the story behind it.

3. A. Leiserowitz, E. Maibach, C. Roser-Renouf, G. Feinberg, and S. Rosenthal, "Climate Change in the American Mind: October 2015," Yale University and George Mason University, New Haven, CT: Yale Program on Climate Change Communication, accessed September 18, 2017, http://climate communication.yale.edu/publications/more-americans-perceive-harm-from-global-warming-survey-finds/.

4. Daniel Cox, PhD, Juhem Navarro-Rivera, and Robert P. Jones, PhD, "Believers, Sympathizers, and Skeptics: Why Americans are Conflicted about Climate Change, Environmental Policy, and Science," Findings from the

PRRI/AAR Religion, Values, and Climate Change Survey, November 21, 2014, accessed September 18, 2017, http://publicreligion.org/research/2014/11/believers-sympathizers-skeptics-americans-conflicted-climate-change-environmental-policy-science/.

5. For an excellent discussion of this and a terrific guide for preaching on climate change, see Leah D. Schade, *Creation-Crisis Preaching—Ecology, Theology, and the Pulpit* (St. Louis: Chalice, 2015), pp. 32, 42.

6. William Sloane Coffin, *The Collected Sermons of William Sloane Coffin—The Riverside Years, Vol. 2* (Louisville: Westminster John Knox Press, 2008), p. 3.

7. "What We Know," American Association for the Advancement of Science (AAAS), accessed September 18, 2017, http://whatweknow.aaas.org/.

8. As pastors struggle to respond to God's call to inspire their congregations and communities to redirect their lives to preserve God's great gift of creation, they will gain both courage and motivation by reading Dean G. Stroud, ed., *Preaching in Hitler's Shadow: Sermons of Resistance in the Third Reich* (Grand Rapids, MI: Eerdmans, 2013).

9. The poet David Whyte explores this understanding of courage in a conversation with Br. David Steindl-Rast that can be found here: http://www.gratefulness.org/resource/crossing-unknown-sea/.

10. Prof. Leonora Tubbs Tisdale, "Speaking Truth in Love: Strategies for Prophetic Preaching," *Reflections* (Winter 2006): 42.

11. Henri J. M. Nouwen, *Love, Henri: Letters on the Spiritual Life* (New York: Convergent Books, 2016), p. 59.

12. Nouwen, *Love, Henri*, p. 78.

13. Nouwen, *Love, Henri*, pp. 87–88.

14. William Sloane Coffin, *A Passion for the Possible: A Message to US Churches* (Louisville: Westminster /John Knox Press, 1993), p. 88.

15. Jim Pierobon, "Why Communicating About Climate Change Is so Difficult: It's 'The Elephant We're All Inside Of'," review of *Don't Even Think About It: Why Our Brains Are Wired To Ignore Climate Change*, by George Marshall, *Huffington Post*, February 5, 2015, accessed September 18, 2017, http://www.huffingtonpost.com/jim-pierobon/why-communicating-about-c_b_6626692.html.

16. "Let's Talk Faith and Climate: Communication Guidance for Faith Leaders," ecoAmerica, 2016, accessed September 18, 2017, https://ecoamerica.org/wp-content/uploads/2017/03/ea-lets-talk-faith-and-climate-web-2.pdf.

17. Climate Nexus' Daily Hot News reported on January 30, 2015: "American Public Doesn't Get Science: There are major discrepancies between public opinion and scientific consensus on issues like climate

change, evolution, GMOs, and vaccines, a new study by Pew Research Center finds. Despite having a high level of respect and appreciation for science, the public disagreed with scientists by 20% or more on eight of 13 surveyed issues, including a 50–87% split between the public and scientists on the validity of human-caused climate change. A large majority of the scientists criticized the education system, and 84% said that public ignorance of science was a major problem." See Seth Borenstein, "Poll Shows Giant Gap Between What Public, Scientists Think," AP News, January 30, 2015, accessed September 18, 2017, https://apnews.com/db5d16d790cc446885b4bf991df5707e/poll-shows-giant-gap-between-what-public-scientists-think.

18. Heather Smith, "Want Everyone Else to Buy Into Environmentalism? Never Say 'Earth'," Interview of David Fenton of Fenton Communications, *Grist* (March 12, 2014), accessed September 18, 2017, http://grist.org/climate-energy/want-everyone-else-to-buy-into-environmentalism-never-say-earth/.

19. Smith, "Want Everyone Else to Buy Into Environmentalism? Never Say 'Earth'."

20. David Abel, "Global Warming to Make Powerful Hurricanes More Likely, Scientists Say," *Boston Globe*, September 6, 2017, accessed September 18, 2017, http://www.bostonglobe.com/metro/2017/09/05/global-warming-make-powerful-hurricanes-more-likely-scientists-say/Q3lUW6iKuGEKvp TOD22sGL/story.html?event=event12.

21. Vimeo of the Rev. Ian Holland preaching while wearing a life preserver over his robe: https://vimeo.com/215718245.

22. Phil Plait, "The Climate Change Elevator Pitch," *Slate's Bad Astronomy Blog*, February 2, 2015, accessed September 18, 2017, http://www.slate.com/blogs/bad_astronomy/2015/02/02/climate_change_elevator_pitch_video_series.html.

8. WITNESSING TOGETHER

1. Martin Luther King Jr., "A Time to Break the Silence," in *A Testament of Hope: The Essential Writings of Martin Luther King, Jr.*, ed. James M. Washington (San Francisco: Harper & Row, 1986), p. 243.

2. Bill McKibben, "The Fossil Fuel Resistance," *Rolling Stone* (April 11, 2013), accessed September 18, 2017, http://www.rollingstone.com/politics/news/the-fossil-fuel-resistance-20130411.

3. A moving account of this momentous day can be found in Stephenson, *What We're Fighting for Now Is Each Other*, pp. 211–15.

4. Thomas G. Long, *Testimony: Talking Ourselves into Being Christian* (San Francisco: Jossey-Bass, 2004), pp. 28–29.

5. Joel Clement, "I'm a Scientist. I'm Blowing the Whistle on the Trump Administration," *Washington Post*, July 19, 2017, accessed September 18, 2017, https://www.washingtonpost.com/opinions/im-a-scientist-the-trump-administration-reassigned-me-for-speaking-up-about-climate-change/2017/07/19/389b8dce-6b12-11e7-9c15-177740635e83_story.html?utm_term=.367a9221982a.

6. Wallace-Wells, "The Uninhabitable Earth."

7. Michael Mann, Susan Joy Hassol, and Tom Toles, "Doomsday Scenarios Are as Harmful as Climate Change Denial," *Washington Post*, July 12, 2017, accessed September 18, 2017, https://www.washingtonpost.com/opinions/doomsday-scenarios-are-as-harmful-as-climate-change-denial/2017/07/12/880ed002-6714-11e7-a1d7-9a32c91c6f40_story.html?utm_term=.36a3ed0d5eff .

8. Jason Mark, "Fear Factor: A Defense of NEW YORK's Climate Doom Cover Story," *Sierra Magazine* (July 14, 2017), accessed September 18, 2017, https://sierraclub.org/sierra/fear-factor-defense-new-yorks-climate-doom-cover-story.

9. John Schwartz, "Investment Funds Worth Trillions Are Dropping Fossil Fuel Stocks," *New York Times*, December 12, 2016, accessed September 9, 2017, http://mobile.nytimes.com/2016/12/12/science/investment-funds-worth-trillions-are-dropping-fossil-fuel-stocks.html?emc=edit_tnt_20161213&nlid=37530612&tntemail0=y&_r=0&referer= .

10. Bevis Longstreth, "Homer Describing Big Oil: 'Lung-Choking, Ocean-Poisoning, Species-Sickening Pitiless Scourge of Humanity'" (paper presented at the Boston Carbon Risk Forum at Harvard Law School on September 29, 2014 and posted on *Huffington Post* http://www.huffingtonpost.com/bevis-longstreth/homer-describing-big-oil-_b_5909420.html).

11. Bevis Longstreth, "The Financial Case for Divestment of Fossil Fuel Companies by Endowment Fiduciaries," *Huffington Post,* November 2, 2013, accessed September 18, 2017, http://www.huffingtonpost.com/bevis-longstreth/the-financial-case-for-di_b_4203910.html.

12. Walter Brueggemann, "To Whom Does the Land Belong?" in *Remember You Are Dust,* ed. K. C. Hanson (Eugene, OR: Cascade Books, 2012).

13. Parker J. Palmer, "We Are Owned by the Wilderness," *On Being Blog*, KTPP, July 11, 2017, accessed September 18, 2017, https://onbeing.org/blog/parker-palmer-we-are-owned-by-the-wilderness/.

14. See David Bollier, *Think Like a Commoner: A Short Introduction to the Life of the Commons* (Gabriola Island, BC, Canada: New Society, 2014) and his column on the website On the Commons, http://www.onthecommons.org. See also Marjorie Kelly, *Owning Our Future: The Emerging Ownership Revolution—Journeys to a Generative Economy* (San Francisco: Berrett-Koehler,

2012). See also Sebastian Junger's stirring book *Tribe: On Homecoming and Belonging* (New York: Twelve, 2016), p. 18, where he suggests that the emergence of private ownership weakened group efforts towards the common good.

15. Walter Brueggemann, *Journey to the Common Good* (Louisville: Westminster John Knox Press, 2010).

9. LIVING HOPE-FILLED LIVES IN A CLIMATE CRISIS WORLD

1. Jenkins, *The Future of Ethics*, p. 316.

2. Cornel West, "Prisoners of Hope," in *The Impossible Will Take a Little While: A Citizen's Guide to Hope in a Time of Fear*, ed. by Paul Rogat Loeb (New York: Basic Books, 2004), p. 293.

3. Rabbi Jonathan Sacks, *The Dignity of Difference* (New York: Bloomsbury Academic, 2003), p. 206. See also http://www.rabbisacks.org/topics/hope-vrs-optimism/.

4. Leiserowitz et al., "Climate Change in the American Mind: October 2015."

5. Jerome Groopman, *The Anatomy of Hope* (New York: Random House, 2004), p. xiii.

6. Groopman, *The Anatomy of Hope,* p. 81.

7. Pastors seeking powerful and practical guidance in how to invite members of their congregation to name and acknowledge their grief about the destruction of creation would do well to consult Joanna Macy and Chris Johnstone, *Active Hope: How to Face the Mess We're in without Going Crazy* (Novato, CA: New World Library, 2012), p. 65.

8. Walter Brueggemann, *Reality, Grief, Hope: Three Urgent Prophetic Tasks* (Grand Rapids, MI: Eerdmans, 2014), pp. 82, 83, 88.

9. Yiming Woo, "Pakistan Digs Mass Graves as Heat Wave Looms."

10. The Center for Climate and Security, "Release: 3 Bipartisan Groups of Military and Security Leaders Urge New Course on Climate," accessed September 10, 2017, https://climateandsecurity.org/2016/09/14/three-bipartisan-groups-of-military-and-national-security-leaders-urge-robust-new-course-on-climate-change/.

11. Nicholas Kristof, "Temperatures Rise, and We're Cooked," *New York Times*, September 10, 2016, accessed September 10, 2017, http://www.nytimes.com/2016/09/11/opinion/sunday/temperatures-rise-and-were-cooked.html?ref=opinion&_r=0.

12. Jonathan Lear, *Radical Hope: Ethics in the Face of Cultural Devastation* (Cambridge, MA; Harvard University Press, 2006). I am grateful to both

Walter Brueggemann and Willis Jenkins for their discussions of *Radical Hope*. See Jenkins, *The Future of Ethics*, pp. 304–6, 324–25; and Brueggemann *Reality, Grief, Hope*, pp. 120–28. See also Charles Taylor, "A Different Kind of Courage," review of *Radical Hope: Ethics in the Face of Cultural Devastation*, by Jonathan Lear, *The New York Review of Books* (April 26, 2007), accessed September 23, 2017, http://www.nybooks.com/articles/2007/04/26/a-different-kind-of-courage/.

13. Lear, *Radical Hope*, p. 2.

14. Lear, *Radical Hope*, pp. 92–94.

15. Lear, *Radical Hope*, p. 103.

16. Jenkins, *The Future of Ethics*, p. 324.

17. This insight comes from Walter Wink, "These Bones Shall Live—Living the Word," *Christian Century Magazine* (1994) (volume and date of issue unavailable).

18. In support of the work of the attorneys general, see Naomi Oreskes and Geoffrey Supran, "What Exxon Mobil Didn't Say About Climate Change," *New York Times*, August 22, 2017, accessed September 18, 2017, https://www.nytimes.com/2017/08/22/opinion/exxon-climate-change-.html?mcubz=1.

19. Kenneth A. Briggs, "Religious Leaders Objecting to Nuclear Arms," *New York Times*, September 5, 1981, accessed September 20, 2017, http://www.nytimes.com/1981/09/08/us/religious-leaders-objecting-to-nuclear-arms.html?mcubz=1.

20. This was the title Henri Nouwen chose for an early book which offered a fresh understanding of ministry for a generation of pastors and priests: *With Open Hands* (Notre Dame, IN: Ave Maria Press, 1972).

21. See Archbishop Desmond Tutu, foreword to *The Green Bible* (New York: HarperCollins, 1989), p. I-13.

22. Martin Luther King Jr., "Letter from a Birmingham City Jail," in *A Testament of Hope: The Essential Writings of Martin Luther King, Jr.*, ed. James M. Washington (San Francisco: Harper & Row, 1986).

23. See "Acid Rain, History, In the United States," https://en.wikipedia.org/wiki/Acid_rain.

24. Tutu, foreword to *The Green Bible*, p. I-14.

EPILOGUE

1. "The Earth Charter," March 2000, accessed September 18, 2017, http://earthcharter.org/invent/images/uploads/echarter_english.pdf.

APPENDIX

1. Bill McKibben, "A World at War," with the epigraph: "We're under attack from climate change—and our only hope is to mobilize like we did in WWII," *The New Republic* (August 15, 2016), accessed September 18, 2017, https://newrepublic.com/article/135684/declare-war-climate-change-mobilize-wwii.

2. Walter Brueggemann, "To Whom Does the Land Belong?" in *Remember You Are Dust*, ed. K. C. Hanson (Eugene, OR: Cascade Books, 2012).

INDEX

ABOUT THE AUTHOR

Jim Antal is a denominational leader, activist, and public theologian. He has been the leader of the Massachusetts Conference United Church of Christ for twelve years. An environmental activist from the first Earth Day in 1970, in July 2017 Antal authored a resolution declaring a new moral era in opposition to President Trump's withdrawal from the Paris Climate Accord. The national UCC Synod passed that resolution with a 97% supermajority. In July 2013 Antal wrote and championed the UCC's resolution to divest from fossil fuel companies, the first of its kind in the country. In 2010 he founded NEREM (New England Regional Environmental Ministries), which organizes various ecumenical environmental activities including the Ecumenical Lenten Carbon Fast. Antal's vocation includes the spiritual discipline of nonviolent civil disobedience. Antal served churches in Shaker Heights, Ohio, and Newton, Massachusetts. In the mid-80s he served as executive director of the Fellowship of Reconciliation (USA), an interfaith pacifist organization. Antal began his ministry as a chaplain and teacher at several schools, including Northfield Mount Hermon and Andover. He is a graduate of Princeton University, Andover Newton Theological School, and Yale Divinity School, where he was Henri Nouwen's teaching assistant. In 2017, Yale Divinity School honored him with the William Sloane Coffin Award for Peace and Justice. Beginning in July 2018, Antal will intensify his work as the UCC's national spokesperson on climate change. Look for him and his wife, Cindy Shannon, cycling through the hills of Vermont, and follow him on Twitter @JimAntal.